EASTERN EXPOSURE

By MARVIN L. KALB

| | | | | | | | | | | | |

FARRAR, STRAUS AND CUDAHY

NEW YORK

EASTERN

EXPOSURE

TO MY MOTHER AND FATHER

CONTENTS

One brisk day in the fall of 1955, the news circulated at Harvard's Russian Research Center that the State Department needed two press attachés to work in the American Embassy in Moscow. Many of us who were engaged in research in the Russian field applied for the jobs. At that time, I was just starting research on my doctoral thesis and I was fascinated by the prospect not only of seeing Russia for the first time, but of doing research in Moscow's Lenin Library—the equivalent of our Library of Congress. A few weeks later, I learned that I was one of those selected for the assignment.

My orders, which called for a quick departure from Harvard and home, scheduled a New York-Prestwick-Bremen-Copenhagen-Stockholm-Helsinki flight and a Helsinki-Leningrad-Moscow train ride. The 5,400 mile journey took four days. I arrived in Moscow on January 28, 1956. For the next thirteen months, I kept a journal. When I returned to the United States, after an extended trip to India and Southeast Asia, close friends who read the journal suggested that it be published.

This journal is an attempt to record a personalized history

of Russia in a year of dynamic change. Moscow buzzed in late January and early February with the news of the historic Twentieth Congress of the Russian Communist Party. Khrushchev delivered his assault on the formerly infallible legend of Joseph Stalin, accusing the Georgian dictator of partial insanity, gross distortions of communist history, and excessive violations of Marxist legality.

The Russian people were not informed of this attack, but they learned by way of Russia's incredibly efficient grapevine that unprecedented shifts in policy and emphasis were being initiated. Leaders who "scorned the popular masses" were charged with building a "personality cult." Modesty was the political watchword. Bureaucracy was attacked as "unLeninist"—a catch-all term for everything bad. The names of historical personalities, which had been buried under the weight of Stalinist fear and suspicion, began to reappear in obscure journals and eventually in the central press. The Russian people began to feel that a huge burden was being lifted from their shoulders. Intellectuals began to think freely again; bureaucrats knew they had to be efficient or run the risk of losing their jobs; teachers started to think about traveling to foreign lands and communicating with foreign colleagues; students took to their traditional role and began to rebel; and finally the ordinary Russian working man opened a gripe attack against the whole Soviet system. He wanted more clothing, more food, and more housing, and he was not afraid to say so. The Soviet leadership felt that this relaxation was a good thing. It sparked initiative and creativity and purged the slothful and inert. This easing of tension spilled over into the international arena. Even diehard communists admitted that it was possible to live alongside the capitalists in peace. Khrushchev himself said war did not have to be inevitable.

I recorded these changes as they happened. There was always an effort on my part to encourage people to express themselves on any subject they liked. I never tried to provoke them into conversation, and I was never faced with any outright hostility, despite the fact that I was an official representative of the United States government. The Russian people were always warm, gregarious, friendly, and curious. On occasion, they were also suspicious.

It took many months of persistent effort, but I finally managed to do research on my doctoral thesis in the Manuscript Room of the Lenin Library. My thesis topic seemed peculiar to the Russians. (It gets a few raised eyebrows in this country too.) I was doing a biography of Count Sergei Semeonovich Uvarov—one of Russia's leading classicists and Minister of Education under Nicholas I from 1833 to 1848. People who have been brought up on a Marxist educational diet believe that Uvarov was a "reactionary." I was told time and again that he tried to "hold up the flow of history." But, whether Uvarov was "reactionary" or "progressive," he was a remarkably convenient way for me to gauge the degree of relaxation in Russia. He opened innumerable conversations, and he gave me a ready excuse to try to get into the Manuscript Room, where his private letters are stored. I became convinced after a while that Uvarov may yet undergo a renaissance even in communist Russia.

When I returned to Moscow in September, after a long trip through dusty Central Asia and the towering Caucasus, the Boston Symphony Orchestra had just completed a successful concert tour. All overt signs pointed to a further relaxation of international and domestic tension. Then Gomulka staged his "peaceful revolution" in Poland, and the bright skies began to get cloudy. A few weeks later, the people of Hungary rose up against their communist oppressors; the clouds became dark and threatening.

People with whom I had the warmest kind of friendship confided that they now were afraid to talk to me in public. Some Russians passed me by as though they had never seen me before. *Pravda* dusted off its most vicious language of the "cold war" and attacked the United States. Finally, Stalin got a new lease on life. His methods were partially restored. Relative freedom in the arts was stifled again, and Russians were warned not "to ape the West." The general atmosphere got very chilly.

I left Russia in early February, last year. Since then, the Western world has been startled out of its smug complacency by a strange hum from outer space. The "backward" Russians had shot a sputnik into orbit around the earth for the first time in history. Khrushchev boasted that the Soviet Armed Forces also had an intercontinental ballistic missile, and our scientists speculated that it was the Russian ICBM that probably shot the sputnik into the heavens, opening for all mankind the new age of space. At this point the Russian leadership enjoyed great propaganda advantages at home and abroad. The Russian people were told that the sputnik is proof of the superiority of the Soviet system. Communist hacks pounded out reams of printed matter, picking apart the capitalist system in minutest detail, almost as though they were trying to convince an unwilling audience of the righteousness of the communist cause.

As I look back now, a year later, on my tour of duty in Russia, I am impressed by four points which refuse to be battered by time:

First, the Russian people do want peace. I was told and I could see that they suffered enormous damage and hardship during the war against Hitler, and they don't want that horror again. That is the major reason why the communist press prints millions of words of peace propaganda every year. If this campaign also impresses the uncommitted areas of the world, so much the better from the Kremlin's viewpoint.

Second, the Soviet economic and educational system has many faults, but it works. Russia is a huge and wealthy country, and its industrial output continues to expand every year. It supplies its people with the necessities of life, and the communists promise that the people will now begin to get a larger share of the profits of industrialization. The peasants, though, are not happy. They still want their own land, and they don't like working for an impersonal state agency.

Third, communist ideology is regarded with mounting skepticism, not only by the youth but also by the intelligentsia. It has lost its revolutionary magnetism. I have heard young people say they would participate in a revolt against communism, if they felt sure the revolt would produce beneficial results for Russia, which is the main source of their strength and inspiration. I believe that the ideology would decay even faster if the Russian intellectual had some emotional and ideological substitute for communism. Now he clings to communism because to abandon it would leave his restless, unhappy spirit without an all-consuming orientation; and there appears to be something in the Russian intellectual that demands a faith as absorbing as Islam was to the Arab of the eighth century.

Finally, Russia very clearly is in a period of transition. One student told me Russia is "between the old and the new." The "old" is communism as practised by Stalin and to a somewhat modified extent by Russian leaders like Khrushchev. The "new" is a vague and distant dream, which will require time to become formulated into a realistic alternative to present-day communism.

I have always believed that the Russian people are much too imaginative to live forever as the docile servants of a bloodless cause. They are no longer the illiterate and inert peasantry that Stalin ruled with iron discipline. They now know how to read, and they are also beginning to think. In a dictatorship, thinking is dangerous.

I wish to express my gratitude both to those who helped guide my training in the Russian field and to those who contributed, directly or indirectly, to the writing of this diary: Marshall Shulman of Harvard's Russian Research Center; Professors Michael Karpovich, Robert L. Wolff, Merle Fainsod, Alex Inkeles, and Richard Pipes of Harvard University; Doctor Isaiah Berlin of Oxford University; Professor Hans Kohn of the City College of New York, who first awakened in me an interest in Russian literature; Ambassador Charles E. Bohlen and all the other fine people at the American Embassy in Moscow; Miss Anna Holdcroft, editor of the former *Joint Press Reading Service,* who offered me countless insights into the Russian mind; Harry Spence, Neville Richards and John Richardson of the British Embassy in Moscow; the corps of United States correspondents in Russia, including Dan Schorr of CBS News, Irv Levine of NBC News, Bill Jordan and Jack Raymond of the *New York Times,* Bernie Cutler of the *New York Herald Tribune,* and Howard Norton of the *Baltimore Sun;* Henry Hewes of the *Saturday Review;* Clifton Daniel and Harrison Salisbury, of the *New York Times,* whose penetrating dispatches from the Soviet Union encouraged me in my own work on Russia while I was still a student; the librarians of the Lenin Library, Historical Library, Saltykov-Schedrin Library, and the Pushkin House; and, finally, my particular gratitude to my brother, Bernard Kalb, who many years ago opened my eyes to new worlds. A separate and special note of thanks to my wife, Mady, who took on almost the entire burden of editing and proof-reading. I am of course responsible for any error in fact or interpretation.

Marvin L. Kalb

New York City
August 1, 1958

I · IN SEARCH OF UVAROV

January 29 : My first full day in the Soviet Union. A surprising incident occurred this afternoon when, despite the 37-degree-below-zero temperature, I decided the time had come to see Red Square. I dressed as warmly as I could, left American House, and walked along *Kropotkinsky Naberezhnaoe* towards the *Gorki* stop on the Metro line. Along the way, I happened to notice a man, dressed very warmly all in black. Feeling security-conscious on my first day in Russia, I glanced about after getting on the Metro and saw, to my left, the same dark-clothed man. He was not at all bad looking, rather young, and somewhat nervous (he kept twitching his moustache). He stood not two feet from me, looking at me, not smiling, dead serious.

At the third stop, I got off, walked out to the street, and spotted the huge and marvelously impressive Bolshoi Theater. I stood looking at it, but the cold made me change my mind about too long an appreciation, and I darted back quickly, only to bump into someone. The same man in black. I suspected he was on my tail. I had heard in Washington that, though times have changed, the Russians might put a tail on a newcomer to Moscow. By the time we reached Red Square, I was certain. He was right behind me, no more than 10 feet away, and no one would follow me around on this freezing afternoon who wasn't assigned the job. I entered GUM's, the fabulous, large Macy-ish department store which fronts on

Red Square, to get out of the cold and to look around. My
man was right behind me. I smiled to him. He did not smile
back. I approached a small stand where a woman was selling
ice cream. I asked her for two cones. I paid her, started to eat
one and then, without looking around but sensing he was
right behind me, I simply extended one of the ice cream cones
back. To my amazement, he took it. How times must have
changed here!

January 30 : A curious contradiction highlighted an otherwise dull, drab day of handshakes. An embassy car brought me
to *Kropotkinsky Pereulok 26*. It was obviously an old building, well beyond its 100th birthday, and a large steep fence
protected it from the narrow *Pereulok,* almost as though in
days gone by it protected the nobility inside from the peasants on the outside. As I entered the garden (an MVD Militia
man stood guard over this building, as over all buildings in
which foreigners live or work), I noticed a plaque nailed con-
spicuously to the front of the building, surrounded by snow
and ice which seemed to leap with dirty black hands towards
the two-storied roof. A bearded face, proud and majestic, welcomed me. Beneath the face were the words: *"P. A. Kropotkin
was born in this house in 1842."*

My mind leaped back to the last time I had read that name.
Perhaps two or three years earlier in Widener library, when
I was reading his *Memoirs of a Revolutionary.* Now I was
startled to see a government which had constructed a powerful, centralized state—perhaps the most centralized bureau-
cratic governmental structure since Genghis Khan's 700 years
ago—pay homage to a man, noble by birth, whose family dated
back to the days of Rurik, whose entire life was passionately
dedicated to the destruction of the state.

Even when Kropotkin returned to Russia in 1917 to work towards what he believed would be an anarchistic Communist society, he was exiled to a small town not far from here to die in 1921 a slow and unhappy death. He and both pre- and post-revolutionary Russia never quite hit it off. Yet, I am told that the incongruous marriage of the anarchism of Kropotkin to the centralism of communism—manifest in this plaque—is a rather common occurrence in Russia these days. The Russians, after all, are their own greatest admirers, and they love even the "bad boys" of Russian intellectual life, like Prince Kropotkin. Therefore, they read and worship not only the Lenins, but also the Turgenevs, the Herzens, the Belinskys and the Kropotkins.

In the Russian political tradition, Communist historiography notwithstanding, there have been at least two powerful currents. One is Communism—or the extremist sentiment which led to it. This is the tradition of the centralized monolith which monopolizes the intellectual and physical lives of its inhabitants. This, I believe, is past its glory. The other is the humanitarian liberalism which we see in Herzen, Turgenev, Milyukov and a flock of other Russian thinkers who consistently placed the cause of individual freedom above all others. The Communists have given enormous encouragement to the reading and teaching of both the 19th century liberal democratic thinkers and the forerunners of Communist totalitarianism.

February 5 : I live at the American House. In it many of the American bachelors live, eat and entertain, not royally but adequately. Our two waitresses who, not by coincidence, are both attractive, young and divorced, each earn 900 roubles a month, which is a fairly good wage, even in Moscow, and they

work every other day. Moreover, they eat here when they
work, so actually they are significantly better off than the
average Russian laborer who earns approximately 700 roubles
a month and must work six days a week for his money. Of
course, these girls are most likely "grade-A" females who have
been carefully screened and briefed as to their duties, which
go beyond serving, and may include on occasion snooping
through personal papers and befriending Russian-speaking
Americans with a view to getting information or forcing them
into positions where they can be compromised. Undoubtedly
for these extra "chores" they are additionally compensated.
One of them mentioned to me that she worked as a waitress
for three years in a decent cafeteria but she quit, she said, because she was pestered by "hooligans" (who seem to be a major
sociological problem in Russia). Young people, she said, are
fascinated by Western dress, and they love jazz, which is the
rage here and can be heard nightly over the Voice of America
English-language broadcasts.

February 6 : I met a middle-aged man who is a television engineer. Normally, he makes 2800 roubles a month, which puts
him in the middle class. His wife doesn't work, because, he
says, she enjoys "just being a housewife." He was quick to add
that he sees nothing wrong with women working, but "they
don't like to." He said that television first hit Russia in 1936,
and that he was one of the first engineers involved in this new
enterprise, which is growing rapidly and fascinating Moscovites. Today scores of them flocked around a new set in ad-
miration and delight at GUM. Their 8 by 9 screen sells for
about 2500 roubles, which at our rate of exchange is $625.

My friend's educational preparation included 7 years of
elementary school, because he's from the country, not a large

city, where 10 years is mandatory. Then 5 years in a *tekhnika*, a kind of trade school, where he studied German, which he has almost forgotten. In any case he said there were now two television stations in Moscow, but the studios plan to open another in May. All told, he counted 27 television stations throughout the Soviet Union, with one in each of the leading cities, like Leningrad, Odessa, Kiev, Kharkov, Smolensk, and Rostov. He did not mention any others, though he did say that Moscow was the only city with more than one station. Their television is fairly good, their productions more than adequate. Programs are heavily weighted towards ballet, plays, and concerts. There are no commercials. Color television, he said, is the next step. He admired what he has heard of American color television. Moscow television, by the way, has a 200-kilometer radius.

February 7 : Three young couples were being married today in a small church located in the Frunzski section of Moscow. I accidentally came across the church and entered to see if it was a functioning one. So many of them aren't. The father of one of the brides became visibly upset when I entered, but the janitor told him that it was all right for a foreigner to be present. Only then was I permitted to remain for the ceremony.

February 8 : On the day that Kruglov was dismissed as head of the MVD, I was driving home in a taxi late at night. The trip was long, and I spoke with the driver, who works in a cement factory during the day and uses a personal car for taxiing purposes after hours to supplement his income, which he finds inadequate. We discussed the dismissal of Kruglov, and I was surprised to discover that he had only vaguely heard of the former MVD chieftain and that the news of his dismissal did in no way affect him. He said that these were affairs of state and that he did not wish to know very much about them. "That is the government's concern, not mine," he said. I got the impression, not only from this conversation but from others as well, that there are two worlds in Moscow. One is for the common people, the other for the government; and it appears that so long as the government does not interfere too much with the daily lives of the people, the people are delighted to leave political affairs to others, to those who represent the other world of policy and decision. To an American, there appears to be political apathy, bred either of fear or indifference—or both.

February 15 : Everyone in Moscow but the Moscovites is buzzing over Khrushchev's speech yesterday at the opening of the Twentieth Congress of the Communist Party. It now appears that he is definitely running the country. How long, I wonder, will this fiction of collective leadership prevail?

His speech indicates that Stalinism is dead only in name. Stalin's policies, now more insidious because they are cloaked in a smile, are being followed, but his name is rarely if ever mentioned. Khrushchev's lack of emphasis on Stalin appears to give an official inauguration to a possible policy of downgrading the former dictator of Russia.

February 16 : An American friend told me that she accidentally found a name, S. I. Stalina, on a poster in the Moscow University building near the Lenin library. That name always evokes curiosity, and we decided to drop in at the University and learn a little more about it.

On the second floor of a building devoted to journalism, anthropology, and philology, we found the following small, hand-written notice, stuck on a bulletin board: "The *Kafedra* of Soviet Literature announces the start of a special course— the theme: Role of the People in the Soviet Novel, Lecturer: Candidate of Philological Sciences, S. I. Stalina." On the next floor, figuring somewhat more prominently on another sloppy bulletin board, we read: *"Notice:* in the second semester starts the special course of Candidate of Philological Sciences, Stalina, S.I. on the theme: Role of the People in the Soviet Novel. Registration for this course held in Literary Office."

In this casual offhand manner, the news was released that Stalin's daughter is very much alive and apparently a promising scholar in philology. Oddly, a huge picture was above the entrance to the room where Stalina's lectures are delivered every Monday afternoon at 3, a picture of the late dictator of the Soviet Union. I asked a Russian girl with Oriental features if she knew anything about the course, but all she answered was that it should be very good, and she said, "Stalina! My, how interesting," and then left. There was no doubt about who Stalina was.

February 17 : I just returned from the famous Moscow Art Theater (the MHAT, as they call it here) where I saw a brilliant performance of "Three Sisters," the turn-of-the-century classic by Anton Chekhov. There can be no doubt that these people can stage a theatrical production equal to the best in the world. I have been told that their productions of Western works are poor, but their efforts on behalf of their own artistic heritage are sensitive and fine.

This is Chekhov with new depths. The Russians feel (and feeling is so very much a part of comprehension in this

country) almost with a sixth sense what Chekhov really
wanted to say, and they say it for him in a way magnificently
new to me.

The theater is old. The seats are straight and wooden and
uncomfortably close together. But there is the smell of history
in this theater, for here Chekhov himself watched his early
productions and helped in the staging and producing. Here,
Stanislavsky and Nemirovitch-Danchenko first unleashed a
new style of drama, though Chekhov was always Chekhov,
not Stanislavsky. Here, too, in the small, antiquated boxes,
set back from either side of a broad stage, sat leading officials
of pre- and post-revolutionary Russia.

Interestingly enough, sections of the theater are reserved
not only for the intermission walks and promenades in which
the Russians love to participate but also for a museum. In
one corner was a copy of the program for the first performance
of the "Chaika" (*The Sea Gull*), another Chekhov classic. On
December 17, 1899, at 7:30 P.M., "Chaika" was first seen. Its
producers were Stanislavsky (who also played Boris Trigorin)
and Nemirovitch-Danchenko (whose son produced the performance I saw this evening).

One observation on the Soviet audience. It is not true, as
many have said, that mostly young people attend the theater.
Both young and old Russians do, and all of them love their
theater. They sat in rapt attention during the performance,
which every now and then was interrupted by the enthusiasm
of a fan who shouted "hoorah, hoorah." This evening the
entire audience rushed toward the stage after the performance and applauded loudly, wildly, happily. There is not the
sophistication in the Soviet theater audience which one finds
on Shubert Alley. What Russians feel inside finds expression
in their cheers, applause, and hoorahs. Many men were crying and applauding and laughing all at the same time. The

mixture of these emotions, so clearly expressed on their faces,
was almost the epitome of the Chekhovian mood. It's a happy
thought that these people worship their literary masters so
much, for many of them carry the message not of the monolith of Communism but of the spirit of freedom.

February 18 : Moscow is a rather strange city from a number of viewpoints. It's perhaps the only major city in the
world where roosters crow their familiar tune all day long.
The tune from the Twentieth Congress is not as familiar as
the rooster's, though, and it appears that the Congress has
indeed launched a crusade against Stalin. Probably the high-
light of today's activities is the heightened attack upon Stalin
and his heritage of "personal leadership." Mikoyan in his
address on Thursday and Malenkov in his today both unleashed severe attacks upon Stalin but on only one occasion
did they ever mention Stalin by name. Instead, they indicated
that since Lenin's death, the principle of collective leadership
has been violated. A "cult" of personal leadership has developed, and it is against the memory of this cult that the present
day leadership rationalizes the unresolved dilemmas of Soviet
society.

The attack upon Stalin started with his death, when Khrushchev, Malenkov, Kaganovitch and Bulganin advanced a
"Leninist" program of collective leadership. Now editorial
after editorial is pounded out to justify the present leadership,
which they claim is "collective," over past leadership principles of the "personality cult." Yet, as the present leadership
pushes the collective leadership principle further and further
before the mass consciousness of the people, the name of
Khrushchev appears more and more. On the coattails of a
vigorous propaganda campaign against a personality cult rides

the small but growing and powerful personality cult of
Khrushchev and his Central Committee. There is something
in the air in Moscow, and it would not be surprising for a big
story to break soon. Big, sensational, explosive, and terribly
significant. The groundwork is being laid.

Yet, despite this new campaign there stands an enormous
monument to the memory of this "tyrant." Side by side with
Lenin, who they now claim believed in collective leadership,
lies Stalin, who they claim believed in personal leadership.
I saw their tomb today. It is in Red Square, and Red Square
is enormous. A long, snakelike line slowly advanced in big
moving semicircles towards the Mausoleum. A strong Siberian
wind, bringing temperatures of 35 below zero, cut from behind the Lenin Museum through Red Square, and out
towards that loud contradiction in architecture, the Church
of St. Basil's. Ivan the Terrible built it in 1552, after his victory over the Tatars at Kazan, as a place of popular worship.
Now the Mausoleum serves for popular worship, and in the
sub-zero cold thousands of people lined up today, as they do
most every other day, to see their two dead leaders—both
theoretically dedicated to the eradication of the differences in
wealth between peoples—lie in a state of Oriental splendor.
Two spotlights cast an unnatural yellow on their waxen faces.
No picture-taking is permitted, and the line must keep moving. If this leadership wishes to destroy the cult of personal
leadership, it had better do away with Stalin, the villain in this
new Soviet drama, because he lies not more than two feet from
Lenin, the hero of this drama. Lying there, Lenin and Stalin
represent a sight which, at least to this Westerner, is at once
awesome and thoroughly revolting.

Across from the Mausoleum is the State Universal Shop,
GUM, where thousands of Russians rush and push seemingly
unaware of Lenin and Stalin across the Square. They are in-

terested in goods to buy, food to eat, and people to meet.
They don't seem in the least interested in politics, meta-
physics, or philosophy. They give every appearance of a
materialistic, grasping community, interested fundamentally
in problems here-and-now. It should be kept in mind that the
average worker in Moscow makes 700 roubles a month. Our
waitress' father drives a truck; he earns 1200 roubles a month.
It is very expensive to live in Moscow, for a Russian as well
as a foreigner, but there are many people here who can afford
these high prices, because Communist propaganda notwithstanding, there is a very definite financial aristocracy in this
town. Alongside a Russian woman in mink one sees a Russian woman in a threadbare shawl.

February 19 : A beautiful, clear, bright Sunday sun shone
through my window this morning, and for the first time in
three weeks the haze which rests on this city lifted. A group
of ten of us drove to the American *dacha,* or summer home,
which is located about 45 minutes outside of Moscow on the
road to Zagorsk. When once you leave the immediate heart of
the city, you enter Russia, for the heart of Moscow, big and
blaring, is not Russia. Russia, it seems, is the small wooden
cottages, or huts, which sit at different points of a wide expanse of white, snow-covered plains, which seem to run with
your eye towards a grey sky in the distance, where sky and
snow melt in a mist. Before a roaring fire and over roasted
weenies, I told about the conversation I had yesterday with
a teacher from the Virgin Lands. I was standing in the Metro,
staring off into space, thinking about nothing special, when
I felt a tap on my shoulder. A happy-faced young man, no
more than 25, asked me in halting but grammatically perfect
English what part of Britain I came from. I told him I came

from the United States. He smiled, and told me that he had studied English and American literature in Moscow University for four years and that he is now teaching these courses in the new Virgin Lands. He told me he had come to Moscow for a month to complete a series of examinations which would result in his getting an M.A., which he confessed he wanted so he could feel secure on his job. (This striving for security seems to be consistent with a growing bourgeois theme in this society. Yesterday I saw a peasant smoking a cigarette in a cigarette holder!)

When he told me that he came from the Virgin Lands, he could not restrain a big grin as he added that there were no virgins in the Virgin Lands.

February 26 : Perhaps the overall significance of this Congress—now in its last week—is a movement away from Stalin and back to Lenin.

There appears to be a growing sense of alarm and frustration about the viability of the Communist dogma. Most Russian intellectuals today who stop to think about their political orientation seem to find the ideology vacant and empty, without any deep significant meaning, and they have fallen back upon Lenin, because they have nothing else. When Stalin was alive, his power was so complete that every word he uttered became a "creative" addition to the ideology. Khrushchev is not the oracle for Communism that Stalin was, and neither is the entire collective leadership of the Central Committee.

If they were to adopt anything outside the basic Communist doctrine, the change would be too radical. Moreover, I do not believe that the leaders are consciously falling back on Lenin as a last resort. Rather, they fall back on Lenin be-

cause within the framework of their present political orientation as well as for the sake of a continued attachment to more
viable organizations like the Asian Communist Parties, they
are unable to seek out and find an alternative political belief.
This sense of frustration will grow as they fall harder and
harder on Lenin, because to a certain extent the Lenin of
1919 whom they have suddenly resurrected was too utopian,
too 19th-centuryish, for existing conditions in this country.
Money and the role of money are crucial cornerstones of this
country's newly founded bourgeois beliefs.

Today, I asked an "information bureau" (a small booth
found on most street corners) where a certain restaurant was,
and I had to pay 30 kopecks for the information that it was
just around the corner. This is a society which economically
is money-conscious, and not socialist-conscious. And the realities of today's Russia conflict shatteringly with the dreams of
1919 Leninism. There would have to be another revolution
to reduce the powerful, rich bureaucracy to the level of common people, the people who sweep the streets. This difference between reality and theory may soon push the intellectual into a slow, growing, conscious effort to find a new
orientation.

February 27 : I went to the Bolshoi Theater last night to see
the third performance of a new Soviet ballet called "Lauren-
cia." *Look* magazine's correspondent Edmond Stevens said
that in many ways it was typical of Soviet-inspired ballet, and
his voice had a weary hum about it. I felt the same way, weary,
for this was a loud and vulgar presentation. The plot centers
on the activities of a small Spanish community. In the hills
overlooking this village stands a castle housing a degenerate,

sex-crazed prince and his equally degenerate, sex-crazed guards. Every now and then, they dash off into the woods with unwilling peasant girls, staggering and falling and behaving poorly. One of these peasant girls, danced by a brilliant artist, Plesetskaya (possibly the greatest ballet dancer in the world after Ulanova) is dragged off to the castle on her wedding night for some physical indoctrination.

But Plesetskaya is not disheartened by the rape. On the contrary, she summons the strength to wake the town into a frenzy of hatred, and she leads the people to the castle. The prince is killed, and the palace is burned, and the finale depicts the entire cast, the epitome of the popular masses, marching, not dancing (by this time, in such a delight of revolutionary fervor, they forget that they are on the stage of the Bolshoi to do a ballet), from one corner of the huge stage to the other, arms outstretched, then upraised, in a full, loud, blaring spectacle of mass strength. The people win, and I couldn't help but wonder amidst the general applause which almost ripped the house down whether the people might not eventually win in Russia too.

February 28 : A friend and I dropped in on the Ministry of Foreign Literature. We wanted to get a feel of what was being translated into English these days for consumption by University and Institute students. No sooner had we entered than an army of little, bespectacled librarians descended upon us to ask for identification and my *dokumenti*. I told them that I had forgotten my documents.

They asked what I was doing in Moscow, and I told them that I was an attaché at the Embassy, an American student working on a thesis, and that out of curiosity I simply wanted to see what was being read and what had been translated into English. Anyway, they made me fill out a card and then permitted me to browse around.

I discovered that there really is no pattern to their taste in Western books. In my quest for logic, I struck a stone wall. For example, they carry Alfred Meyer's book on Marxism, by no means a leftist biased interpretation of the movement—in fact, the second half of the book is a depiction of Marxism in decay—yet they have not a single book for general publication by E. H. Carr, whose generally deterministic view of the Bolshevik march to power falls more into line with accepted Communist dogma. Trevelyan is in full supply, but they have very little of Toynbee.

They have an extensive collection of American literature. All of Hemingway, Steinbeck, Dos Passos, and of course, the "greatest, most progressive" writer of them all, Howard Fast. William Steig, the cartoonist, is complete. Lots of Thurber, but no Perelman. Vol. 1 of Karpovich-Vernadsky is there, on ancient Russia, but their account of Kievan Russia and the Mongol period is absent. *The U.S.S.R. and the Capitalist Countries* published in 1938 under the authorship of L. Mekhlis, Y. Varga, and V. Karpinsky has been there since 1939, though Varga was in disgrace for many years after the war. Merle Fainsod's first book on *Government and the American Economy* is available, but his book on *How Russia is Ruled* cannot be obtained. There is no Richard Pipes, B. Wolfe or R. Wolff, or B. Moore, but Harry Truman's first volume of *Memoirs* is read. Carlton Hayes' *History of Europe* is read, but there is not a single one of his works on nationalism. The last three works by Hans Kohn can be read—on *The Future of Austria, The Making of the Modern French Mind,* and *The Mind of Modern Russia,* but all the other works of Kohn, in which his strongly anti-Russian bias is evident, are not available. Copies of the *New York Times* for the previous six months are on file.

A slight pattern of discrimination was evident, but not one that was clear-cut and sharp. A large exhibition of Heine's works, stressing his democratic nature, was highlighted here, as elsewhere in Moscow. Marx's statement that he was the "most democratic, humanitarian German writer" of his day headlines all the exhibits.

February 29 : My waitress told me today that if I wanted to get some material for my doctoral dissertation on Uvarov, I had better go down to the Historical Library, which is a very old building located on *Starosadsky Pereulok, dom 9*. I got there at about 7:30 and found a long line of serious-looking Soviet students waiting to register for permission to use the library. This is SOP for everyone. I went to the end of the line, and within a few minutes my turn came. The librarian, an old, old woman who undoubtedly knew Tsarist Russia as well as Communist Russia, asked me my name without raising her eyes from the application form. I told her, but when she heard my accent, not the purest Russian accent this side of the Volga, she looked up, seemed very puzzled, and asked which of the people's democracies I came from. I told her I was a student from the United States. She grew cold and reserved, and moved as far into her seat, away from me, as she could.

"What university?" she asked.

"Harvard," I answered.

Her face grew a little whiter. *"Dokumenti, u vas?"* she asked.

"Yes," I answered, and showed her my *diplomaticheskaya kartochka*. This threw her completely. She didn't know what to do, and a whole crowd of students had grouped around us.

"*Tovarisch,*" she said, "come with me," and she led me through the crowd to a quiet room, crowded with exhibits on Heine, Lobachevsky, and Dostoevsky, not to mention a huge one on Red China. I waited there for fifteen minutes. The door was open, and the crowd moved in front of the open door. Soon, a brigade of four librarians moved through the crowd, into the room, and the chief librarian asked me what my subject was. I told her. She smiled.

"Why do you want to study Uvarov? Why not Lenin?"

I told her a great deal had already been written about Lenin, that I wanted to do my doctoral dissertation on Uvarov. She said, "Good!", led me to the reading room, gave me a desk and a card catalogue and asked me to select some of the books I wanted to start on. Within one hour after entering the library, I was doing research, and the material was top flight. Soon I was brought an official admittance card and was told not to be bashful, but to ask for anything I wanted. She returned my *diplomaticheskaya kartochka,* and I got down to work. One of the correspondents who has been here a long time told me that he thought I was the first member of the American Embassy, or the first American for that matter, who had obtained a card to this particular library. I am very delighted even now, as I write, even though it is late and I am very tired. My research has begun.

March 1 : Just returned from a beautiful performance of Romeo and Juliet, danced with exquisite artistry by Ulanova. I have never seen ballet like this. The staging, dramatic effects, and Ulanova's talents are incomparable. Voroshilov and Vincent Auriol occupied the seats of honor this evening, and unfortunately the audience gave them more vigorous applause than Ulanova and Zhdanov, her partner.

March 3 : This afternoon, I stopped by at the *Trest Pokho-ronovo Obsluzhivaniya* (Bureau of Records on the Dead), lo-cated on *Vetoshny Pereulok, dom* 11, just across the street from GUM, to find out where Uvarov was buried. I knew that he died in Moscow in 1855, and wanted to find out where he was buried. I discovered that there is a large monu-ment to his memory in Leningrad, and I was told that the house in which he lived might still be standing, near the Nevsky Prospekt. Afterwards, I went over to the State Mu-seum, which is a large red building, standing directly oppo-site the fantastic (still fantastic and never tiring) St. Basil's Church. The woman in charge of the historical materials sec-tion of the museum—a very old woman who spoke better French than I Russian (all women in museums seem to be very old)—referred me to Hall 30 where Uvarov's famous in-struction for Nicholas I on "autocracy, nationalism and orthodoxy" sits, under glass cover, for all modern and "pro-gressive" Soviet youth to smirk at—and they do, as they pass on these organized tours of forced culture.

When I returned to my French-speaking Russian museum keeper, I asked her if it were possible to see all the material on Uvarov. I told her that I was an American student, and she was very cordial. She referred me to the *ucherny sekretar,* or learned secretary, who told me that she had a great deal of material on Uvarov's son, who was an outstanding arche-ologist, but that on Uvarov, the father, she had practically nothing. I was disappointed, and I told her—hoping that it would get me somewhere—that I had come a long way for this information, all the way from Harvard, and that if I returned without material, I couldn't complete my doctoral thesis. As soon as I mentioned doctorate, she suddenly became very solicitous, asked me how long I've studied, what subjects, whv Uvarov, did I like Harvard.

We got along well; in fact, we spoke for better than an hour, and when I left she gave me her assurance that she would do everything in her power to see that I gained admission into the historical archives to work on this dissertation. She told me to check back with her on Wednesday for the answer. If I get in, I am sure that I shall have a great deal of material to work with and that I will certainly be establishing some kind of precedent. When I told a correspondent friend of mine that I had gotten this far in my quest for admission into the archives, he could only lean further back in his soft chair, draw hard on his pipe, and utter that three years ago, it would have been impossible to have gotten through to the *ucherny sekretar*.

March 6 : On Sunday, I went through the Lenin Museum, which is an enormous pink-faced building of post-revolutionary vintage located between Revolution Square and Sverdlov Square. There are over twenty *zals* or halls devoted to exhibiting Lenin's life, and I think it is the only place in Moscow which is free. Upon entering, everyone checks his coat, hat and rubbers at either one of two huge checking stands near the main entrance. After ten to twenty people have grouped in the main hall, a tour guide approaches, generally a woman in her thirties, or so the ages ran that day, to begin the tour.

The picture one gets of Lenin clings pretty much to preestablished truth. Lenin was a great revolutionary from the day of his birth. He read Marx instead of the Russian comics. He was courageous, brave, and terribly Russian. Beset on all sides by imperialist hounds, he had few people whom he could trust. They were generally those Communists whom

Stalin decided, probably in the thirties when the Museum was opened, that Lenin could trust back at the turn of the century. In the last ten *zals,* Stalin plays more and more of a role, until finally, he moves to a position of power, as Lenin's disciple-in-arms, and compatriot.

I was especially interested to see how the guide would handle Stalin, but the official tour stopped to all intents and purposes in 1922, when Lenin suffered his first stroke. The guide left us at this point and we were permitted to wander through the remaining *zals* by ourselves. Not by coincidence, in these *zals* Stalin played as prominent a role as Lenin, and in the last three or four *zals,* the dominant role—the time when Lenin was completely incapacitated and lived in Gorki while Stalin ran things from Moscow as Secretary General of the Communist Party. Probably the guide didn't wish to speak about Stalin too much, if at all. In the earlier *zals,* if Stalin was mentioned, it was always with other names, such as Kirov, Molotov, Kalinin and Kaganovich. Frequently, our guide had simply drifted past portraits where Stalin and Lenin were depicted as revolutionary coworkers even back in 1905-1907. She did not mention a word about him. There could be no doubt that the guide was making a very deliberate effort to avoid references to Stalin. Her reticence about mentioning even his name gives a good indication of the ways and means employed here to prime citizens on political drifts. In fact, it may be that within the next few months the Museum will be "redecorated" in such a way that Stalin's role in the pre-revolutionary movement and his associations with Lenin (who is now the holy-of-holies) become quite casual and secondary. Moreover, it's possible that Trotsky, the impetuous and flamboyant Trotsky, who has been denied his place in the Communist hierarchy by a jealous and psychotic Stalin, will be brought out of mothballs and his role as organizer of the Red Army be at least mentioned. Even other old "purged" Bolsheviks, like Kamenev and Zinoviev, Bukharin and Rykov, Tomsky and Piatakov may be resurrected.

Certainly, from the speeches of Mikoyan and Pankratova at the Twentieth Party Congress, there is some indication that the history of Russia over the past thirty years will be rewritten again.

March 8 : Today was the day I was to find out whether I am to get into the archives. The answer was disappointment. The *ucherny sekretar* joined the Soviet pass-the-buck parade. She told me that she herself could not grant permission to enter the archives. Secondly, she mentioned that she is not at all certain about the regulations. Finally, she didn't really know where material on Uvarov would be housed. She then suggested as a final gesture that I might try the Historical Library. I told her that I knew about the Historical Library—that, in fact, I was a member of that library—but I was interested more in straight source material. I wanted to see his letters, his papers, his home. I wanted to see Uvarov firsthand. I told her that I was most disappointed with the treatment I had been receiving.

Apparently, her heart was not made of stone; softening, she suggested I might try the Central Archives of the Soviet Union. She gave me no indication that a direct personal plea would be successful, but her tone of voice and a peculiar twinkle in her eye led me to believe that possibly I might have more success with a direct appeal than indirectly through her.

March 14 : So far Moscow has produced a record of my unsuccessful attempts to crack the wall of stubbornness and bureaucracy which seems to stand between me and Uvarov. Before I arrived, I doubt that the Soviets ever gave more than a passing nod to the former Minister of Education. His name seems to have been linked irrevocably with the reactionary reign of Nicholas I. He is regarded as a true precursor of Pobedonotsev and Leontiev. He did little, it would appear, of any merit. The Soviets even ignore that under his administration significant advances were recorded in the field of Russian education. I have spent many days and nights roaming the bookstores of Moscow in search of material. To date, my efforts have been crowned with a remarkable lack of success. I got two books on *an* Uvarov, but this Uvarov turned out to be his son who, under his father's direction, became the most brilliant Russian archeologist of the 19th century. The manuscripts cost a great deal (as everything does here in Moscow—at our rate of exchange a chocolate bar last night at the theater cost $4.50) but they resulted in frustration. Nothing on the father at all.

I study at the Historical Museum, but here too the material is adequate only for a college term paper. So with frustration welling up within me and with the knowledge that I have already been in Moscow close to two months, I decided that today, fresh from four hours of translating an especially dull *Pravda* article for the Embassy, I would make an effort to crack the famous Central State Archives. Even under the Tsars, this was an impossible task. Under the Soviets, it would be equivalent to, say, breaking into the Chase National Bank, or better still, Brink's. And because Brink's once was broken into, I thought that perhaps the Archives might too.

It was not just crazy nerve, however, which prompted me to adopt this course. In a sense I felt justified because of two or three public statements and editorials which have appeared of late in the Soviet press. For one thing, a leading editorial in the magazine, *Partinaya Zhizn* called for "unveiling the dusty shelves of the state archives to the clean light of scholarship."

Moreover, Education Minister Pankratova's speech and sections of Mikoyan's and Khrushchev's at the Congress seemed to indicate that history was going to be set right and I wanted to get in on the ground floor before the rush with my man Uvarov, who I reasoned could not possibly be as vicious a monster as, say, Trotsky. In this frame of mind, I set out for the Central State Archives, located on *Bolshaya Pirogovskaya Ulitsa.*

It turned out to be a large, very Soviet-looking building in the grandiose Stalin tradition. (I felt it somewhat ironic that the Archives building, built in Stalin's taste, would be unveiled in a sense for his destruction.) I may have appeared brave and self-confident, as I opened the heavy metal door and strode quickly to the main desk, but my stomach was doing strange somersaults. I was plain frightened; and when the young guard who stood beside the desk informed me, after I had asked him if this were the Central State Archives, that this was the MVD, I died quietly inside, though I managed to maintain—I think—an external appearance of composure. I had heard that two or three years ago, this might have been grounds for arrest.

But, I tried to look brave as I asked the next natural question: If this isn't the Central State Archives, where are they? He asked me why I wanted to know, and I explained to him that I was very much interested in writing a biography of Uvarov and that I had been informed that the Central State Archives had a wealth of material on him. He told me that in that case I could do research there, if I got a *propusk,* or a pass, and I could get a *propusk* right around the corner. I felt encouraged, and I hurried off to the *propusk* desk.

There I once again explained the purpose of my visit to another guard, who asked me politely to wait in the next room for a moment. I did, in a dark, depressing chamber. Five minutes later, a head librarian or archivist came into the room. She was a large woman, in the Russian style, with thick rectangular glasses and a pleasant smile. I explained to her that I wished to do research on Uvarov. She asked why Uvarov when I could do a good biography of Lenin. I told her that many people have already written about Lenin, that many still would write about him; moreover, I added, I was more interested in pre-revolutionary Russia, and since I hoped to be a teacher one day, I was interested in a man with very different pedogogical views from mine. She answered that though she disagreed with my choice of a topic, she saw no reason why I could not be granted a *propusk*. I thought I'd scream; I felt that I had cracked the Archives, on one of those flukes which got me a card into the Historical Library. I was thrilled!

As the librarian was about to grant the guard permission to fill out a *propusk,* she asked me where I was from. I told her the United States. And the poor woman's jaw dropped. Regaining her composure with great effort, she told me to wait there for a moment. She stopped and whispered to the guard to watch me, but I overheard her. I had a fleeting impulse to run from the waiting chamber into the corridor, through the door, and towards the Embassy, but the guard simply looked at me, and I realized that I had better just wait. I did.

Ten minutes later, a tall, rough-looking man approached me, shook hands, and once again asked me what I wanted. I repeated for him what I had told the librarian, the second guard, and the first guard. I wanted to do research on Uvarov. He told me that there has been a regulation in effect since

1948 requiring all foreigners who wished to do research there
to send an official request (from the Embassy to which they're
attached) to the Ministry of Foreign Affairs. If the MFA
looked favorably upon the request, the MVD would be informed, since the Central State Archives are under the direct
control of the MVD. I asked him when he thought I could
start my research. He politely, but more firmly, repeated
what he had said once. I decided not to delay, and I set straight
off for the Embassy to see our First Secretary.

On the way I could not get over the fact that (1) I was not
arrested, which I might have been three years ago; that (2)
if I were not an American,—I might be doing research right
now at the Archives. I was flattered at the progress in my
spoken Russian (the librarian had assumed that I was a Soviet
citizen, or at least a "proud" member of one of the satellites).
Finally, if I should gain admittance to the Archives, it would
be a real coup. Very few get into the Archives. This was a by-
law under the Czars, and the Communists have not been
averse to following some Czarist examples. It should be a good
gauge, I felt, for measuring the extent of the easing-up which
the country has been experiencing these last two or three
years. I arrived at the Embassy and told the First Secretary
exactly what had happened. He seemed very interested and he
told me that he would talk to the Ambassador about this request personally and see what could be done.

March 16 : I had been told that the only Jewish synagogue
in Moscow was located on *Bolshoi Spasoglinishky Pereulok,*
a small street located about five minutes from Nogina Square,
which in turn is located about ten minutes from the Kremlin. I decided to visit the synagogue. I wanted to attend
a Russian Jewish service and I wanted to speak with Russian

Jews. I took the Metro at the Gorki Park stop and traveled four stops to Derzhinsky Square, named after the first head of the MVD.

The trip took about ten minutes, and I had time to reflect on the plight of the Russian Jews. I thought about stories I had heard about the situation at the turn of the century. The Tsar had under his dominion about 4,000,000 Jews, which was about 4,000,000 too many for his taste. Some Russians and Ukrainians felt the same way, and they organized clubs, whose purpose it was to cleanse Russia of all harmful influences, like liberalism, progress and Jews. Many pogroms took place, and Jews were killed by the thousands. Many, in protest against the prejudice, joined liberal organizations; some even revolutionary organizations. Not all were dedicated to change. Some, still clinging to their old communal beliefs, wanted to be left alone and to have as little to do with *goyim* (gentiles) as possible. In a sense, they were reactionaries; they opposed efforts for change, because in the efforts, they saw more pogroms and hardships and deaths, and they wanted none of these things. Then, the revolution occurred, and suddenly in the flush of red victory many extremist Jews found themselves in positions of authority. Trotsky, Zinoviev, Kamenev, Rykov, and the list grows. Stalin fixed himself in power, and through an odd series of events, some connected directly to Stalin, others to impersonal historical movements and circumstances, Jews were quietly removed from positions of prominence. The Nazi-Soviet Pact was a signal for Molotov to take over from the Jewish Litvinov. Two to three million Jews were killed in Russia during the war. Most of them were not in uniform.

Then, the war was over, and people the world over wanted peace and a return to normalcy. But Stalin was not normal. In 1948-1949, a campaign against the "homeless cosmopolitan" broke out viciously and hard, and invariably the "homeless cosmopolitan" had a name similar to Goldberg or Schwartz. Cartoons which would have made Hitler proud appeared in the Soviet journals. Anti-semitism, an old disease in Western Russia, which had been waiting to erupt for many years, broke out, and the consequences were ugly.

Meanwhile, Jews in Russia were flocking to the synagogues, and one Passover soon after the founding of the infant state of Israel, Bess Meir, then Israeli Ambassador to the Soviet Union, appeared at the Moscow synagogue, and close to 300,000 or 400,000 Jews, the entire Jewish population of Moscow, swarmed *Bolshoi Spasoglinishky Pereulok* to see her and sing the praises of Israel. To Stalin, this was heresy, for this was a foreign allegiance. Soon after, the campaign was intensified. Stalin's life drew to a mysterious close, but before he died, he set the stage for what might have been a bloodbath of not only Jewish but even Orthodox blood, even Communist blood. Fantastic charges were made against "Jewish doctors" who planned to take the lives through medical "treatment" of leading Soviet officials. Even Zhdanov, Stalin's closest associate before he died in 1948 and the Communist most closely associated with the anti-cosmopolitan campaign, was said to have been killed by these "Jewish doctors." Harrison Salisbury, the *New York Times* correspondent in Moscow at the time, says the streets were quiet and slaughter was in the air. It smelled blood, as the Russians might say. But Stalin died on March 6 and, soon after, the "doctors' plot" was denounced as a fabrication.

With these thoughts, I traveled to Derzhinsky Square, walked south down the *Serova Prospekt,* made a left turn on *Maroseyka Ulitsa,* then took the first right, which is *Bolshoi Spasoglinishky Pereulok.* The streets were icy. It was getting dark and people were rushing somewhere, and I was walking toward a Jewish synagogue in Moscow. It all seemed very much like a dream. I walked down the curving, dark street, looking from one side to the other, but before I knew it I had come to the end of the block, and I still hadn't spotted the temple. I walked back. Still no luck. I knew it had to be on this street, and so I walked back a third time.

It was then that I noticed an old building, which looked like a Greek temple, with large pilastered columns, six of them. It was dark by this time, and the street was very quiet. I could see no lights in the temple, and it looked as if no one was there. I walked up the eight steps of broken concrete and noticed, right above a center door which was locked, some Hebrew letters. A small door to the left was partially open, and I entered what I now felt certain was the synagogue. The hallway was grey and musty.

An old, old lady saw me enter, and she approached me and asked if I wished to pray. I told her that I did, and she took me inside the main congregation room. As soon as she opened the door for me, I heard the melodic chant of a Hebrew prayer, which sing-songed its way into every nook and corner of the high-ceilinged room. The congregation consisted of about fifty or sixty men, whose average age must have been about fifty-five; they were welcoming another Sabbath in the ancient Jewish tradition in the capital of world atheism. I sat down in the rear, but a man came over to me, asked me where I was from. I told him America, and he smiled warmly and led me up to the altar, got a chair for me and a *makhsa,* a prayer book, and asked to join in the service.

It didn't last long, perhaps half an hour, but it was one of the most emotionally exciting experiences of my entire life. These Jews prayed like no other Jews—or, for that matter, Christians—I have ever seen. They prayed hard, and they seemed to say each prayer as though this conceivably could

be the last time they would say that prayer. And they seemed
to speak right to God. The Cantor sang in front, on the plat-
form, but he wasn't necessary, because these people needed no
intermediary to God. They were on very good terms with the
Almighty. They had spoken to Him many times, in private,
in public, and they spoke to Him again, passionately, deeply,
warmly, and with total dedication. When the ceremony was
over, I realized that I had tears in my eyes, and I couldn't
help it. I listened to them wish one another a happy Sabbath,
and I joined in and wished people to my right and left a happy
Sabbath too, and perhaps for the first time in my life, I understood what the words meant.

The President of the temple asked me later if I wished to
speak to the Rabbi, and I told him I would be very happy if
I could. I was introduced to the Rabbi, a very old man with
a long grey beard, and we spoke in Russian. He asked me
more questions than I felt I had any right to ask him. He
asked questions about the Jews in America and how they
lived. I told him as much as I could. I told him why I was in
Moscow, and I told him about Uvarov too. He seemed to disagree with my choice, and when I told him that it was my
impression that Uvarov was no lover of Jews, he smiled,
but said nothing. He told me that the synagogue was open
every day for services, and he made a special point of telling
me that next Monday, the start of another Passover, the synagogue would be packed with people, to over-flowing. I wished
him a happy Sabbath and thanked him for the opportunity of
seeing a Jewish service in Russia. These Russian Jews filed
out of the synagogue, where they all looked like Jews, into the
streets, and within one minute, they seemed to vanish into
the huddled Russian people who walked this dark, small
street.

March 19 : Dramatic charges are being launched by the Central Committee of the Communist Party against the memory and legacy of Joseph Stalin. The charges are quite specific: (1) Stalin is said to have "murdered" three-quarters of the membership of the 1934 Congress of the Communist Party; (2) he is said to have brutally slaughtered nine-tenths of the Red Army officer corps in the great purges of the thirties and thereby seriously affected the morale of the military just prior to the start of the second World War; (3) he is accused of ignoring intelligence reports from Germany and warnings from Churchill that Hitler was going to attack Russia in 1941; and finally (4) he is accused of having concocted the "doctors' plot" himself as a perverted excuse for initiating a new blood bath of the Communist Party leadership. In addition to these four specific charges, it is believed that at some time during the Twentieth Congress Khrushchev launched a vicious attack against Stalin as a man. He is believed to have called Stalin a madman, driven by a persecution mania. Further reports indicate that throughout the Soviet Union, these charges are now being discussed. 30,000,000 people are said to be involved in the discussions—in other words, all the party members, the Komsomols, and leading non-party government workers.

Apparently, these charges are taking on a nationalistic flavor. People who have recently returned from Tbilisi in Georgia have reported that riots took place there ten days ago in protest against this defamation of Stalin, a Georgian by birth. Moreover, someone who returned just yesterday said that all over the city Stalin's picture hangs, and hangs proudly and unashamedly. The Georgians are not interested in seeing Stalin, one of theirs, blasphemed, perhaps because in his downfall they see a new attack upon Georgians in general.

March 21 : I spent three hours this afternoon in search of Stalin and, if I hadn't known what he looked like, I would not have found him. For Stalin is being buried, there is no doubt. Some of his pictures have already been removed from the Tretyakov Galleries; this was reported in the press. The famous picture of Stalin with Voroshilov on the Lenin hills looking down upon Moscow has disappeared.

Today I was witness to greater political black magic. I went to the Lenin Museum again. This museum was built by Stalin for one specific reason: he wanted to prove to the Russian people that he was in a kind of direct succession to "the old man" and he had pictures painted which showed the young Stalin tutored by the older and infinitely wiser Lenin. Stalin appears time and again. Yet, throughout the entire tour, though his face stared down upon our little group and our braggart of a guide, not once was his name mentioned—not even as one of a series of revolutionaries. He simply never came up in the course of the tour, though Khrushchev did four or five times. The guide would simply avoid pictures with Stalin and Lenin. And perhaps, because Stalin's face appeared so frequently, but his name was not mentioned even once, he was the most important person on this tour. At one point, I happened to be passing *zal* 21, which has been "closed for repairs." A worker opened the door at just that moment, and I looked in. Two huge pictures of Stalin were being removed from the walls. I had the peculiar feeling that I was witnessing the rewriting of a small piece of history.

March 27 : I spoke last night with an important Western Ambassador, who made a number of guarded references to the incidents in Georgia. He mentioned that a friend of his had

been in Tbilisi during the reported "riots," but this friend
had seen no evidence of rioting. Whatever did take place was
more in the nature of an orderly demonstration of Tbilisi citizens who gathered in the streets, walked through the main
square, shouting and carrying pictures of Stalin. The former
dictator's pictures were also prominently displayed on the face
of many buildings. But this visitor's impression was certainly
not that of a riot. In fact, he told the Ambassador that he was
not really certain that something out of the ordinary had happened, because he has seen many such "sponsored" demonstrations before. This, he later found out, was the first "un-
sponsored" demonstration in many years.

March 28 : An explosive article appeared in *Pravda* today;
spread brazenly across the bottom half of the second and third
pages—the inside fold—it buried the Stalin era. The many
pictures of the former dictator, who died just over three years
ago on March 6, which still hang in the Metro stations, the
museums, the libraries, and the offices, are the lingering re-
membrances of "the personality cult." Soon, all of them will
be removed. For Stalin was hacked to death today. Sparing
praise for his fine "creative" additions to Marxism-Leninism
in the early period of his reign appeared, haltingly, throughout the article. But later in his life, the article makes clear,
he abandoned all modesty. He not only did nothing to stop
adulation; he encouraged it. Alongside the development of
this "ego-maniac" grew the Soviet state, one almost superim-
posed on the other. Soon, the State's progress was hindered by
the personality cult. Only now that the cult is being destroyed
is progress being resumed in a vigorous manner. *Pravda* continues:

"The personality cult means excessive exaltation of individual people, the endowment of them with supernatural traits and qualities, the transformation of them almost into miracle workers. At that time, Stalin won popularity, sympathy and support in the Party, and became renowned among the people. However, there gradually began to appear those traits and qualities in Stalin's practical leadership which later developed into a personality cult. . . . With the passage of time, this personality cult assumed more and more ugly forms and seriously damaged the cause. Marxism does not deny the role of outstanding people in history, the role of the leaders of the working people in guiding the revolutionary-liberation movement. The most important of these principles is *collective leadership*. The personality cult and the practice of leadership which took shape under its influence in the final period of the life and activity of J. V. Stalin, inflicted great damage. When combating the personality cult, it should be remembered that the petty bourgeois anarchist views which deny the role of the leaders and organizers of the masses are alien to Marxism-Leninism. It is also well-known that the Communist Party has upheld and still upholds the principle of one-man management in production enterprises and military affairs."

In short, Stalin was emasculated, and in his place, standing as guardian of another personality cult, is the dead Lenin, who, alive, would have despised such a cult.

March 29 : This evening I met Volodya, a thirty-year old graduate student at the History Institute in Moscow. A major in English and American history, Volodya speaks English fluently and is now preparing a master's thesis on Franco-Russian relations before World War II. He is about 5′ 10″ tall, slight of build, with a longish face and aquiline nose, dark, intense eyes and an open smile. I had the feeling he might be an Armenian—he simply did not look Russian—but he would only say that he was born in Moscow. Many times, during our conversation, I got the impression he was a member of the Communist Party; in any case, he knew Communist dogma very well, and he defended the Communist position, through every twist and turn, with beautiful facility.

We met by rather odd circumstance—I was introduced to Volodya by a cab driver—and we walked up and down Gorki Street for close to two hours. We talked about Ulanova, whom he adores, and the United Nations, at which he scoffs. A stiff wind reduced our appreciation of the "Broadway" (Gorki Street is sometimes referred to as Broadway by Russia's young set) crowds, and we decided to have a meal at the Grand Hotel.

The food and the conversation were wonderful. A small Russian band tried its hand at playing American popular music, which the Russians call "jazz," and a chubby woman, who might have worked on a collective farm last week, attempted to sing the blues. Both were highly unsuccessful, but the Russians seemed to love both band and singer.

Volodya, though, seemed as unimpressed as I. He asked about my reactions to Russia, and I ticked off some generalities about an American in Moscow. I was doing most of the talking, Volodya most of the listening, but in his quiet, confident way, he impressed me. He is a complete intellectual, a product of the Soviet educational system. He speaks English, French, and German fluently. He is intensely interested in every period of history, and his familiarity with Uvarov astonished me. He knew details of British history which might surprise Churchill. He went into some details of President Grant's administration, which were more than mildly embarrassing.

He revealed that he had been a member of the Soviet UN delegation about five years ago, that he had been in New York for seven months. He wanted to attend the Conference of Historians in Rome last year but couldn't. He spoke very highly of Harvard Professor Langer's *The Undeclared War*. Volodya said that the Director of the Institute of History corresponds with many American historians.

Volodya was very interested in a possible exchange of scholars and students, "who have common interests which rise above politics" and on the basis of which "mutual trust and understanding could be developed." He said: "The foreign policy of the Soviet Union has not changed at all.

"We have always favored peace," Volodya said. "I think that America's policy has changed. We were so friendly during the war. Then President Truman changed the atmosphere, and relations were poisoned between our countries."

"You're right," I answered, "you're right. Our foreign policy has changed. But then, we were growing more and more disillusioned with Russian policy, and we decided that we had to stop the spread of Communism." I stated that America wanted the world to remain free and not to be subjected to a Communist strait-jacket.

Volodya then suggested that I eat my soup, which was getting cold.

After a while, I asked Volodya what history meant to him. He said: "History is the examination of the objective facts of a given period in order to understand the vast forces at play." I agreed. I then asked him if I might ask a further question. I suggested the possibility of a student trying to do a piece of objective scholarship on the 1905 Russian Revolution. The student would have to have available all the documents relating to this period. Volodya agreed. I continued: "Trotsky was a very prominent man in the Petersburg Soviet in 1905; in fact, for a while, he was Chairman of the Soviet. Could this hypothetical student read Trotsky's speeches?"

Volodya did not answer. He seemed for the moment to be listening to the band play "Love and Marriage," which is a big favorite in Russia. His eyes wandered restlessly over the crowd of vodka-drinking Russians. "Volodya," I said, trying to break into his reverie, "Volodya, you know that Trotsky was a very important figure in the Russian revolution. Could an average student study Trotsky, or his influence upon Soviet Russia? And, if not, can you still claim that Soviet scholarship is objective scholarship?"

Volodya still could not look me in the eye, and, when he did, his eyes were no longer hard and defiant. They were soft and apologetic. "You've raised an interesting question,—one which we have been raising too." Volodya obviously did not wish to continue this trend in our discussion, but his smiling refusal offered clear proof that Soviet scholarship in many critical ways still remains the handmaiden of the Communist Party.

When Volodya did resume the discussion, he said: "The Russians do not want war. This I swear. They hate war." I answered that the American people also do not want war. But, I added, that until we were convinced that the Soviet leaders do not want war, we would remain strong to repel any sudden Communist attack. Volodya protested that "B" and "K" had made many friendly overtures in the past three years. "These are sincere, friendly gestures." I told Volodya that it is true that Soviet Russia has changed her manner, but I was still unconvinced that she had changed her goals.

April 2 : This past weekend I went on a short trip about 100 miles northeast of Moscow to Vladimir, Suzdal and Bogolyubov with some Embassy personnel and an American correspondent. We left on the 12:40 A.M. train and arrived in Vladimir at 6:30 Saturday morning.

The station is set in a valley, and it is the ugliest part of town. A long, sharply-bending road leads from the station up the hill. To the left on the summit stands the old Kremlin of Vladimir, and from its walls the Russian prince had his men shoot arrows into the approaching, slant-eyed Mongols from the east in 1238. In those days, Vladimir was the capital of Russia. Kiev was in sharp decline, and the new cities of the northeast were in the ascendency. The son of Vladimir Monomakh, Yuri Dolgoruki, started Vladimir on its road to glory in 1132, and from then on it was the outstanding city of Russia, rivalled only by Rostov and Suzdal, until 1238, when Batu's hordes put an end to the glory of the Vladimir principality—indeed, as they put an end to the glory of old Russia. Only with the growth of Moscow, a century and one-half later, did Russia once again begin to regain its former prestige and power. Now, Vladimir is blessed only with haunting symbols of its former greatness, and as we walked past the white walls of the old Kremlin, just as the sun rose to throw golden shafts over the top of the wall, on our way to the new Vladimir hotel (finished only in January of this year), we were all amazed at the decay. Vladimir is not a one-horse town but it is obviously not the capital it once was.

After breakfast, when the sun dropped behind a black cloud, Vladimir wore a frown and seemed most unhappy. But a friend and I left the others and we dashed off to see Vladimir before it fully awoke. As we walked into the quiet main street (*Ulitsa Frunze*), we had the feeling we were sneaking up on a sleeping, old woman, and we almost walked on tip toes not to disturb her. Our first discovery came when we tried to see the interior of the Kremlin. A guard stood at the door, which is not unusual, and told us firmly that we could not go in to see the interior part. We asked him why. He said that there was nothing to see. I asked him if it were possible for us to see nothing, but he didn't see any humor in that comment and insisted that we leave. After we did, it struck me suddenly that he was no ordinary militiaman, but rather an MGB trooper, because he wore the special red epaulettes of the MGB (the Ministry of State Security). Moreover, as we walked around town all day, we noticed a great many similarly dressed troops, far too many for a city with Vladimir's small population.

Comparing notes later in the day, we decided that behind the walls is a school for training MGB troops. But early in the morning, much too fascinated by the atmosphere of the old city, so different from loud, ostentatious Moscow, we didn't think about the significance of this discovery. We were too busy rushing over to see the beautiful, astonishing *Dmitrievsky Sobor*, built in 1194-1197, by Vsevolod III, for his personal family. It too, like the Kremlin, sits on the back of the city, and it sits majestically, alone, oblivious to the MGB machinations which its five graceful cupolas overlook. To its left is the huge palace which Catherine the Great built for her convenience whenever she wished to leave St. Petersburg for a quiet rest. But it seemed out of place next to the Dmitrievsky Sobor, and it was located, and this was even more unfortunate, between the Dmitrievsky and the Uspensky Sobor, built ten years before by Vsevolod for all the people of Vladimir.

This cathedral is truly a splendid achievement. The old frescoes of Andrei Rublev, done in 1406, still grace its tall, strong walls, but only in the rear of the church. The front has been redone (restored, the Russians say) in a hideous, un-Rublevian fashion, and for one who has seen some of the great Rublevs in the rear of the church, the restoring was enough to make one anti-Communist. A service was being conducted there, and it was impossible not to be deeply touched by the strength of the religious conviction of those in the church. Most of the people were old—only three young people were present—but they prayed with a quiet power, and they made one feel confident that somehow, Communist efforts notwithstanding, religion will not die in Russia. (Just yesterday *Komsomol Pravda* ran a long article chastising the many Komsomols who get married in church and who immerse themselves in holy water.)

Saturday afternoon was devoted to an excursion to the lonely and majestic Church Pokrov Bogoroditsy Na Nerli. The church is located on the outskirts of Bogolyubov, now a small village about 35 kilometers from Vladimir. This backwater town was once the home of Andrei Bogolyubov ("Love of God"), the grandson of Vladimir Monomakh, who ruled the Vladimir principality from 1157-1174. In an effort to free himself from the growing power of the old Russian Boyars, Prince Andrei followed his father's example and moved the seat of his principality from Vladimir to Bogolyubov. As his name indicates, he was a very devout ruler, and in the distance, at the mouth of two small rivers, set on top of a hill overlooking this river intersection, he built a small, squarish, single-cupola-ed artistic masterpiece. The church is now barren. The echoes of the last prayers died many hundreds of years ago in its small interior but the ghost of its dignity guards this church proudly. From it one looks onto miles of Russian countryside, unbroken, beautiful, and, no doubt, just as it was 800 years ago.

Nat Davis, an Embassy officer, and I went out there alone. The others left earlier, but never made it to the church. Nat and I decided to walk from the road to the church. The skies were dark and threatening, and our two-mile hike through high drifts of snow took close to an hour. When we finally reached the door of the church, we were standing on a hill overlooking the snow-patched plain. No one was close by. A dog barked loudly, but his bark was a lonely bark, for its echo died in the song of the wind. We were alone, and suddenly the sun broke through a small break in the clouds, and the bright light splashed a warm, gold on the white walls of the church, which then was silhouetted against the background of a black sky.

While Nat raced around trying for the best camera shot, I stood off at a distance. I couldn't help but recall an hypothesis of the late Sir Bernard Pares, who knew this country better than most Westerners of his day or ours. He had written that in Russia the sky and the earth meet, and the two become one, and in the minds of the simple farm-folk, who still comprise most of this country's population, a mystical belief was formed that somehow they were closer to God than other people. The belief was verbalized by the intellectual, and it was easy to see the inspiration standing there on the hillside, next to the church.

Nat and I returned to the hotel about 7 P.M. that night, and walked into our room to find the others deeply engaged in a conversation with a Russian, about 25 years old. He said he had heard Americans were in town, and he wanted to meet them. He had come to the hotel to talk with us, for no other purpose. He simply wanted to meet us. He spoke frankly, easily. He was a boxer (not professionally—there are no professional sports in Russia, he said), who came from Suhumi, in Georgia; he had been assigned to Vladimir to teach physical culture.

Vladimir, he said, was quite dull. There was no excitement. There was a growing feeling of stagnation. He liked Americans because they were "exciting." He liked the way we walked and talked, he liked our casualness. He said: "I am sick and tired of Marusia, the tractor-driver. I've had enough. Propaganda, propaganda, propaganda. That's all we hear. I've had enough of Marusia, the tractors, and the plans. I want music, jazz music. I want to dance. I want to relax. I want to have a good time. Let's not talk about politics. Let's talk about things which will bring us closer together."

He said later that the sort of propaganda dished out by the Party was okay "for the peasants, but not for me. I am an intellectual. I don't believe most of what I hear." He told us he earned 1000 roubles a month teaching gymnastics. His wife is a psychiatrist who had recently finished school. She earns about 1500 roubles a month. He admitted that their marriage was a common-law marriage. They never bothered to register it. He said this was rather common amongst the intellectuals of Russia. He mentioned further that at a recent conference in Moscow of Russian psychiatrists, it was admitted that psychiatry in Russia lags drastically behind Western psychiatry. He said that most of the experiments were based upon Pavlov's theories. One of the ways Russians have of curing alcoholism is to feed an alcoholic a mild poison which would make him throw up, at the very same time that he is given alcohol. He admitted that this cure worked well for a while, but soon the alcoholic was having long lost-weekends all over again. This problem of alcoholism was a real problem for the Russians, he said. It was terrible after the war, and now it is still quite a headache for a sober-minded leadership.

At this point, some of us left the Russian and went to the theater to see the new Soviet play *Odna*. It was written by S. Aleshin, and it is a bad play. It is remarkable, however, in one way—it tries to prove that in many cases love is more potent than the solidity of the family and the dictates of the Party. A Party man, middle-aged and successful, runs off with the wife of his assistant, leaving a wife and a sixteen-year-old daughter. The play ended with the deserted wife, who remains "odna," or alone, reciting a long speech that a husband is after all not the most important thing in the world in a society where everyone—including middle-aged mothers—have all the opportunity to develop their natural innate abilities and still have the feeling that they are contributing much that is creative to society. As I listened to her long tirade, I recalled a poem which ran in *Literaturnaya Gazeta,* about two months ago, on the very same theme. It evidently made the point that though your husband leaves, don't fret, honey, because here in Russia you can still fulfill a valuable function.

When we returned from the play, we met our Russian friend in the street. He told us that we were going to have lunch at his house, and that his wife was going to make shashlik. When we returned to the hotel, we were told that he had had dinner with the three Americans right there in full view of all the other Russians. This was a remarkable thing, but the hour was late, and we suspected that he would not show up the following day at 11 a.m., the time for our appointment.

The following day was a bright, beautiful day, and I set off early in the morning for the town market. The market—a kind of bazaar—was set on a large field at the other end of town from the hotel. Hundreds of townsfolk were there to sell and buy wares. As I entered the bustling market, I saw the sellers line up, each with his little item to sell. The buyers simply walk alongside the line, stop, bargain, then either buy or move on. Peasants also had come to Vladimir to sell the products of their *usadba* plots. Little piglets sold for 200 roubles. Large pigs for 400 roubles. The one cow there for sale had no price-tag, and I couldn't find out from the owner how much he wanted. In fact, I had enormous difficulty conversing with any of the peasants. One woman, though, wanted to sell me a large duck for 65 roubles. One old man had an old pair of rubbers to sell. A woman asked him how much. He answered 72 roubles. She said I'll give you 70. He said no.

After the would-be purchaser departed, a woman standing near the old man, said, "Are you crazy? Why didn't you let your price down two roubles." To which he answered very proudly. "My price is 72 roubles." Another woman was buying a coat for her son. It cost 750 roubles, which was an average price, and she was sold on the coat, except for one thing —she didn't like the style of the pockets, which were square; she wanted slit pockets.

As I returned to the hotel, eager to meet our Russian friend, I became involved in a conversation with about six Russians on a street corner. A young assistant mechanic on the railroad, who stuttered badly, and whose stuttering grew worse as the conversation grew more and more touchy, wanted to know about America. He wanted to know specifically why we "did not want peace"—why in the face of "universal condemnation of war," we still followed a "policy of war." I told him this was untrue. He told me then that he went to school for seven years (which all rural children in the Soviet Union are required to do), then had two years of specialized training, before he went to work on the railroad. He refused to say how much money he earned. Then, as we continued to talk about prices and wages, he asked point blank if Negroes were permitted to work in the United States. I told them that of course they were. He seemed very dubious.

Another fellow popped up (by this time the crowd had grown to about 50 people) and said that he read that Negroes are "treated like dogs" in the United States. I told him that this too was untrue. He said that "Here, all people have equal

rights. Tatars, Georgians, Uzbeks. In the United States, Negroes and whites are treated like two separate people." He
wanted to know why. I asked him where he got his information, and he told me the press. I asked him if it had ever
occurred to him that the reporting might not have been accurate. He seemed amazed and blurted: "Our papers always
tell the truth."

A third man joined in. "All the world has protested against
hydrogen bomb tests in the Pacific Ocean, and yet you persist. Why?" When they were informed that the Russians too
are conducting experiments with hydrogen bombs, they did
not believe the news. I told them that the admission was made
two months ago in *Pravda*. They still seemed quite sceptical.

Gradually, I tried to get their reactions to the efforts to
bury Stalin. I spoke about the Congress, saying I had been
in Moscow at the time and found much of it very interesting.
They nodded in agreement. I asked them what they thought
about the personality cult. (Some of the people disappeared
at this question—others joined the crowd.) One man volunteered that in Russia the "people are the heroes; they are the
creators." A man hopped in with another question. He wanted
to know about the balloons being launched from the West
with "spying, intelligence" equipment. He said they consti-
tuted a "threat to the people." I answered that these were
meteorological balloons, not for military purposes at all, and
that we had stopped launching them as soon as we heard about
the Russian complaints. We shifted back to the "cult." "We
believe in our government," one man said; then he added,
smilingly, "at least that's my opinion at the moment." Marx,
Engels, Lenin were all modest men, they said, almost a direct
quotation from the *Pravda* article which appeared last week.
Stalin wasn't and he encouraged self-glorification. When
asked if there was any assurance against the rise of the cult

again, a man answered "We believe and trust our government." "But," I asked, "where were your present leaders when
Stalin was alive? Why didn't they do anything then?" There
was great hesitation and distress throughout the crowd. One
man finally broke the silence. "There is an old Russian prov-
erb: better late than never." With this, the crowd grew very
tense. At just this moment, a funeral procession moved slowly
down the block. We all took off our hats until it had passed.
The conversation had been mercifully interrupted. One
young man came over to me and said: "I am a believer. I can
tell you truthfully. I know that God will help us all, all, no
matter—and will wish us well. God can do such things. God
be with you. Excuse me. Goodbye."

Our Russian friend did not show up, so we all left for
Suzdal, which is located about 45 kilometers northeast of
Vladimir; it was our destination for this Sunday afternoon.
The road no longer bore the marks of Batu's chargers, but it
was undoubtedly more suitable for horses than for our courageous little car. We passed the villages of Pavlovskaya (just
outside the town stands a church in bad repair, which was
used as an observation tower by the Mongols in 1238 as they
advanced on the then notable metropolis of Suzdal) and
Borisovskaya along the way. The latter now is home to an
average-sized *sovkhoz* (state farm). Both are small towns; each
has a large prominent church, neither of which has been functioning since 1922. The landscape is open, wide, and here too
the horizon melted into whiteness with the sky.

Before the revolution, Suzdal had 36 churches. Not one of
them is in use these days, though one old lady strongly hinted
that come Easter one of them will be used for services. The
people of Suzdal were warm and friendly and there were no
monuments to the city's glorious historical heritage, except
for a small museum located in the center of town, the site

of the former Kremlin, which was destroyed by the Mongols. Most of the churches are now used for storing grain. Outside of one, I asked a young man if he could tell me whether it was possible to see the interior. He answered that he for one is not in the least interested in religious matters, that he was a representative of the near-by *sovkhoz* and a member of the Komsomol.

Suzdal also has three old monasteries, one of which is used as an electric power station, another seems to be a training ground for MGB troops, and the third we did not even see. Most memorable about Suzdal, which appeared to be a small, run-down village on the whole, was our farewell send-off. The entire population—led by a spokesman, who identified himself as a cabdriver—surrounded our car, and we became engaged in a long conversation, the essence of which was that these people did not want war. They said that they loved the American people, and that the Russian people were a good people. One young man pleaded for greater exchange and understanding between the American and Russian people.

The conversation was spontaneous and warm, and very friendly. One old man grabbed my hand and held it throughout the conversation, mumbling every now and then that the Russian people did not want war, and please to convey the love of the Russian people to the American people, whom they loved very much. The whole scene was very touching, for after a while this man started to cry as he gripped my hand. After an hour, we finally managed to get into the car and drive back to Vladimir. For about ten minutes, we were all very quiet. We were deep in our own thoughts, and the old man's eyes, full of sincerity and love, burned an impression in me I shall not forget.

When we returned to Vladimir, our Russian friend, who had disappointed us earlier in the day, was waiting for us. He said that his wife was afraid to have us over for lunch, was indeed afraid to meet us at all. Our friend, though, took us out to dinner in the hotel restaurant, paid the check for the six of us, and we drank one toast after another dedicated to things like peace and friendship. He promised to meet us in Moscow "one of these days."

After we h ' returned to Moscow, we discovered that soon after we had left Vladimir, he was arrested and kept in jail for twenty-four hours. The magazines which we had given him—*Life* and *Time*—were taken away from him.

April 5 : "The Communist party has been victorious and is victorious through its loyalty to Leninism." Under this headline, the second in what appears to be a series of articles dedicated to the rewriting of Stalinism appeared in today's *Pravda*. It added nothing to the first article which was published last Wednesday. For the first time there was public recognition of the serious effect that de-Stalinization could conceivably have upon this country—at least, from the viewpoint of the present leadership. The article admitted that "at the same time, one should not overlook instances when individual rotten elements try to make use of criticism and self-criticism for all sorts of slanderous fabrications and anti-Party assertions." Certain individuals "used internal Party democracy for speeches of a slanderous character directed against the Party and its Leninist foundations."

The present leadership has opened a Pandora's box, and even they are uncertain at the moment of the surprises which might pop up. They have started a small snowball slowly downhill, across an expanse covered with snow, and this snowball may pick up more snow—if the present trend is continued for any length of time—until some time in the future it may roll down from the Russian countryside, huge and frightening, a sort of modern-day, white Pugachev, and smash into the walls of the Kremlin and drown the system in a storm of white fury.

April 6 : More insight tonight into the Russian intellectual's mind. I met Volodya again—a candidate at the Institute of History associated with the Academy of Science. Our discussion indicated that he apparently enjoys real status at the Institute of History, for he told me that he was the Secretary-General of the Soviet Historical Committee, which sent a delegation of scholars to Rome last fall and which will play host next year in Leningrad to a new conference of international scholars of history. Professor Donald MacKay of Harvard is the chairman of the American contingent.

During our talk, he asked me many questions about the level of concentration on Russian affairs in the United States, and he was very surprised at the depth and penetration of our studies of the Soviet system.

"In Russia," he said, "there are more people who know the English language but fewer who fully appreciate the American scene."

He said that he was firmly convinced that the Russian leaders do not want war—that Dulles is the strongest man in the United States—that Eisenhower seems "to drift off into the haze"—that American foreign policy is dictated by a small group of bankers and industrialists who because of their position in society wish to continue the arms race in order to increase their profits—that he favored greater and greater exchanges between scholars and students of the United States and the Soviet Union—that he believed Dulles and Adlai Ste-

venson differ only very slightly—that people like Corliss Lamont are true disciples of peace.

When I pointed out to him that the "substructure" of
Lamont, Dulles and Stevenson was very similar, but that their
"superstructures" differed so drastically, and I then asked him
how he would explain this obvious contradiction in Marxist
dogma, he smiled—as he had done last week when I asked him
about writing a history of 1905 without reference to Trotsky
—and answered feebly that there were exceptions. We drifted
to a discussion of Herzen, and I asked him what the present-
day Soviet historians thought about Herzen. He answered that
they thought him a "progressive," but that on occasion he was
so confusing that it was difficult to stamp him one way or the
other. I told him that it was my impression that Herzen never
gave up his faith in the dignity of man, that all men must be
free, as individuals, not as members of a society which wants
and professes freedom for all. "History follows no libretto," I
quoted Herzen as saying, to which Volodya answered that
"we" have a different view of Herzen. Man arrives at freedom
for all first, before each individual gets freedom, he said. I
said that Herzen wanted freedom for the individual before
he would buy freedom for the mass of society. We argued for
hours, and though he did not succeed in convincing me, nor
I him, I can't escape the feeling that some of my points were
well taken, for he could only smile, helplessly. In any case, we
promised to meet again.

As I left Volodya on Pushkin Street, as people jostled back
and forth noisily, I felt that the future of Russia rests in the
logic and emotional strength of many Volodyas, who are
capable of recognizing a fact, without relating it to a reli-
gious-political dogma. In him sits the destiny of Russia in
this century. He will either strip away the political and ideological nonsense and reconstruct his country so that it may

live genuinely in peace with its neighbors, or through panic
and fear he will unleash its newly-gained power and throw the
world into an ugly catastrophe. The Volodyas can do either.

April 8 : Mysticism and sensory perception are hazardous
tools for anyone with pretensions toward objective scholarship, but this is a country where feel, touch, smell, sensation
are important realities. These are days of enormous change in
Russia. One gets the feeling that there is a great ferment eating away at the structure of this society.

Today in front of the Metropole Hotel, a middle-aged man
was arrested. Six militia men were necessary to throw him into
an MVD car. He was screaming at the top of his lungs—in an
argument with a friend—that Stalin was "a good man and you
are a fool if you think differently." A man standing nearby
mumbled to his wife, "He's a Georgian, what can you expect
from a drunken Georgian?"

Last night, in the Uzbekistan Restaurant, a young Russian,
who is a "master of basketball," and who travels frequently,
told me that a Communist was a person who "has a car, a
family, a dacha and lots of money every month." When I
asked him who the greatest living Communists are, he answered, "Khrushchev and Bulganin are the greatest living
Communists, because they have cars, families, dachas and lots
of money." He went on to say that he believed war was inevitable, and it would come inside of two years. Why? Because,
he answered, "capitalists want to come here, and the Russian
Ivan might not like Communism, but he loves Russia, and
he will crush the invader, as he has done before." Later, he
added: "Russia is not really Western; we wish we were, but
we have only the glass of the West without its essence."

These people are confused, troubled, and uncertain. One

young Russian girl told me she felt the entire attack upon Stalin has made this a very dangerous time. "One can never tell what will happen in such troubled times," she said.

April 11 : Volodya waxed eloquent last Friday in his very emotional Russian way about the *Vsemirnaya Istoriya* which the Institute of History of the Academy of Sciences is now publishing. I decided after work this afternoon to go down to the bookstore he pointed out and sign up for this ten-volume series, the first volume of which has just been issued. I discovered that each volume costs 40 roubles (ten dollars at our exchange), and I would have bought the first volume were it not for the fact that I had to lay out an additional 40 roubles for the last volume also, a volume which, at the saleslady's own admission, probably won't be published for another four years at best. Apparently, you cannot purchase one volume; you must sign up for all ten with an initial payment for the first and the tenth. I would have, but I did not have enough roubles.

Feeling low, I wandered off towards Moscow University to try to gain admission into the University as a listener in their courses on Russian history. I went straight to the Faculty of History office. The *dekan* (similar to our university department chairman) of the History Faculty was not present, but his secretary informed me that I had to have the permission of the Assistant Rector of Moscow University, a man named Lavrin, before I could attend courses. I checked at the Rector's office. He was not in. He has office hours only on Friday afternoon from 1 to 6 p.m. I made an appointment to return at 2:30 Friday, and for some reason or other, I was feeling very confident. Once again, in a kind of never-ending battle against Soviet bureaucracy, I felt as though I had won a skirmish as I left the Rector's office and walked past the statue of Herzen which stands to one side of the old Moscow University building.

April 13 : Today is Friday the thirteenth, but as I walked past Herzen's statue again, I envisaged no difficulties. I felt sure that I would be listening to Russian history classes in Moscow University before another week was up. The reason for my optimism is hard to pin down to specifics. It is wrapped up once again in a feeling I had, possibly stemming from the general relaxation in Russia these days. This time, though, I was severely disappointed. The "feeling" turned out to be rooted in quicksand, and soon I was being dragged down into the mire of Soviet bureaucracy and fear. The Rector's secretary brought me over to his office. I had to wait for about a half hour. I finally met him. He is a tall man, with a badly scarred and battered face, and with a direct, friendly, and stubborn manner. I explained to him that I wished to listen to courses on Russian history. He said that normally his assistant, Mr. Nikolai Ivanovich Mokhov, takes care of such issues, but that Mr. Mokhov is on vacation. In any case, he answered, I had been misinformed. He did not have the power to grant this permission. He outlined the necessary procedure for me. First, the Embassy would have to write a letter to the Ministry of Higher Education, which would then grant its permission to the Ministry of Foreign Affairs, which would then grant its permission to the Ministry of Internal Affairs, which finally would grant its permission to the Assistant Rector of Moscow University, Mr. Lavrin, who would then contact me. I was very discouraged, and quite frankly asked Mr. Lavrin if he felt there was any chance at all of a decision being reached within a year. He seemed quite offended, said that within a week I should hear, but he added with a smile that he gave no guarantees. I told him that Moscow University had invited professors and students from Harvard to study and lecture at Moscow University, and if the University was sincere in this invitation, why was it that he himself was suddenly unable to grant permission for a simple thing like attending courses on Russian history, courses which concern the first part of the 19th century, before Communism had even begun to make a ripple in European political waters. He answered that the exchange was a completely different matter. I might have agreed in a better frame of mind. He said in Russia there was no provision for auditors in classes, and it would be in that category that I would have to be placed. Moreover, I am an American. This fact, he admitted, required special permission. I then asked him what he envisaged this exchange to be. He answered that a Harvard professor would lecture at the University and that students would attend classes and study much the same as any other students. I asked him if they would be granted access to the archives. He did not answer my question, but simply repeated what he had just said. I felt as though I had run up against a stone wall. I felt exasperated and, looking at the huge picture of Stalin which hung on the wall behind his desk (at just that moment Stalin seemed to be smiling at me in a kind of sly, contented way), I shook hands with Mr. Lavrin, left, and walked back to the embassy.

This evening I met Volodya again, and we had a discussion which was friendly but touchy and thus enormously revealing. I had always known that Communists had a completely different mentality, but knowing this in the abstract and meeting it head-on are very different matters. I told Volodya about my encounter with Lavrin, and he said that he did not understand the latter's stubbornness, but then he added that on this question of exchanges, there are a great many more critical problems and issues, which require much patience to solve.

Tonight we decided to talk about ethics and morals, and Volodya explained that he believed that ethics were tied closely to concrete situations and did not exist in a vacuum. If an event ran counter to the interests of the Soviet state, as interpreted by the Communist Party, then this event would be opposed and would be condemned as unethical and subject to extermination. He said he could easily understand where I would disagree with him. I still had hopes, though, that by specific example I could convince him of my logic. I brought up the horror of the murder of millions of kulaks and peasants during the collectivization drive. I told him I thought this unethical. I could not see disagreement, but Volodya, explaining nicely and gently to me, as though I were eight years old, "showed" that kulaks were interested in restoring capitalism. Their interests were opposed to the interests of the state at that time. They were "ethically eliminated," though he did admit that this was not a pleasant thought.

What was frightening about Volodya's discourse was his sincerity. I couldn't believe my ears at first, but he was completely earnest. Volodya spoke his mind and heart, and both were slaves of the Communist dogma. I told him (by now rather upset at Volodya and Lavrin) that he reminded me of a religious fanatic, who holds a fixed set of beliefs and who never deviates. Volodya only smiled, almost condescendingly.

I felt sorry for Volodya, because in America he would be a top-flight scholar. In Russia, he was successful only in spouting the last three *Pravda* articles about Stalin. My mood must have come through, because Volodya asked why I had become so quiet. I did not feel like answering. Suddenly I saw no hope of rapprochement with this Communist offspring —or, for that matter, of seeing him again. But I didn't say a thing. I only smiled and answered that I wished to know only one thing: was he really serious? Volodya seemed offended. "I am very serious," he answered. "I know that Communists will triumph all over the world. Only now it can be done peacefully, because Comrade Khrushchev said so at the last congress. But now we should try to improve our relations in a cultural sense. This we can do with the West, because in the West, culture can be divorced from politics. In the Soviet Union culture is a part of politics."

I left Volodya more convinced than ever that Russia can be a baffling experience.

April 17 : I didn't know Anna Guzik last night but, after seeing her this evening, I shall never forget her. During the thirties, before the Yiddish stage was closed for myopic Communist reasons of bigotry, fear, and foreign policy, Anna Guzik was the Al Jolson, Eddie Cantor, and Sophie Tucker of Russian Jewry. She was a fine, talented performer, "with a lot of heart."

Tonight, at the Stanislausky Moscow Dramatic Theater Anna Guzik made her long awaited return to the Russian Yiddish stage, and she was Al Jolson, Eddie Cantor and Sophie Tucker all over again, and then some. The theater was packed, and the Russian Jews who mobbed the galleries were all dressed well in honor of the occasion. Her appearance on the stage must have been like the dawn after a long, dark, cold night. And she dispelled the clouds—aided by M. Chaibovsky, G. Svetlov, and M. Yakubovich—with old favorites like "Stempenyu" by Sholom Aleichem, "A Mother's Heart" (better known on the lower east side of New York as "Mien

Yiddishe Momma"), and a rendition of "Dzhonny" (also
better known as "Johnny, You're the Man for Me"). There
were others too, and everyone loved Anna, and from the look
on Anna's face after the show, Anna loved tonight too, and in
one number when she screamed out, "Now we must be grateful and live again," everyone cheered. Tears flowed down the
joyous faces of the men and women in the audience. The theater was crowded with young and old people, and everyone
seemed to enjoy her songs and they seemed to understand Yiddish. (At her rendition of "Mien Yiddishe Momma," they
cried openly and unashamedly. It was a moving performance,
one for which these people have waited close to two decades, if
not longer.)

Anna will perform again tomorrow, and then once again on
the twenty-third, before she returns to Leningrad. It would
appear that if only for the while, the curtain has been lifted
from the shoulders and heads of Russia's Jews.

April 21 : Dinner this evening with a friend at a small Russian restaurant (as distinct from Georgian restaurants, or Armenian ones) offered new insight into the Georgian mentality.
Two young men, dark and attractive, asked if they could join
us at our table. We of course consented. We exchanged very
little in the nature of conversation for about an hour. My
friend and I were involved in a long discussion of Georgian
nationalism, which had come up in an article this past week
in *Zarya Vostoka,* the Georgian newspaper printed in the Russian language, which pointed to strong upsurges of "bourgeois nationalism" in Georgian literature. One of these young
men asked us if we would drink vodka with them. We did. We
toasted nothing special, and then my friend, who speaks excellent Russian, asked them if they were Moscovites. They

answered that they only live in Moscow temporarily, but that they are Georgians. I told them quickly that we had just been discussing Georgia, and one of them admitted that he had thought so. Apparently, he understood that much English.

The other Georgian said: "Moscow is considered to be the capital of the world. For us, Tbilisi is the capital of the world." I was tempted to ask them what they thought about reports of riots in Georgia, but both men seemed nervous, and I hesitated. They told us, however, that everyone in Georgia knows the Georgian language, that everyone is quite proud of Georgian history. I asked one of them how long he had studied Georgian history. He said three years. I told him that I had studied this history too, and was impressed with it. He told me that during the time of Queen Tamara, Georgia had 12,000,000 people. "Now we have only 3,000,000 but we'll have more. Many nations, especially Turkey, have tried to subdue Georgia, but none of them has succeeded entirely, nor will they." His friend told him to be careful, and both men looked around them in a guarded manner. At that point, one of them suggested that they leave, and they did.

April 22 : A group of us from the Embassy drove out to Zagorsk this afternoon. Zagorsk is about 50 kilometers from Moscow, and it is the site of the Troitsky Monastery, probably the largest landholding monastery, if not the largest landholder, in old Russia. Its dominions were vast, and inside its high walls, priests were trained. They still are in Zagorsk. We saw their school, and we saw them perform an elaborate pre-Easter service this morning. I counted 19 students, but there might have been more, since not all of them necessarily participated in the services. The monastery itself was founded in about 1340, about the same time that Ivan Kalita ("Money-

bags") established Moscow as the major political center in
northeast Russia. Its walled fortress played a major role in
the defensive strength of Moscow during this period, and
through the 17th century. Its greatest glory in Russian history
was its gallant 16-month defense of the outskirts of Moscow
against the Poles during the Time of Troubles. It is said that
as many as 30,000 Poles were killed outside the walls of the
Zagorsk Monastery during this period. The white-stoned
Troitsky Sobor is the outstanding church in Zagorsk, of the
six or seven major churches within the walls.

In the Zagorsk museum—once a church, but converted to a
museum at Lenin's order in 1920 (everyone in Russia today
celebrated the 86th anniversary of the day of Lenin's birth;
red flags draped all major buildings in Moscow)—I bumped
into a young Russian, who smiled, excused himself, and
asked if I were an American. I told him that I was. He told
me, pulling me off to one side, that he was a former lieutenant
in the Red Army, that he had been awarded the Red Star
Order, which he then proceeded to show me. He said he was
afraid to talk to me, but had to, because, he said, he had
something very important which he wished to discuss with
me. He took me into the men's room of the museum, locked
the door, and took out from under his coat two folders of
personal papers. These papers, he said, were all the records
of his father, who now is dying in a hospital. He proclaimed
himself to be anti-Soviet and anti-Communist. He said that
once he listened to the Voice of America and the BBC. Now
he can't because the Russians jam these broadcasts, but he
wanted me to take these papers which are in effect a case
study of a Soviet citizen, and broadcast to the entire Soviet
people how unpleasant things are under the Communists.

I told him I could not take these papers. He then appealed
to me to help him leave the country. I told him that under

present circumstances I was in no position to help him at all. He said that he was an expert mechanic but he had not been able to find work for three months. He said he was penniless and had not eaten for two days. I gave him some money, which he did not want to take because, he insisted, I would believe that he was only giving me a line. I told him to take the money.

He told me that he had seen pictures of Bulganin and Khrushchev leaving for Britain, and he spat on the floor and said, "Bulganin and that man from the Party are both fat, because they have good jobs. I am thin and have no job. This is a cursed country. Please take me with you!" I asked him if he were not afraid to be seen talking to me (by this time we had made our way out into the streets) because it was obvious that many people saw us in conversation. He said that if he were thrown into jail, what difference would it make? There was little I could say. I felt just as I had the day before, when I was told that two of those rioting Georgian students were killed in the main square of Tbilisi. This is a system which needs a Stalin. I can not shake the feeling that further relaxation will reach a point of no-return.

April 24 : The little pieces of evidence on the uprisings in Tbilisi are beginning to take shape. A number of American correspondents have just returned to Moscow from a week of looking and talking "in the darker alleys of Tbilisi," as one put it, and the picture they draw of the critical events of March 9 is very revealing. Apparently, on March 4th, a group of students asked the Rector of the State University in Tbilisi for permission to stage a demonstration the following day to commemorate the third anniversary of Stalin's death.

This request was refused, on the basis of a 1955 state decree which sanctions such demonstrations only on the birthdates of great figures, but not on deathdates. The following day, hundreds of students lined up in front of the enormous statue of Stalin in the central park of Tbilisi. Similar gatherings took place for the next three days, with each day more and more people participating. According to one diplomat, two students were killed on the morning of the 8th. Thus far, no troops had interfered with any of these demonstrations. No violence appears to have taken place.

On the 9th, the Communist Party staged its own demonstration in honor of the unveiling of a statue of Lenin. On this day, troops, army troops—not security troops—took over the city, lining the streets with machine guns and tanks. Speeches were made by officials of the Party, but no one was permitted close to the center of town, which was walled off by a mass of troops. After the ceremony and throughout the day, small outbreaks took place. Young students, many of them apparently still in our equivalent of high school, stoned cars, disrupted communication and transportation. There appears to have been some element of organization at this stage of the demonstrations, for most attacks which took place were aimed at communication and transportation networks. That evening, railroad cars pulled into Moscow from Tbilisi with broken windows. Back in Tbilisi, close to 11:30 in the evening, several thousand young students marched "in a human wave," as one Georgian later described the scene, on the post office. Down the block from the post office stands the Council of Ministers building. Both buildings were guarded by many hundreds of Red Army troops, but in front of the Council of Ministers building, machine gun installations had been established. The troops guarding the post office called out to the young protesting student group to break up the mob and go home. Apparently, they shouted back that they wished to send a wire. Some say the wire was to go to the United Nations, calling for help against the Russians; others say they wished to wire Moscow and Molotov asking for a halt to the de-Stalinization. Whatever the reason, they did not disperse and the troops opened fire directly into the mob. A conservative estimate of casualties is 100 dead, many of them shot in the back trying to rush off.

For the next week, Tbilisi had a midnight curfew, and the Red Army held it in an iron grip. Tanks patrolled the streets, as did armed soldiers, crushing the greatest rebellion against Soviet power since the *Bashmachi* outbursts in Central Asia in the twenties.

I heard an unconfirmed rumor tonight that in an issue of *Military Messenger,* to be released tomorrow, the charge has been made that Stalin was the greatest threat to Russia in 1941, not Hitler. All military disaster in 1941 is laid at his doorstep. Military intelligence knew about the attack, but he did nothing. The army is calling for stern revenge against the former dictator.

May 1 : For a month now, Moscow and all of Russia have been preparing for May Day. It would be impossible to estimate the cost. Millions of workers were involved in making posters, stands and platforms. Flags and decorations have been pasted to the walls of the major governmental buildings and hotels, and Moscow wears a halo of red; for all flags and banners are in red. Buildings framed in lights are common, and if anyone forgets—as though this were possible—millions of May First signs in neon lights and banners appear all over the city. May First is a Tuesday, and, according to the newspapers, the "workers voted" to work on Sunday in exchange for Monday as an off-day. This action gave them three days off in a row, since May 1 and May 2 were declared public holidays. Any Russian who works today is supposed to get double-time, and in some cases, triple-time. The real reason for the Sunday-to-Monday switch is that government officials apparently thought it foolish to open the factories and the electric power just for Monday, after having closed them normally for Sunday.

The area of Moscow around Revolution Square, which takes in the National Hotel, the Moskva, and the Metropole, and of course Red Square, was roped off by a line of MVD troops by 7 a.m. this morning. We arrived at the National at 6:30, and sat by a dirty window sipping black Nescafe and waiting for the parade to start. Only certain foreigners are invited into Red Square for the festivities. These include the corps of correspondents and ambassadors, wives, families, and the top service attaches. Therefore, many of us were forced to look through the unclean windows of the National at the grandiose spectacle.

Starting at about 8 a.m., crowds of demonstrators and marchers gathered along the four main streets leading into Revolution Square. Straight up Gorky Street—a mass of human beings, all carrying their modern-day ikons—pictures of Lenin and Marx (I saw only one small picture of Stalin). A similar spectacle was seen on the Makhovaya, alongside Moscow University, the large avenue which fronts on the Council of Ministers building, and on the long narrow avenue which runs alongside the Kremlin wall across from the National Hotel.

At exactly 10 a.m., guns roared the opening of the festival, and Marshall Zhukov, riding in an open car, made a saluting tour of the Moscow garrison troops which stood at rigid attention in Revolution Square. He drove back into Red Square, and delivered a short address, aimed at highlighting

Soviet intentions for peace. Forty-nine jet fighters zoomed overhead, and from Gorki Street the columns of troops, in transport carriers, pulling heavy mortars and large guns, moved across Revolution Square, into Red Square, passed the reviewing stand, on which stood the Presidium. Following the military demonstration, which was very short (lasted only eight minutes) and a sign that the Russians consciously played down military prowess in an effort to convince Westerners of their sincere appeals for peace, the human columns started converging on Revolution Square from their four avenues of approach. They marched by for four hours, a long, seemingly never-ending stream of people. After three hours of watching, I began to realize how strange it really was: this was the first parade I had ever seen where there were almost no spectators.

May 2 : The rainy weather yesterday afternoon cut down festivities somewhat, but today it was lovely, and millions and millions of Russians walked the streets, arm-in-arm as is their way; some danced, some sang, some were drunk. They were letting off steam. And though the militia men were standing nearby in case anything occurred, the mood was festive and gay. Some Westerners like to ask the question, in the middle of a well-timed puff on a pipe: why was the mood so gay? The reason possibly lies in the simple fact that the average Russian worker got three days off in a row, and he was delighted. I spoke with many Russians on the streets and invariably their reaction was one of apathy for May First and great delight with the weather, the no-work, and the vodka. Communism seemed to be the last thing on their minds.

May 3 : Isaac Stern, the brilliant American violinist, showed the Russians tonight in the large hall of the Conservatory that in addition to hydrogen bombs, we have artistic talent, too. A highly critical audience turned up. The hall was jammed, and a mood of excitement ran through the crowd. I felt that this was one audience which would have been delighted to leave the performance convinced of their preconceptions about the "shallowness" of American culture, but Stern did not permit this to happen. He was much too good, and soon he won the Russians over completely by announcing his own encores, and in Russian, which he speaks very well. When the Russians, excited and entranced, clapped their hands rhythmically, crying for a fifth encore, Stern came on stage, motioned to the audience to calm down, and said: "I am the first American artist in a long time to appear in Russia, but I hope that many more will be coming along soon. Thank you very much. *Spasibo bolshoi.*" David Oistrakh, who knows Stern, was backstage to congratulate him on his great success, as were Ambassador and Mrs. Bohlen, many representatives of Soviet music and culture, and a flock of American and Russian journalists. I got the impression that Stern did more good than fifty conferences to improve relations between Russians and Americans. During intermission, I discovered that the Russians had never heard of Copland and Bloch. They were cool to Copland, though Stern played his work brilliantly, because, as one Russian music lover explained, "There is a great deal of rhythm in Copland, and we don't understand rhythm too well; rather, we appreciate something more melodic. Perhaps, we shall get used to it in time, but now we are simply confused." Bloch's music, which has a fine ring of the East, with mournful, melodic sections, was extremely well received.

May 5 : In the past three weeks, a pattern has been developing in the provincial newspapers. Writers, not by accident, have been stressing three main points of dissatisfaction, in addition to the now hackneyed attacks on the personality cult. (1) Soviet legality must be strengthened; (2) the level of cultural activities has been too low; that is, composers and writers, seek their inspiration in the distant past rather than in contemporary themes; (3) the educational program has been deficient in far too many ways, especially in the teaching of the Russian language in central Asia.

The emphasis upon education, culture and legality is like three broad avenues which all converge on the youth, for it is the youth and their direction and their thinking that is crucial to us and to the Soviet Communists. The future of Russia lies with its youth. It seems that the gradual disillusionment which like a dark spring cloud is moving across young Russian minds is a consideration which is foremost on the Kremlin list of unfinished domestic business. The youth have been guilty of hooliganism. Reports of this appear in the papers almost every day. The youth marry unsatisfactorily. Thirty divorce cases are reported in *Moscow Evening News* nearly every day, and this is insignificant in comparison to the total number of divorces in this country in one year. Youth cut classes. Youth attend church services. Youth think these days, and thinking in a closed system has the strange tendency of either destroying the system in one violent gesture or compelling a gradual change in a more open-society direction.

May 10 : An interesting taxi ride this evening. The driver told me that most cab drivers in Moscow earn roughly 750 roubles per month. They work a thirteen hour day every other day. These drivers have a certain norm to meet, as do all the workers of this country. Every cab driver is expected to bring in 250 roubles every day that he works, and 3,500 roubles every month. He is permitted to pocket all tips. If a driver is able to hustle more than 3,500 roubles in fares every month, he is awarded a bonus in proportion to the additional amount.

I asked him how many drivers were able to exceed the norm, and he answered that he for one did not, and he believed that few others actually did. Many of them, were forced as a result to seek supplementary employment on their off-days. He seemed very interested in the living conditions of American cab drivers, and I told him that their position was somewhat better than the condition he described as common for the Russian driver. I told him that I even knew several cab drivers who owned their own cabs, houses and personal cars. He seemed very surprised.

May 12 : Notes on the medical system. Each district in Moscow has its own polyclinic. Service in this clinic is free to everyone who works and to those who with good reason can not. If an individual does not work, he will rarely be given free medical assistance, though I have heard of instances where non-working individuals through "pull" have obtained free medical help. The dependents of working people are, of course, able to get medical aid free. All operations are free as well, though of late a six-rouble-per-day tariff has been instituted to pay for food and bedding in the hospital. Fewer in number are the pay-clinics which exist throughout the country. Here, it is understood that treatment has a more personal flavor; doctors take a direct interest in the patient. Instruments are more up-to-date, and the clinics are less crowded. The usual visit costs roughly 12 roubles. The pay clinics are able to send patients to state hospitals for free operations, if the diagnosis so warrants.

To the best of my knowledge at the moment, there is only one operation for which there is a fee—abortion. Until recently, this was an accursed term in Russian medicine and ideology. Abortions were sanctioned only when doctors felt the woman's life was at stake. There were a number of reasons for the strictness of this regulation, but among the most important were a/ the government was interested in a continued increase in the population and b/ abortion, which indicates a restriction of the natural population growth, smacked too much of Bishop Malthus and his theory about the population increasing at a geometric ratio and the food supply at an arithmetic ratio. The Communists, who at least in theory have always held that shortages are man-made, the imposition of an exploiting class' will over the exploited, could not therefore have sanctioned abortion. Now, the Communists have changed their mind, and, I have been told, shortly before the convocation of the 20th Party Congress, they legalized abortion. Soviet women can have abortions as easily as they can have their teeth removed. Doctors caution against abortion on a first pregnancy, but only for medical reasons.

For example, an abortion costs roughly 100 roubles, plus six roubles a day for the five days in the hospital. (Russian doctors calculate that a woman can go home after four days in the hospital, plus the day of the operation.) If a woman simply does not have the money, she might find it cheaper in the long run to have the child. A woman now receives sixty days off with full pay before and after giving birth.

Why *legalized abortion?* First, illegal abortions undoubtedly were carried on and at a brisk pace. Second, Russia is no longer the vital Communist society it once was, and is capable of drifting further and further from orthodox Marxism, the leaders believe, with impunity to themselves and the system. Third, they may believe that the housing shortage combined with a continued shortage of food in the urban regions makes it advisable that the steady 3,000,000-a-year increase in the population be reduced.

Concerning doctors and their responsibilities to the state: when a student has completed a medical institute, he is required to work for two years in a public capacity, normally at a very low salary scale in comparison to Western doctors, roughly 1,000 roubles per month. In these two years, all of his activity must theoretically be dedicated to public functions, and he is a very busy man. He works in the free polyclinics, he makes calls, he can not have private patients. Once he has fulfilled his debt to society, he is *theoretically* free to engage in private practice, but the cost of establishing himself in an office with equipment is often prohibitive. Moreover, there is a shortage of medical supplies, so that the state gets first call on all equipment. However, he can continue to work for the state, on a regular basis, and in his spare time care for private patients. One of his most critical functions while working for a free polyclinic is that he alone has the right to sign medical excuse slips from work. Doctors in pay clinics do not have this "right."

Summing up, medical service in Russia has always had a more public orientation than in our country and, as a result, it should not be surprising that Russian doctors stay in public service longer, and almost voluntarily.

May 14 : A senior official of the MVD, who prefers to remain anonymous, reportedly told a member of a visiting French delegation during a trip to the Tula corrective-labor camp that all internment camps in the Soviet Union will be abolished within the next 18 months. In the future, he said, there would be only two types of camps: ordinary prisons and corrective-labor camps. Only those prisoners convicted of serious political offenses (undefined at this stage) will be deported to the East. A special Soviet commission, it is said, has been established to review the sentences of people convicted of political and counter-revolutionary offenses. The commission has allegedly been ordered to complete rehabilitation of innocent people by next October. These disclosures, of course, have not been revealed in any official decree. If they turn out to be true, however, this would be a major step in the direction of liberalizing the internal structure of this system.

May 19 : A pointed reference in *Turkmenskaya Pravda,* the newspaper of the Central Asian Turkmen Republic, about the imposition of one culture upon another. Before the Revolution, the paper boasts, there were only two publications in all Turkmenistan in the Russian language. Now, there are six republic newspapers, six *oblast,* two city, 44 *raion,* 10 branch newspapers and 10 journals—all in the Russian language. The newspaper omits any reference to how many Turkmen publications there are now in the Republic, or how many there were before the Revolution. In the same article, an indication of the breadth of newspaper dissemination in the Soviet Union: as of December, 1955: there were 7,200 newspapers in 57 languages, (48.4 million circulation—7 million more than in 1952), 1760 journals (with circulation of 360 million), 52,967 book titles (with circulation of one billion copies). There is no doubt that this is a fabulous advance over similar statistics in 1917. It would appear that on occasion Communist propaganda serves only to defeat its own purposes. The fact that many more people read, that the classics of the

19th century are circulated broadly (and it should be recalled that they circulate many ideas of a free and democratic content), could conceivably operate as a kind of fifth-column within Russia. An alert, sharp mass of young people does not necessarily make the best human fodder for totalitarianism.

May 24 : French Foreign Minister Christian Pineau has been traveling around the Soviet Union the last few days, after the departure of Prime Minister Guy Mollet for Paris on Sunday morning. The Franco-Russian talks, from the tone of the Russian press, were a blazing success but, from what I have heard from French correspondents, it was hardly that. The French came here basically for Russian support for their North African policy but they ended up with a rather hazy, confusing statement that the Russians "hope" the French act "in a liberal spirit" in deciding the North African question. In any event, Pineau visited Leningrad, Kiev, and Erevan, the capital of Armenia. He was scheduled to remain in Erevan only until 3 this afternoon, when his plane was to depart for Moscow. Atmospheric conditions, though, kept the plane from leaving at 3 p.m. Pineau did not leave until 6 p.m., when the skies cleared. At 3:15 p.m., four Armenians were arrested. The connection between the weather, the arrests and the time factor provides a cutting insight into this political system, which these days wears the guise of liberalism cloaking a political totalitarianism, still dynamic and vicious.

When Pineau arrived yesterday, hundreds of Armenians mobbed the Erevan airport to greet him. They were the representatives of many other hundreds of Armenians who had returned to the Soviet Union within the past three years after living for twenty, thirty years in France. After WW II, the Soviet government had suddenly appeared respectable, and these Armenians were told that if they returned home, they'd have everything they wanted. They would relinquish their French citizenship and reassume or adopt Russian citizenship—rather, Soviet citizenship. They decided to return to Armenia. After three years, they had had enough, and these French-Armenians were jamming the Erevan airport to ask Pineau to please help them all get back to France. Pineau said he'd do what he could. Four men represented the hundreds at the airport and it was these four who were arrested at 3:15, today, 15 minutes after Pineau was supposed to have departed from Erevan. When I heard this story this evening, I could not help but think about our Russian friend from Vladimir, who was so nice and pleasant to us and who thirty minutes after our train pulled away from Vladimir for Moscow was arrested.

May 26 : I visited the chief Moscow television studio this afternoon with Dan Schorr of CBS News and spent three hours there. Television is a subdivision of the Ministry of Communications. As such it is considered strategic, and this TV building is guarded by armed troops, some of them women. A typical Saturday night's entertainment was on the agenda. At 6 p.m., a children's show; at 6:30, a young pioneer show; at 7:30, a live show from Vnukovo airport on the new Russian jet passenger plane; at 8:00, the Afghanistan ambassador spoke; at 8:30, a documentary on K's and B's visit to Britain, which was a fine documentary; at 10 p.m., the news; at 10:30, a concert, vaudeville kind, of dancing and singing. At midnight, Moscow television signs off. The evening's entertainment is over. There are two stations in Moscow, but a young man who is now the chief engineer of the main Moscow studio (there is just one other) and who graduated from the Leningrad Institute for radio and television engineers five

years ago, told me that within the next two years a third chan-
nel would be installed in Moscow.

May 27 : Forty blue-frocked, enthusiastic, but somewhat bewildered young Chinese Communists had their legs pulled
last night at the Metropole Hotel, but they didn't know it.
In fact, when they finally got to bed, they must have felt warm
and excited in a delightful, naive intimacy with their Communist dream. At 3 this morning, they arrived in the lobby of
the Metropole, tired, puzzled and more than slightly lost.
They had traveled all the way from Peking. Now they were
in the Socialist paradise, the country associated with Lenin,
Stalin, and even the devil Trotsky. A young American happened to be sitting in the lobby, collecting his thoughts after
a rough day of sightseeing, the ballet, and a late dinner. His
room was too warm, and his mind too active. He was busily
cursing the Russian bureaucracy to himself, when he saw this
flock of young Chinese, all dressed in blue, like good little
schoolboys off to school on assembly days. Nobody from the
Metropole staff was there to meet them, and our American
friend, unable to hold back a good speech when he feels one
coming, burst out in Russian: "Comrades, on behalf of the Socialist paradise, on behalf of the Communist Party and the Soviet government, on behalf of the International Workers'
movement, I welcome you to the kingdom of Marx on earth; I
welcome you to Soviet Russia." The young Chinese were
terribly impressed. Our orator, first now beginning to feel his
oats, continued, now ascending a table top: "Our friends from
the brotherly Communist Party of China, under the inspired
leadership of Mao Tse-tung, pupil and son-in-arms of the
great Lenin, who as everybody knows always hated the de-
testable Stalin, whose cult of the personality was alien to the

spirit of Marxism-Leninism, are always welcome to this land where everyone is free, where everyone works for the future brilliant emergence of Communism, where women have equal rights with men to dig ditches, drive trucks, and use tractors. Thanks to the industrious Soviet people, the Soviet Union is now truly a land of paradise. Therefore, on behalf of the Communist Party and the Soviet government, I welcome you." The Chinese applauded. The leader, a young man of about 20, deeply intense, approached the American, who spoke beautiful Russian, and answered, also in Russian, that they were delighted to be there, that this is the culmination of a life's wish. The American then took them to the *dezjurny*, got a key to a large dormitory-like room on the fourth floor of the hotel, and went so far as to tuck them all into bed. The Chinese thanked him a great deal. When he left their huge room, he sat down on the floor and wept.

May 28 : The Leningrad Theatrical Company performed Dostoevsky's *Humiliated and Insulted* this evening at the MXAT in Moscow, and it was splendid. Not only was the essence of the story portrayed honestly, fully, but the acting was superb—far and away, the best that I have seen here in Russia. Scenes with strong religious flavorings and heavy Dostoevskyan mental probing abounded. The cross was visible in every scene.

May 31 : It was the Queen's birthday today; Elizabeth II of England is 30 years old. Bulganin and Khrushchev were at the British Embassy for the party. I saw them close up for the first time. I spoke with them for a short time. Khrushchev looks like a short, fat, strong, peasant-type leader. He has practically no hair. He has bad teeth. His trousers were baggy. He laughs heartily, and seems to have a good sense of humor. He was speaking with Isaac Stern, who is leaving Russia tomorrow after a successful stay, when Stern asked him about the Moiseyev dance group, which is supposed to come to the United States. Khrushchev said, "No Russian will submit to fingerprinting. That is only for criminals." An American official who stood nearby pointed out that this was a law of the land, that just as Americans observe laws here, Russians must learn to observe laws in America. Khrushchev said that the law should be changed. Bulganin, who was standing nearby, agreed. Molotov, also nearby and eavesdropping, said he too agreed and that "there were some intelligent Congressmen who would initiate legislative action." Khrushchev roared a huge, false roar of approval, and said, "This reminds me of a story which we heard before the Revolution. It seems that a young official, on leaving a government building, leaped into a *droshki* (a horse-drawn carriage) only to meet with an accident, which sent him sprawling in the street. His head cracked against the curb, and his brains fell out on the road. He thought nothing of it, left his brains on the gutter, and marched off. An old lady ran after him and said: 'Sir, you lost your brains.' 'That's all right,' he answered, 'I am a member of the Duma.' " (The Duma was the Russian Congress before the Revolution.) Khrushchev has little respect for Congress, and I gathered from the sneer in his voice that he also has very little respect for representative legislative organs in general.

June 2 : Two big news items today. Molotov lost his job as Foreign Minister of the Soviet Union; Tito arrived. The fact that Molotov, who signed the Communist doctrine which ex-

pelled Tito from the Cominform back in 1948 for deviationism, is bounced, and that Tito returns to the Soviet Union for
the first time in ten years, is no simple coincidence. B and K
were obviously searching for the best time to drop Molotov,
since his retirement has been rumored in Moscow for close to
a year. The timing was beautiful. Molotov was the lamb
slaughtered to appease the god who has returned to the Communist "paradise." And Tito's return was a triumphal one
indeed. The streets were lined with well organized mobs, all
shouting happy slogans. The Kievsky station was bedecked
with the state flags of Yugoslavia and the Soviet Union. His
train arrived promptly at 5. All the Soviet leaders, including
Molotov (leaders fade away these days; they don't just disap-
pear) were there to greet Tito, whose bearing is proud,
straight, very military. Tito alighted from the train, made a
short speech, and then stood by to watch the honor guard parade past. It did, but strangely enough, on the face of their flag
was a huge picture of Stalin, and as the flag was carried past the
spot where Tito stood, a brisk wind, as though ordained by the
dead dictator himself, unfurled the flag in one rapid, quick
snap. Stalin stood looking down at Tito. His ghost walked a
troubled, distraught afternoon. He was all over . . . in every
speech, in every gesture of all-abiding love . . . even on the
flag and in that mysterious wind. There was an Italian reception this evening, as well. Two Soviet leaders were there. One
was Molotov. This is the new look. Shepilov, the ex-editor of
Pravda, the new Foreign Minister, made a big pitch for Italian
friendship on his first day on the job. Nothing unusual, since
this is Italian Independence Day.

After the reception, my brother Bern (who's on his way to a
Southeast Asia assignment for the New York *Times*), and I
saw the best of the Turkmen dances, which were hardly
Turkic, poorly performed and unimaginative.

June 17 : Yasnaya Polyana is about three and a half hours
from Moscow by car. It is large, lovely, beautiful. It consists
of two large buildings, one smaller one, lots of peasant huts,
and Tolstoy's grave, a simple mound of earth bedecked in
flowers. One large house is two-storied, and Tolstoy lived in
it most of his life. It is white and pretty, and everything seems
as though Tolstoy just stepped out for ten minutes. The place
was mobbed, as many, many Russians come to pay silent
homage to their great writer. He wrote all of his major works
right in the center room on the upper floor, the one which
has a fine balcony in front of it. Down the road a little is the
small *Literaturnyi Dom,* where Tolstoy ran his own school,
teaching the peasants' children his special brand of Gandhian
religion. He had about 70 students. Now, the building is a
monument to Tolstoy's relation to modern Russia. As I passed
one lecturer telling her starry-eyed group of Russian peasants
that Tolstoy greatly valued Gorki's work, that he thought
Gorki a great artist, I turned around and asked my guide if
this was true. He said (outside after we had left) that this sort
of propaganda was for them (pointing to the peasants) not for
you (pointing to us). He said that in fact Tolstoy thought
Gorki a rather crude writer.

Tolstoy inherited Yasnaya Polyana after the death of his
wife's grandfather. The estate consisted of 1,000 hectares of
land. When he died in 1910, he gave away 700 hectares to the
peasants, free. The remaining 300 hectares make up the present Yasnaya Polyana.

During World War II, the Germans set fire to part of the
big house, but neighboring peasants spotted the blaze early
enough to put it out without too much damage to the building. Each part of the house adds new dimensions to certain
parts of *Anna Karenina* or *War and Peace.* Each tree has a

history in the huge black and white, tall, straight forest which covers most of the land. One tall oak, the story goes, stood somberly along the pathway as Prince Volkonsky approached it one day. He was thirty years old, and he thought his life was over. His mind was overcast with heaviness and darkness. The dark tree made an unhappy impression. He passed it. Soon after, he met Natasha along the path, and he lost his heart to her. When the two of them walked the same path back to the house, they approached the same dark oak, but now it was a dark symbol of a happy future.

The thousands of peasants who crowd this shrine every holiday may not have any hopes about a bright tomorrow, may not have the vaguest inkling as to the true significance of Tolstoy, but they love him, and they appear contrite, humble, happy just being at Yasnaya Polyana, and I felt the same way this afternoon.

June 19 : The Moscow River is a filthy, slow-moving body of black water these hot June days. Along its banks young men and women tell one another their life-stories, their sorrows, their dreams—if they have any. Others just walk the bank, much the same as I did this evening, to escape the heat of a closed, hot room. The breeze may be dusty and the river filthy, but it's cool.

I decided to take a little boat ride up and down the river. Sleek, white boats run regularly, serving as a kind of river bus. I tried to buy a ticket, but a young man, short, dark from the sun, who spoke a poor English and too colloquial a Russian, stopped me. He asked if I was from America. I told him I was. He grabbed my hand and, gently but firmly steering me over to one side of the crowd, out of earshot, asked me if I would not consent to take a ride on his boat.

I told him that I would love to, but couldn't because of a prior appointment. This was not true, but I have learned from past experience that every now and then (possibly one out of twenty cases—the percentages were much higher about two years ago) a Russian who is too friendly gets into trouble, and this fellow tonight seemed very nice, perhaps even too friendly. He then suggested that we take a short walk, which I thought was okay and much less public. We walked through Gorki Park, which, in the evening, is packed with young couples, who laughingly dash off into the bushes, in search of fun, a break in the routine, an escape. He told me that he was born in New York in 1928 but he returned to the Soviet Union with his parents in 1936, an unhappy victim of his father's desire to die in Russia. His father is not yet dead, but my friend told me that he wished he were. He said he wanted to return to the United States. He said he detested the Soviet Union; he detested its clumsiness, its inefficiency, its undisciplined power. He said, "There are millions who work but nothing is produced. Millions and millions of roubles are spent on consumer items, on industrial equipment, but we see so little in proportion to the labor and money which goes into the production." He said, as we parted, that he wished to see me once again—only he wished to see me in New York.

I departed, feeling a little lump in my throat, hoping that his wish would come true. There is such disillusionment, unhappiness, and bewilderment among the youth, that I ask myself: how can this system continue, on any long-range basis, without the support of youth?

June 21 : The Russians can be a very warm people. They are a simple people, for the most part, not blessed (as one friend put it) "with the curse of civilization." When a Russian likes you, he likes you at once. He doesn't size you up, carefully, tactfully, as we are prone to do. He simply likes you, and he likes you carelessly, tactlessly, happily, completely. This afternoon, I felt in a kind of nature-ish mood, and I took a walk through one of the most unnatural parks in the world—Gorki Park. It was packed, as usual. I took a seat on one bench. Soon, a young Russian girl sat down next to me. She started to read. I glanced over and noticed that she was wading her way through *War and Peace*. I asked her if she was enjoying the book. She told me, rather abruptly, that she was. She didn't seem to wish to continue our short-lived friendship; I was mistaken. Rather suddenly, she turned around and asked me the usual: where was I from? The USA, I answered, and one question led to another; before either of us was aware of it, the conversation drifted away from the literary sphere.

Soon this girl, whom I had met not more than ten minutes earlier, was telling me all about her life, where she was born, where she now lives, what Institute she attends. She told me that some gypsy friends of hers had told her that she has sad eyes and that her future would never be a happy one. I said, rather gallantly I felt, that she was very attractive and she should not feel that way. She told me that she had been dating a general's son, but his father and her mother had put an end to this affair. When I asked her what the objections were, she told me that it is a rare thing for a general's son to marry *out of his class*. For this reason, the general opposed the relationship. Her mother objected, because she wished to save her daughter heartache. "Your father is a truck driver," her mother had cautioned. "A general's son will not marry you." I asked her if there actually was this very class-conscious orientation in Russia these days. She answered that this situation has existed for many years. It had made her very unhappy but, as she confessed at our farewell soon after, she has become accustomed to the distinctions now. The "class-lessness" of the Soviet Union was too much of a fantasy even for the humblest of Russians.

June 26 : The Shah of Iran arrived in Russia today, the first package of royalty to grace the Soviet Union since the early twenties. The Shah arrived with his wife, an arrestingly at-tractive woman, and the usually Victorian editors of *Pravda* couldn't resist what may have been *Pravda's* first cheesecake. The Shahrina shared the front page spotlight yesterday with her husband, and, by noon, there wasn't a copy of *Pravda* left on the stands.

In any case, whether the Russians like the Shah, his royalty, or his wife, they turned out en masse last evening outside the Bolshoi Theater, where a special performance of *"Bachi-saraisky Fontan"* was staged for the Shah and his family. They wanted to catch a glimpse of royalty, and they did. Thou-sands of Russians mobbed the entrance way, necessitating the presence of an almost equal number of security troops. The crowds shoved, pushed, screamed their happy delight. They were seeing royalty and beauty and the associated pomp, and they loved every minute.

June 28 : Reports have reached Moscow of continued dis-turbances in Georgia. Little descriptive information is avail-able, except that Red army troops still are patrolling sections of Georgia, in an effort to keep the lid on the welling Geor-gian resentment of Stalin's "desecration." This latest manifestation of unrest might be associated with the publication in the *New York Times,* the *New York Herald Tribune* and certain British newspapers of Khrushchev's secret speech, in which he takes off against Stalin with bitter hatred and passion. The actual publication of this document (everyone has known about it for some time now, but few had actually read it) is certainly an eye-opening testimony to the thorough bankruptcy of a totalitarian system of government. It paints Stalin as a fiend, a psychotic monster, who unleashed torrents of injustice throughout the world, and especially throughout the Soviet Union. It is hardly a document which could endear itself to the average patriotic Georgian, and the Georgians are a fiery and dedicated people. Though they too might have suffered a little under Stalin, they did not suffer as brutally as all of the other peoples of the Soviet Union. Moreover, Stalin is one of theirs, and Khrushchev isn't.

Metropolitan Opera star Jan Peerce returned to Moscow yesterday afternoon after a spectacularly successful tour of the Ukraine, and he performed brilliantly this evening at the Conservatoire. During intermission, the father of Piatagorsky, the famous cellist, walked into Peerce's dressing room, and embraced Peerce. He put his long, thin arms around Peerce's shorter, stockier frame, and he wept. "I am so happy to see you. I am so happy," he said. He spoke in Russian, and I interpreted for Peerce who speaks no Russian. Piatagorsky is an old man, 81 years of age, but a fine, trim figure nonetheless. He has a shock of long gray hair, which seemed uncombed for the last few years. He has a big, handle-bar kind of moustache, also gray, and his whole appearance was one of pride and confidence. He said that his sons did not come to see Peerce, because they were busy. "I am not busy. What have I to do at my age? I have my pride; this, this is mine." He told us that he has not seen his cellist son for 38 years, and this is the first time that he has had the opportunity to meet and talk with someone who knows his son so well.

He is a delightful, charming, wonderful old man, and we all fell in love with him.

June 30 : Russia these days is like a hurricane of change. One change tumbles down upon another, and the spectator is left dazzled, bewildered and dizzy. The Lenin Testament was published in today's issue of *Communist*. The possible consequences are fantastic. For the first time in Soviet history, the "Testament" (so-called, because Lenin, struck down by the first of a couple of strokes, was no longer able to participate in state activities) has been published. Lenin is now officially on record as damning Stalin and praising Trotsky. More than this, he makes highly favorable comments about people like Bukharin, long regarded as just about as "evil" as Trotsky. The "testament" gives Lenin's assessment of the composition of the Politburo of that time. It would appear that all of Soviet history is in for a solid house cleaning, beginning with the "arch-fiend" Trotsky and running through the "right-wing, capitalist" Bukharin, who once told the peasants of Russia, "Enrich yourself."

Last night, a Russian told me that the Russian press is not sensational like the American press. Yet today's publications alone have left me breathless. Russian papers are spectacular in the most unspectacular way. A small item on the back page of *Pravda* today gave the Communist view of demonstrations which took place yesterday and the day before in Poznan, Poland. On June 28, an International Fair opened in this Polish city. Many international businessmen, representing countries throughout the world, were there. So were hundreds of representatives of the Communist world. No sooner had it started than "destruction" took place, which, said *Pravda,* "bore the character of a broad and carefully prepared provocative-diversionary action."

Western business observers reported that trouble really began when a mass of protesting workers converged on the city square. The headquarters of the Communist Party was attacked. The prison was set on fire. Trams were overturned. People were killed. The people who attacked the headquarters of the Communist Party are theoretically Communism's greatest friends, the proletariat. Workers at the Stalin Locomotive and Engineering Works were unhappy over revised work schedules and pay reductions. Soon, shooting was heard, and tanks were seen lumbering through the streets of Poznan. Armed soldiers appeared on the streets shortly thereafter. All communications to the town were cut, and aircraft diverted to other points. It is impossible to state with accuracy whether this was a passive demonstration which got out of hand or a well-planned uprising, though today's *Pravda* claims it was the latter.

Last week, students were striking and demonstrating throughout Czechoslovakia. College strikes took place. Reports from the scene indicate that in many cases the police stood by helplessly as the students, carrying placards instead of books, mobbed the streets of many towns in Czechoslovakia.

It is difficult to grasp the full significance of the change which has taken place in Russia and the satellites since the Twentieth Party Congress. We are too close to the source to draw back and out of the environment and contemplate the events. They pile up day after day. The one thing which seems to make sense at the moment is what a Russian cab driver told me, as we drove along the Moscow River toward the American House, after I had told him about the Testament: "Indeed, it is surprising, what is going on here. It is even amazing, even funny, to us, because we were here three years ago. You weren't. It is like a peaceful revolution, a quiet major change is taking place." Even better, though, is what a young Russian girl told me last night, "*Now,* we are not afraid to think or ask questions."

July 1 : A story making the rounds these days is that during Khrushchev's no longer secret speech, which he made in the great Kremlin palace just before the close of the Twentieth Congress, a note was passed up to him. It read: "Why didn't you do something about this while Stalin lived?"

Khrushchev reportedly read the note, smiled, and asked: "Who sent this note up here?"

The hall was dead quiet. No one raised his hand. No head turned.

Khrushchev smiled again: "That's why I did nothing."

July 4 : Independence Day in Moscow. It's a strange feeling.

July 7 : I'd like to write this in the mood I feel, but I fear this will be impossible. For I've just returned from my first Russian date. We went to hear a Polish jazz band perform in Gorki Park at the Zelyony Theatre. I picked her up and took her home after the concert. These are all the facts; yet, it is an amazing event—a human testimony to the lengths the leadership has gone in relaxing domestic tensions.

Tamara is a relatively short girl, by our standards. She looks kind of fluffy and peaches and cream. Like many Russian girls, there is nothing artificial about her. She comes from Khuibyshev, where she is a candidate for the Masters degree in an engineering institute. She was born in Khuibyshev, though she was raised in Russia-Poland, the area ceded to

Russia in 1939. When the war exploded in 1941, she quickly lost her brother and her father. She now lives with her mother. She is in Moscow for consultation with her professor. She says she is too busy for much fun, and I believe her. She puts in about 10 hours a day at lectures and laboratory work, and keeps a second job as a laboratory assistant to make enough money so that her mother, who is ill, will not be forced to return to work.

One of the Secretaries at the Embassy met her in one of the three Khuibyshev theaters about a month ago. When Tamara came to Moscow yesterday, she decided to call him at the Embassy. He arranged the date for me.

I picked her up at the Moskva Hotel, spent about 15 minutes talking with her about jazz, which we both knew very little about. We then took the Metro to Gorki Park. Like many others, we were late to the concert, and the mob we were a part of converged on the theater about twenty minutes after curtain time, but just in time to hear the announcer present "Summertime" from *Porgy and Bess*. We got our seats during a five-minute break, between "Summertime" and "Love and Marriage." The theater was over-crowded. The music was commonplace but novel in this country. (I marveled at how different the Poles are from the Russians, in taste, clothing, and Poznan daring.)

Soon, we were just another couple in a beehive of couples. The sky was clear above, and when the concert finally was over, we walked towards the Metro again, arm in arm, like all the others. Unlike the others, though, we shook hands outside the entrance to the Moskva. We shook hands because Tamara was a little nervous about inviting me in at midnight. There was nothing wrong with this, but my ego was hurt; she was not afraid of me—just of the hotel authorities.

July 10 : The market in Moscow is a large, sprawling, open-air arrangement, where peasants come to sell their produce. Many foreigners go to this market, because of the more varied selection of goods there than in the state stores. Moreover, the food is fresher, because it comes right off the farms which surround Moscow. This sort of food bazaar functions on a straight capitalist principle: prices are determined by supply and demand. When the state stores run out of cucumbers, you probably can find them at the peasant market, but at a jacked-up price. Incidentally, last week, the Council of Ministers published a decree to the effect that urban owners of livestock must relinquish their property to the state. It seems that too many peasants have been fattening their stock (usually one or two cows at best) with food purchased at state stores at low prices for sale in the peasant market at higher prices. Their incentive was too capitalistic, apparently, for the Party leadership. In any case, I went down there this afternoon with a girl from the Embassy who wanted to buy some fresh vegetables. I was off at one counter, while she was at another. I heard a louder than normal roar from her "counter" and went over to see what was happening. Apparently, she had been mistaken for a German, and the peasant behind the counter asked her (she does not speak much Russian at all) if she was a German. She asked him to repeat his question. "Are you a German?" he repeated. "Are you a Nazi?" he asked. She understood the word "Nazi," and quickly showed her U.S. passport.

"I am an American," she answered. When he heard the word American, his entire disposition changed, as did the disposition of all the Russians who had gathered around the "counter." "American, American," he said, and he smiled broadly. "All of us Russians remember the Americans and all their help during the war against the Nazis. We suffered from that war. We suffered a lot, and we do not want another war. But we know that the Americans do not want a war either." Cries of approval went up in the crowd. The counterman put his leg up on the counter and rolled up his pants. He had a wooden leg. "That is why I don't like Nazis. I don't like them because they made us suffer. But we always have liked the Americans, even when we were told that you were bad, evil. We remember the war. We love the American people." He started filling her bag with potatoes, carrots and cucumbers. "Here, take this food. We don't want money. Please just take this as a gift." She accepted the gift and thanked them all very much. Before we left the market, the counterman shouted: "Why don't you come to my house tonight for supper? I make a very good borscht." We told him that one day, we hoped real soon, we would. We left the market with the most meaningful bag of vegetables in Moscow.

July 13 : Many things American have been seeping into Russia of late. In addition to music, jazz, books, Americans, there are also some old superstitions. Today is Friday the thirteenth, and a Russian, who works at the Embassy, did not show up for work. He told his superior yesterday that he would not even leave the house on Friday the thirteenth. "Who knows what can happen to a person on Black Friday?" This Ivan does not even sign his pay check if his name happens to fall on the thirteenth line.

July 14 : An evening with Arkady Raikin is like a major operation on Soviet society. Raikin, who is a top-flight Soviet

satirist from Leningrad, slashes Soviet Russia to pieces, and
the thousands who flock to the Estradny Theater at the Ermi-
tazh Park just love him. Raikin's act is a series of skits, each a
masterful insight into the system.

First: a writer appears at the office of a publisher. He is a
writer who writes what the Party wants, and has many books
to prove it. He earns a great deal of money, and he enjoys most
of all the "advances" which he receives before he even writes a
line. "Where is the first chapter?" the publisher asks. "I haven't
done it yet, because I want another advance." "But you have
already had two advances, and we haven't seen a line." "Without a lot of money, words come very slow. I am no Sholokhov." The reference to Sholokhov, the brilliant Russian
author of *Quiet Flows the Don,* who hasn't published a line in
over twenty years, as a kind of quiet protest against the regime
inflicting its criterion of art upon an artist, was especially revealing. Russian writers of sensitivity and genius, like him,
have refused to write what the Party wants.

Second: The chief of a local fire station sits, quite bored,
at his desk. The phone rings. He lifts it up, very slowly, very
annoyed. "Yes . . . a fire . . . interesting . . . hmmm, the
whole house is burning . . . what kind of a house? . . .
wooden, hmmm . . . how did it start? . . . match? . . .
strange! . . . oh, you want me to send a truck . . . wait a
minute . . . I'll see if one is available." He picks up another
phone, slowly, very slowly, and speaks to his aide. Minutes
are passing. He shows no concern over the fate of the burning
house or the owner's appeal. "Ivan, hello, how are you? . . .
and the wife? . . . good . . . oh, she's at the dacha . . .
good, it's nice weather . . . (all in a very bored voice . . .
the other receiver is off the hook . . . the house is still burning) What's that? You have an anecdote? (His whole expression changes . . . he gets excited . . . interested . . .)

Is that right? (he listens and starts to laugh uncontrollably) . . . Is that right? Husband comes home and finds wife . . . (he can't speak . . . he is laughing too hard) . . . Oh, that is funny . . . Say, Ivan, why did you call me? Oh, I called you. Oh, my God, the fire," and then the fire chief hangs up on Ivan, and once again reassuming his tired, bored, annoyed air, he drifts off into a quiet droning kind of voice, as he picks up the other receiver. "Yes . . . I hear you, still burning (very bored) . . . oh well, what can we do? . . . Oh, you want a fire truck . . . hmmm . . . (seconds pass quietly, as he picks imaginary threads from his jacket) . . . Let me see. What's that? . . . The house has already burned down . . . then why call me?" . . . and he hangs up furiously. In six months in Moscow, I have yet to see a fire engine roll by, in a great big hurry to a burning house.

Third: A young dandy, cane in hand, arrives in the house of the girl he proposes to marry. He is a student at the Institute which her father runs. The girl is very wealthy, and she has a high position in society. The dandy wants her for two reasons: money and position. He would take any girl, who was this academician's daughter. That a person marries for wealth and position occurs in our society, the Communists would say, but not in theirs. Yet it does, as Raikin demonstrated, and the audience loved it. It reminded me of the story a Russian girl told me—that her mother wouldn't let her continue seeing the son of a general, because the general would never permit his son to marry out of his station. This country is more "bourgeois" in many ways than ours.

Fourth: A "hooligan" is brought before a jury of his peers. The judge rants about his irresponsibility, on the job, towards his wife, towards his daughter. He drinks too heavily. He is a disgrace to Soviet society. A woman from the audience screams out: "And how about you on the jury? Did you show him sufficient concern? Does he know how to behave? Did you help him correct his errors? What did you do, Komsomolka (turning to one girl in the jury box), did you care for his child?" The questions continue. The drunk gets bolder and bolder. Finally, he gets up and addresses the entire courtroom in a bellicose tone. "You are at fault, not me. Leave me be. (Everyone begs his pardon.) You made me a drunk and now you want to persecute me. Send me to jail? No, you should be sent to jail." Everyone is thunderstruck. They realize their guilt. They beg his pardon. He leaves the courtroom, no sentence, no punishment, with the jury and judge racing after him imploring him to be kind to them. The skit was not only a protest against hooliganism which is a big problem in this country but also against the mild punishment meted out to hooligans.

Fifth: A manager of a factory addresses his five foremen. "We must make more use of criticism and self-criticism (parroting the new Party line). We must be honest in our criticism. We must conceal nothing. Now, start giving me criticism." One man gets up, rather sheepishly, and says: "In my shop, labor discipline is perfect. Everyone works well. Everyone is happy. I'm sorry, but I have no criticism." The second man says in effect the same thing, so does the third and fourth. The fifth man (Raikin) gets up, and says: "We must be honest in our criticism. I agree. I must tell all. (Everyone applauds. Good, they say.) We have no shortcomings in my group. None at all. In fact, we have no shortcomings in any group in this plant. In fact, we have no production."

Sixth: One official sits at his desk. He is tired and bored. He is also lazy. A petitioner approaches him and requests politely that he approve his request for leave. No response. "What will you give me if I do? One hundred roubles?" "Okay, here's one hundred roubles." The official gets the money, then signs his approval. The petitioner then says: "This is very bad. A Soviet official accepting bribes. How is this possible? I shall call the prosecutor." He dials the number, but before he can relate this episode of corruption, the official offers him two hundred roubles not to report him. The petitioner agrees, only to have the official make an attempt to call the prosecutor to inform on the petitioner. Bribes run back and forth; finally, the petitioner has no more money, and the official ends up with all his money and his clothing.

Seventh: The writer and the publisher return, still arguing about more advances. Writer: "How can I write anything about contemporary life? That's what you always ask me for. Don't write about the past. Write about today. But how can I write about contemporary life, when I don't know what is yet going to happen in our contemporary life?"

Because I do not believe that Raikin functions as a free artist—his criticism is too devastating—I believe that the government sanctions his satires of the Soviet system as a kind of escape valve for the Russians' pent-up feelings against the bureaucracy.

July 15 : The Baptist Church on a Sunday morning is an unforgettable scene. It is overwhelming, because it is so real, so true, so unaffected, so sincere. A delegation of 26 Baptist and Congregationalist ministers from home came to Russia last week. Today, they participated in the services. Four of them spoke. Most of what they said managed to provoke a tear from every Russian in the church, and they swarmed the church tightly to pray to God. A New York minister said that Russians and Americans are united in their love for Christ (woman in white kerchief cries aloud "Yes, you are right, we

beg you, we love Christ, we love mankind in the image of
Christ and what he said"); that all men are the same regardless of lingual differences, or differences in color, (women and
men, old and young, cry silently, everyone wiping his eyes,
smiling almost as they cry); that all of us oppose injustice and
war, and that those united in a love for Christ should unite
in opposition against perpetrators of injustice and war. (All
shake heads in agreement. All are crying. All realize the
meaning of the last sentence: that Americans must not judge
Russians, and Russians must not judge Americans; that only
God can judge us.) Everyone stood up as he concluded. "We
beg you, return. God be with you." The minister also said that
he did not know Russian but he knew the hearts of every one
in that church by looking at their faces. This was certainly
true. The average Russian in that church loved these Americans, as the Americans loved them.

July 16 : A young student from the University of Moscow,
with whom I spoke this afternoon, told me that he is not certain about the current trends in Russia but he is convinced—
indeed, he has an enormous pride—that his country is a
great country, that Communism has brought incalculable
advantages, that regardless of the political change which
might occur, the might of Russia would always be respected.
"For this," he said, "we Russians have Stalin and the Party
to thank." "Stalin," he admitted, "undoubtedly made enormous errors. Yet," he continued, "he also made great contributions to the development of Russia. Now, you in the
West must look up to us." This student felt that he had to
offset his unstated self-consciousness before a foreigner by
extolling the power virtues of Russia. This attitude, it would
seem, is a rather common reaction among the young people

of Russia. Intellectually, they seem to be in a state of uncertainty, unsteadiness. Their one prop is Russia, which they love dearly.

July 23 : Klin—a small Russian town—is located about 86 kilometers from Moscow on the Leningrad road. It had its first big day on May 5, 1892, when Peter Ilyich Tchaikovsky decided to settle down on its outskirts in a large, red frame house. The great Russian composer lived in this house until October 6, 1893, when he moved to Moscow and then to St. Petersburg for the opening performance of his Sixth Symphony. Two weeks later, on October 25th, Tchaikovsky died in Petersburg. But the fifteen months that he lived in Klin were happy months for Tchaikovsky. Not only did he finish his Sixth Symphony there, but he had the feeling for the first time in his life that he had a home. "I myself do not know how terribly attracted I am to Klin, but I can not imagine myself in another place," he had once said.

Tchaikovsky's house was modest. His work desk was a simple wooden table, situated about two feet from a cot-like bed. There was a garden, in which he was very fond of walking, talking, resting. An expert guide, who delightedly offered a group of us countless insights into the man's character, told us that Peter Ilyich was a very generous person. No man ever left Peter Ilyich in need of money. She explained that though Tchaikovsky made a great deal of money in his life-time, he left very little when he died, simply because he gave so much of it away, to poor families, to struggling young musicians. He even established a scholarship fund for the Moscow Conservatory of Music, where he was once a professor of music. She delighted in telling the story of Tchaikovsky playing the castanets at a Moscow performance of Rimsky-Korsakov's

"Capricio Espagnole." It seems that Rimsky-Korsakov was practicing with a rather undisciplined group of musicians on the afternoon of the day his piece was to have its debut. Tchaikovsky had heard about the rehearsal, and he came down to the hall simply to listen in. The castanets player refused to play the instrument as Rimsky-Korsakov wished, and he walked out on the rehearsal. Rimsky-Korsakov was in deep distress. When Tchaikovsky saw this, he told Korsakov not to fret, that come time for the concert that night, he himself would play the castanets for the performance. When he appeared on the stage that night, he received a standing ovation from the members of the orchestra before the performance even started. It is said that "Capricio Espagnole" has never been played so well.

Our guide also loved the story about Saint-Saens and Tchaikovsky arguing over how part of the Swan Lake Ballet should be danced. Anton Rubinstein, the great pianist, was there, and he suggested that each of them dance the part as he believed it should be danced. Both Tchaikovsky and Saint-Saens danced the entire male lead role in Swan Lake to prove their points, and Rubinstein is said to have remarked later that each was an excellent dancer.

Tchaikovsky's entire life was music. While a professor at the Moscow Conservatory, he got married, but was divorced soon after. The marriage was a complete failure and apparently upset him greatly, for he rarely had much to do with women after that experience. Our guide dodged every question in reference to her—to the point, in fact, where she has become a kind of unknown *femme fatale* in my imagination.

Tchaikovsky was a hard worker. He was of the school which believed that genius could produce one great work but many solid works could be produced only by regular work. So, Tchaikovsky worked about seven hours a day regularly, but he never worked at night. After I had recorded my impressions in the visitors' notebook, I had the pleasure of meeting his nephew, his sister's son, who is about 86 years old, tall, distinguished, with an excellent command of English, and piercing blue eyes. His eyes were so alive, they looked as though they belonged to a much younger man. He said that he had been living at the house in Klin for over twenty years. He liked it here. He likes the feeling that people from all over the world still treasure his uncle's music. With him, I had the refreshing experience of knowing what it was like to talk with a representative of the 19th century Russian intelligentsia.

Before we left to return to Moscow, though, we decided to have a picnic lunch in Tchaikovsky's garden as he might have done himself. While sitting there, we got into a conversation with an old man and an old woman, who live in a home in Klin. They were fine old people who were hungry for information from the United States. When we told them we were Americans, they were incredulous. "It doesn't seem possible. A few years ago, we thought we'd never be able to meet Americans again." The old man explained that he had lost both his legs during the war, that since the war he has lived in Klin. We shared our lunch with them, and when I offered the old man some soda, which we had bought in the small *buffet* behind the house, he could no longer restrain the tears. He cried openly, with a deep, sad happiness. The woman explained that both of them were Jews. She said that people in Klin do not like them, that their existence is a lonely one. She went through the now old story of the persecution of Jews in the late 1940's and early 1950's, and she then went on to tell us an interesting story about how a whim of her father's prevented her from coming to the United States. She said that in 1904, her mother had wanted to emigrate to the United States but that her father had thought Russia better than the United States. "If it were not for him, I'd be an American," she said, with great sadness in her voice.

Our ride back to Moscow was filled with choked feelings about these two old, lonely, pathetic souls. When we returned to Moscow, our mood changed. Moscow is so big, so gaudy, so much like a department store window for all of Russia, that we wanted to return to Klin. We stopped at the Metropole before going on to the Embassy for coffee and cake. We were in a blue 1955 Chevrolet, a car which normally would not get a second look at home, but one which simply bowls over the average Russian. I stepped out and was instantly surrounded, right there on the street, in front of the Metropole, by a mob of about 50 young men and women. They wanted to know the price of the Chevrolet, whether it is considered a good car or a cheap car, how I liked Moscow, what other cities had I seen, which I liked best, did I like Moscow's more recent architecture, did I like Moscow University, whether I thought a Tadjik fellow, standing nearby, looked Negro, whether I felt that Russia had any culture at all, why it was that the United States had so few theaters, where I had learned my Russian, whether Harvard was better than Columbia, how much the average American worker earned, how I thought Russians lived, would I make a comparison, any comparison, between living conditions in America and living conditions in Russia, any comparison at all.

What was especially striking was this interrogation took only ten minutes, and they wanted a straight answer all the time. They would not be a party to diplomatic zigzag talk; they wanted my opinion. The militiaman, standing on the outskirts of the mob, didn't seem in the least concerned about breaking up the meeting. In fact, he seemed to be listening almost as intently as the others, but he did not ask any questions. This mob question period confirmed two clear impressions: one, the average Russian does not give complete credence to what *Pravda* says about the United States. Second, the Russians have an inferiority complex. For instance, the Russians asked me about the price of the Chevrolet. I said it could be bought new for about 2,000 dollars. One man said, "Oh, that's 8,000 roubles, and that is not at all expensive." Another man shot up: "Don't be silly, a dollar is really worth 12 roubles, not four roubles. That's just what our government says." Others nodded in assent. "But," the first fellow insisted, "I read that in the newspapers." "Good God, you don't believe that, do you?"

The second impression was the result of a series of questions asking me to compare both social and cultural conditions in the United States and in Russia. When I told them that I believed the Russians have an impressive culture, they seemed only partially satisfied. They liked the reference to the culture but they were unhappy about my sidestepping any mention of their social conditions.

"Tell us something, anything, about how we live. Do you like our houses? Our streets? Our new university building?"

I told them that I couldn't say anything about that, that it would be impossible to make a comparison of living conditions because of the vast difference in social and economic systems. When a few of the people in the group quietly noted that to persist in asking this kind of question was "impolite," the conversation broke up. I excused myself, shook hands with at least fifty people, and got back into the car and drove off.

July 24 : The incidence of crime in the Soviet Union must have shot up considerably. If not that, then certainly the reporting of crime has shot up considerably. The provincial press has suddenly blossomed out with case after case, de-

picting crimes which range from brutal murder, to rape, to
banditry, to theft, to "squandering of state property." And
this rash of crime reporting must be catching, for of late the
major Moscow newspapers, including *Pravda* and *Izvestiya,*
have also gone in for crime reporting in a big way. I asked
an old Russian who works down at one of the hotels near
Red Square if he had any opinions on why crime reporting
has gone up so considerably. "This is a warning. There are
many hooligans, much crime, much stealing and murder.
These are warnings that the state knows about the crimes, that
if it wishes to, it could punish the offenders very stiffly."
When I asked him if he felt that crime has been on an up-
surge in the Soviet Union recently, he said: "I think that
crime has gone up a lot. People are not as well disciplined as
they once were." He didn't wish to comment, though, whether
he thought this relaxation of authority, which he feels is the
motivating factor for the increase in crime, is a good thing or
an evil thing, which should be stamped out. Whether there
actually is more crime today than there was years ago is impossible to say. These records are locked up. No published
statistics on this problem exist, to the best of my knowledge.
But certainly the old man was right when he said that this is
a government warning to the youth to keep in line.

Undoubtedly, Bulganin and Khrushchev must both be
somewhat distressed by the reaction at home to the de-Stalinization. Khrushchev, in Sverdlovsk yesterday at an agricultural
conference, and Bulganin, two days ago in Warsaw, both
warned that "a principled and disciplined struggle" must be
waged against "opportunist vacillations." "It would be er-
roneous not to note," Bulganin said to bubbling Poland and
all Communists, "that in connection with the struggle against
the cult of the individual, not only have hostile and opportunist elements become more active, but unstable and vacil-

lating people in our own ranks have also come out into the open. These people, misled by hostile propaganda, at times incorrectly interpret individual propositions connected with the cult of the individual, and this has found its reflection in some press organs of the socialist countries, Poland included." It is no easy job running a totalitarian government in a half-totalitarian, half-free manner. In fact, it might well be that a slight movement in the opposite direction has already been started. No mention of terms of 'Party democracy' or 'norms of Party life' or other cliches indicative of the thaw have appeared of late in the press.

Hungary has swung into line. Rakosi has been fired for the worst crime imaginable these days in Communist countries. He committed the crime of having followed the "personality cult." Poor fellow, after having murdered, and gotten away with it; after having lied, distorted, fabricated, and gotten away with it, he gets tripped up on having tried to establish a little "cult" of Rakosi in imitation of the old man in Moscow.

July 27 : The flight to Kiev tonight was like riding an express elevator from the first floor of the Empire State building to the twentieth, then dropping suddenly back to the tenth, only to shoot up to the fiftieth a moment later. It was my first experience in a Russian plane, and it was harrowing. First of all, there are no safety belts. Second, people smoke on take-offs. But the Russians apparently felt they were on a roller coaster, because they seemed to love it. In any case, inside of three hours, we landed at the small airport in Kiev. An Intourist Zim waited for us, along with a guide who spoke horrible English, and we were whisked off very quickly to the Hotel Intourist in Kiev.

The hotel is located on Lenin Boulevard. I was given a

room with a balcony overlooking the boulevard, and as soon as I stepped out onto the balcony I knew that I wouldn't be able to fall asleep immediately and I decided to take a long walk. There aren't many lights in Kiev at night, but there were enough to reveal a city with a distinct and proud figure. Kiev is a city of cobble-stoned streets, trolley cars and hills and a great deal of green. It is very different from Moscow, and this was apparent even at first glance. Moscow is like a woman who is never sure if her seams are straight. Kiev knows they are straight. Couples walked the dark streets arm-in-arm, hugging one another, kissing one another, teasing one another. There is a greater sense of ease, of comfort, of relaxation. The girls all wear bright colors. They seem taller and far more attractive than the girls of Moscow. They are also very dark from the sun. Their entire appearance, like their geography, is much more south, more warm, more demonstrative. Even the odor of Kiev is different.

I began making Kiev's acquaintance by strolling down the *Vladimirovska* towards Bogdan Khmelnitsky Square, site of the majestic St. Sofia Cathedral. This avenue, like all the others I saw this evening, is tree-lined with a park on every block. The benches of these parks, by the way, were occupied by young couples, who wouldn't run a bad second to the clinch scenes in front of a Wellesley dormitory late any Saturday night. It was too dark to see much of the church, but the gold dome on top of the bell tower, which looks down upon the wide Bogdan Khmelnitsky Square, is tremendously impressive.

I thought it was interesting that at 1:30 a.m., the trolleys were still busy. One seemed to bustle along every minute or so, and there were people standing on every street corner.

Back at the hotel, I had a snack with Patrick O'Regan, First Secretary at the British Embassy, a delightful and highly intelligent veteran of almost three years in Russia, and Leo Haimson of the University of Chicago History Department. O'Regan told the best story I've ever heard about modern day Russia's drive to recapture its past. (The Russians are "restoring" about every old church in the country.) Last winter, he was in Vladimir, and he dropped in on one of the great, historic churches of the city to see the beautiful religious frescos of the past. Instead, he discovered an old Russian chipping away furiously at a wall covered with a still visible old Rublev. When O'Regan saw chunk after chunk of this art dropping to the floor in a pile of rubbish, he grew terribly upset. "Why are you chipping off the frescos?" he stormed. "I am not chipping off the frescos, you fool; I am restoring them," the old man answered.

We were all tired from the trip, the vodka, and the food, but Leo insisted that he had one better story. When he was in Leningrad last week, he was given permission to visit the storehouse of the Russian Museum. He expected to find discarded works of Russian painters. In a sense, he did. He saw hundreds of old pictures of Joseph Stalin.

We went to bed.

Before we did, we ordered breakfast for 9:30 a.m. I wanted to have some oranges and, since they are very scarce in Moscow, I thought I would ask the restaurant manager if Kiev had oranges. He answered in a very offended tone: "Of course, we have oranges. We have everything. This is Kiev."

July 28 : The bright Ukrainian sun charged through the windows this morning and rushed me out of bed at 7:30. For the first time in many, many a morning, I literally leaped out of bed, got dressed, forgot to shave, and went down the steps to the lobby of the hotel two-at-a-time, something I also hadn't done in many, many a morning. I asked the first person I met which way to the *Krishchatek*—the main street of Kiev. I knew, but I asked anyway. "Down the street. You can't miss it," a happy-faced young Ukrainian answered in Russian. I thanked him very much, and started off at a brisk pace. I noticed that he followed close behind, so I deliberately slowed down and waited for him to catch up. He walked alongside me for about a block without saying a word, but staring at me almost continuously. "You are an American, aren't you?" he asked.

"Yes, I am."

"I knew this. I could tell by the way you walk. We don't walk as freely here as you do." He was referring to my careless, duck-style of walking that used to make my Army sergeant wince. Obviously, he didn't wish to say more, because with that he melted into the crowds.

The *Krishchatek* is the Gorki Street of Kiev. The area around the *Krishchatek* was thoroughly destroyed during the war, including the street itself. In 1946, it underwent major repair. Buildings, big, ugly and Soviet, were thrown up on either side of the street, which was widened to become, as one Kievan later in the day told me, "the widest avenue in the world." (When I asked him how he knew, he answered that so it had appeared in the press. And when I told him that the *Sadovaya* in Moscow was wider, he said, "The *Sadovaya* is not an avenue, it is an extended square!") It's hardly that, but it is very beautiful. Trees grow on either side of the *Krishchatek,* and, alongside the trees are pretty red flowers. Despite the newness of parts of the *Krishchatek,* it has the flavor of antiquity and the mellowness of age. Unlike Gorki Street, the *Krishchatek* has a lived-in look.

By 8:30 a.m., hundreds of people were rushing along the avenue. Queues formed in front of all of the food stores, waiting to get first crack at the short supply of dairy products. A line which stretched the whole length of the block waited for the *Univermag* to open. Two little boys sat down on the curb, unwrapped an old newspaper, took out a couple of hard-boiled eggs, and started to take off the shells. They bit into the eggs, and then burst into laughter as they noticed me watching them. The eggs ended up all over their shirts, and their teeth looked yellow.

I walked back to the hotel for breakfast. The manager of the restaurant wasn't there. A woman had taken his place. The oranges we had been promised so indignantly weren't there either. The woman manager said there simply weren't any to be had.

O'Regan, Haimson and I ordered a big *Zis*. (That's wrong. Last week, Zis's were officially renamed Zil's in the latest snub to the memory of Stalin. *Zis* means "plant in the name of Stalin." *Zil* means "plant in the name of Lukhachov.") We set off for the famous Kievopechersky Cathedral and its monastery.

The monastery is located on the high, right bank of the Dnieper. From a distance, its huge gold domes glisten in the sunlight, as they reach for the highest point in the sky. A wall surrounds the monastery, and runs up and down the mountains. As one approaches the monastery from the north, the wall looks like a huge yellow snake frozen against the green mountain. The cathedral, called the *Lavra,* was built in bits and pieces, starting in about the tail end of the 10th century. The *Lavra* received a lot of attention during the reign of Yaroslav the Wise, who ruled from 1019 to 1054, ushering in the golden age of Kievan history. He spent fortunes to make Kiev the most beautiful city in the world, and I think that at this time someone once described it as "the glory of Greece." The *Lavra* was the first center of the Ortho-

dox Church in Russia. It was a great sanctuary, and the mountains on which it was built were honeycombed with passages.
The famous Russian Chronicles were written here.

Today, much of the famous monastery is a museum. Some
small churches in the *Lavra* still function, and all the services I saw were overcrowded. What the Russians have not
been able to destroy spiritually, the Germans succeeded in
destroying physically. The old and once very beautiful
Uspensky Sobor, which was located right in the middle of the
monastery, at its highest point, a brilliant monument to
Kievan culture, was destroyed in 1941 by the invading German army. Pock-marked walls still attest to the vigorous fighting which took place there. All that remains is one corner of
the church. The rest has been reduced to rubble. I watched
as one old lady humbly approached the front of the nonex-
istent church, bowed down before it, touched her head to the
dirt, and crossed herself. She got up with tears in her eyes.

It is easy to become transported in time in the *Lavra*. Especially so, when you walk through the caves. The passages of
the caves are very low (they weren't even six feet high). There
are no lights. Candles are sold before the descent into the
caves, one rouble apiece, or whatever the traffic will bear. The
money goes to support the church. The caves twist and turn,
deeper and deeper into the mountain side. It grows cooler, as
you go deeper, but the air is not clear. One body after another
is set in small alcoves off the passageway. They are placed in
glass-encased coffins. Many of the Russians who went along
with me kissed the coffins, and wept bitterly. I was there out
of curiosity. But most of the Russians who went there were
performing a very important, very significant, very deep,
and very personal religious rite. An old lady told me that the
monks who died here would enter the caves themselves. Once

they did, this signified that they had given up their earthly existence. They remained in the caves to die, and when they wanted to die, they simply stopped eating and prepared themselves for their paradise of death.

There is a section of Kiev called the *Podol*. It is the oldest section of Kiev, the section least destroyed by the Germans possibly because they deemed it least significant to destroy. In a sense, Kiev is really three Kievs. The first is the central section around the hotel. It is all new and built since the war. It is all Soviet. The second is the section around the monastery. It is very old. The third is the *Podol*—possibly, the oldest Kiev, the Kiev which directly fronts on the river and which was and is the market place of the city. We asked our driver to take us there. "Why see that?" he asked. "There is nothing interesting there. It is all old." We kept insisting that he take us there, until finally he told us that he is not supposed to take us there, that the *Podol* is not part of the Kiev excursion tour. His insistence only increased ours. We broke him down, and he took us there. But he refused to stop anywhere. He only drove us through an area of incredible poverty, filth, and misery. Slums unparalleled in my experience. The streets were cobble-stoned and littered with garbage. Pushcarts lined the main street of the *Podol,* a street called the *Nizhny Val,* the Lower Bank. Nothing that Dickens described in 19th century capitalist London could hope to match the reality of the socialist *Podol.* We were thunderstruck, and our driver realized at that point that he might have made an error, for he drove us out of the *Podol,* after we had scarcely arrived.

Our driver, who makes 1,200 roubles a month, was more than relieved when we told him that our next stop was the St. Sofia Cathedral. "Of course," he cried in relief, "that's the place to see. That is interesting. That is old, very old. That is

really better than the *Podol.* I still don't know why you
wanted to go there in the first place."

St. Sofia is really the Russian equivalent of the famous St.
Sophia in Constantinople. I haven't seen the Constantinople
Sophia, but the Kiev Sophia is a beautiful church. It is huge.
From a distance, the gold cupola stands like an arresting
beacon of antiquity. "Last year, they put 16 kilograms of
pure, pure gold on top of that cupola," our driver told us.
"Here, we take good care of our past. We show great concern
for the past. Our Party always has." I couldn't help but laugh
—and I know this was not polite—for the first thing that came
into my mind was O'Regan's story on Soviet "restoration" of
the past.

The church was built in the early part of the 11th century.
During the war, it was battered but not destroyed. The outside of the church was restored last year, remarkably in keeping with the model of the church I later saw in a guidebook.
But the inside had not been restored, and we all were thank-
ful for that.

Later in the day, we set off for the theater on Franka
Square to see a Ukrainian musical comedy, but after one act,
we left. The singers appeared to have left music school before
the end of their first lesson, and the dancers who would have
tipped any scale at 200 charged around the stage like dizzy
elephants.

There is a small restaurant off the Lenin Boulevard on the
Krishchatek called the *Abkhazia.* Haimson and I went there
and sat down at a table with a young man. The band started
playing fast native dances. Unlike what Moscow bands play,
there was no "jazz" here, just jazzy native dances. Two dark,
mustached and very drunk men got up from a table in the
corner and started to dance. The young man at our table

glanced first at the dancers, then at us, and he said "Georgians" in identification, and almost in the same breath, "speculators." I asked him how he knew they were speculators, and he answered that all Georgians were.

After we told him that we were from America, he was at first astonished and then started ordering vodka. Before we knew it, we were all pretty high. Everyone else in the restaurant was too. I got the impression that the Ukrainians are a very spontaneous people, very powerful physically and very simple. They seemed to be inhibited by no bonds of sophistication, and it struck me that a man like Khrushchev can best be understood after an evening in the *Abkhazia*. Our young friend turned out to be a Pole, born in Kiev, married to a "pure Ukrainian." He is a swimming instructor, who spent three years in German concentration camps during the war. He told us that he had had an opportunity to remain in the West but preferred to return to Kiev. The pull of nationalism, his wife and baby were stronger than the lure of the West. He has another child, whom he described as "postwar." His first, he called "pre-war." He said that a swimming team which he coaches had been preparing for the Olympics now for four years. He was confident that the Ukraine would win the *Spartakiada,* which is opening this week in Moscow, a mass athletic competition of all the republics and *oblasts* of the Soviet Union. His wife, he said, had won the individual women's swimming trophy last year, but that she was not participating in any function this year.

He drifted off at this point to a discussion of the Olympics, and he said that there was no doubt in his mind that the Olympic competition would be between the USA and the USSR, a contest to determine which country had the healthiest people. "You simply can't deny the political significance," he said in answer to my protestations that the Olympics were regarded as a sports event, pure and simple, in the United States, that we do not put the same emphasis and stress upon sports at home as they do here in the Soviet Union. "Hogwash!" he retorted. "If a country like Hungary wins an event, it means that the people are strong, that they are healthy. This reflects on the political structure of the government." Using his logic, I asked if the Finns, who repeatedly win some of the great international titles, had a better economic and political structure than the Soviet Union as a result. He sidestepped my parry by ordering another round of vodka. He asked if he could try one of my Pall Mall cigarettes. I gave him a whole pack. Before he picked it up, he smiled sheepishly and asked: "Do you think I'll be arrested for taking these American cigarettes?" I told him I didn't think so, that a great deal had changed in Russia. He shrugged: "What's the difference? Nothing can frighten me any more, after the Germans, after . . ." he stopped speaking, but it was obvious that he meant Stalin and Stalinism. "I've lived through a great deal here, in Germany, all over. Nothing can frighten me now." When I asked him how he thought recent conditions were, he only shrugged his shoulders, and said, "Not bad, but not really good, not really as it should be."

Later, he insisted upon driving us back to the hotel. On the way, he told us that there are a great many "bad people" still "amongst us," especially those with a higher education. "I don't trust those smart ones who are around us these days." When we approached the hotel, he stopped talking, thanked us for our company, and asked us to come back again and again. We thanked him too. He said he would always keep the package of cigarettes as a remembrance of our meeting. Then he added: "My wife won't believe me in any case. She'll say that I stole the cigarettes from some foreigner."

July 29 : Haimson and I battled Intourist for almost two hours, before we managed to get their permission to rent a motor boat (they call a motor boat a scooter) and take a long ride up and down the Dnieper. I don't believe that Intourist in any sense objected to our riding around the Dnieper. It only objected to paying for our trip. Haimson, who is in Russia on an Intourist de luxe arrangement, insisted that Intourist pay, and after the morning was almost over, Haimson won, and Intourist was 70 roubles poorer.

Anyway, the trip on the Dnieper this bright July morning was more than worth the wait. It was wonderful. We saw literally thousands of Kievans rushing to get down to the beaches. It seemed like the BMT in Brooklyn any hot Sunday noon, and the beaches along the Dnieper, most of them on the lower bank of the river, were as jammed as Coney Island ever was. The people brought fishing rods, lunch baskets and more than one bottle of vodka. They were there for the day, and they were determined to have fun. The little nooks of beach and rock were filled with young people. All were bronzed from the sun. Most were tow-haired. All were laughing. They seemed to be a happy people. Communism was very far away from them this morning on the hundreds of small beaches which front on the Dnieper. It certainly had little in common with the hundreds of Bikini bathing suits I saw, and if I may take the liberty of paraphrasing John Fisher (*Why They Behave Like Russians*), Marilyn Monroe wouldn't get a second look on a Kiev beach.

Haimson left for Odessa after lunch, O'Regan returned to the *Lavra*, and I went back to the *Nizhny Val*. I walked from the hotel, up the Vladmirovka, passed the St. Sofia church, to the Andreevsky church. This church is situated on what an old man, standing in front of it, called the peak of Kiev, the very highest point. Actually, it is the highest point, but what adds greater dimension to its location is the fact that just behind the church is a steep, sharp drop of about two hundred feet, directly into the pit of the *Nizhny Val*. It is in a sense contradictory—the beauty of Andreevsky towering over the fallen, filthy figure of the old *Podol*. I walked along a narrow, steep, bending alleyway from the church to the *Podol*. Even the odor changed. The *Podol* smelled like sections of Moscow, unlike the rest of new Kiev. The streets are old, the houses pathetic, rickety and wind-blown. The people are dressed in rags. I felt this was Gorki's *Lower Depths*. The *Nizhny Val* runs off this alleyway towards the river. The same pushcarts were there. I heard many languages besides Russian. I heard Armenian, Yiddish, Ukrainian and Georgian, but most of all I heard Yiddish. One rarely hears Yiddish in Moscow, but in the *Podol*, it is the common language. I found out that most of the people who live there are Jews. The *Podol* is the Jewish ghetto of Kiev.

One Jew approached a small covered pushcart, selling blankets.

"How much is the blanket, Yankel?"

"Seventy-five roubles, Moishe."

"Give it to me for 65."

"Don't be silly, you know it costs 75, that is the state price."

"Yankel, don't talk to me about state prices. How much is it?"

The fact that I overheard the conversation meant nothing to either buyer or seller. They were involved in a big financial deal, fencing carefully, avoiding too great a violation of state economic rules. All the bargaining I heard was certainly more reminiscent of Delancey Street twenty years ago than anything I've read about in *Pravda*. Oh, by the way, buyer got blanket. Cost—69 roubles.

One old Russian, who was selling his ax (he had it for forty years, but now he needed the money and felt he was too old to use it anyway), told me that he thought there were more Jews in Kiev than anywhere else in the Soviet Union and more Armenians in the *Podol* than in the Armenian Republic. He probably exaggerated.

The peasant market in the *Podol* is a scene of unbelievable poverty. Most of the people were barefoot. Old peasant women sell rotten potatoes and wilted vegetables. The meat looked as if it had come from animals killed sometime "prewar." The smell was horrible. What was crushing, though, was the terrible, beaten, battered look on the people's faces. They looked mad, angry and frightened, most of all frightened. They seemed to be involved in a constant battle to outwit the other fellow in this most Darwinian battle of the fittest I've ever seen among people.

In a certain sense, the *Podol* is possibly the last ghetto in Eastern Europe. It has one synogogue, located on Shchekobitsky Avenue, a small, poor synagogue. There was once another synagogue but it was converted into a "theater for young audiences" in 1949, when Stalin felt one synagogue was more than enough. A young Jewish man was kind enough to point out the synagogue to me. He was twenty-eight years old, one of the thousands of Jews who were scattered throughout Russia during the German onslaught and who returned to Kiev in 1944. Like so many other young Jews in this region, he spoke Yiddish as fluently as he spoke Russian. He also knew a little Ukrainian. He flatly denied that an anti-Semitic uprising had taken place in Kiev in May of this year, as the *New York Times* reported three weeks ago. He said: "If anyone calls me a dirty Jew, I can turn him in to the authorities. Things have become much better since Stalin died. Legality is stronger. We are relatively content."

When we got to the synagogue, we saw a funeral taking place. Scores of Jews followed an old truck which stopped in front of the temple. Four young men carried the casket into the synagogue, and a short religious ceremony took place. The immediate family of the deceased followed behind the casket as they brought it outside once again and placed it on the truck. They were in deep grief, and two younger men supported an old woman who had cried so much she didn't seem to have the strength to walk. As we watched this sad spectacle, an old, old Jewish man approached me and asked me in very good English: "How is Harry Truman?" I told him that Truman was in good health. "Could you please tell me how Margaret is? Is she married?" I told him that she had just married a famous foreign correspondent for the *New York Times*. "Thank God," he said, and with this seemed to vanish in the large crowd which gathered around me after the funeral procession had pulled away from the synagogue for the cemetery, located up on a large hill, where hundreds of thousands of Jewish victims of the Nazi racist madness are buried. I was asked many questions about Jews in America, about American life in general. One Jew, obviously a tailor, felt the material of my suit with two very experienced fingers. Then, he turned to a friend nearby and said: "Huh, we made this style here thirty years ago!" Something, I'm sure, Brooks Brothers won't be too happy to hear.

August 1 : The Russians have an inferiority complex of long standing. Baron August von Hauxhausen wrote about it in the early 16th century, and a whole host of Western travelers to Russia have concurred through the centuries. Story after story supports this theory. One of the better recent ones is offered by an American who traveled through Central Asia.

He was in a train compartment with a Russian. They started talking about one thing or another, as the train rumbled through the deserts. During a lull in the conversation, the American pulled out a little transistor radio and started listening to it. The Russian looked at the object very carefully, and then blurted out: "Oh, my God, we've got one of those." Then, he leaned back in his chair self-contented. Several moments passed until, somewhat contritely, he pulled himself up, leaned forward, stared at the transistor again, and asked sheepishly: "By the way, what is it?"

August 2 : A friend just back from Odessa told me that a group of French Armenians who participated in the airport demonstration which greeted French Foreign Minister Pineau in Erevan over a month ago were in Odessa in hopes of meeting French tourists, who, they heard, would be visiting the Black Sea city. Since their demonstration, which resulted in the arrest of the ring-leaders, the leading members have been out of work and thrown into a frenzy, searching furiously for a means of getting out of the Soviet Union. My friend said five of them approached him and begged for assistance. They told him that the four ring-leaders were still in jail. Families had been split up. Jobs were impossible to get. Social and political ostracism had set in on them. They reported being followed constantly, spied everywhere. One of the five men looked mad. One young fellow had been turned in to the authorities by his mother, who also came from France but who likes Soviet Armenia and dislikes her son's efforts to escape it.

August 5 : The Spartakiada opened today. The Spartakiada is the Soviet version of the international Olympics. The best athletes from the 16 republics of the Soviet Union and the

major subdivisions of the Russian federation have gathered
in Moscow to flex their muscles before 100,000 spectators at
the new Lenin Stadium, located on the other side of the Moscow River from the Lenin Hills and the now not so new Moscow University. (Until two months ago, the authorities were
not convinced that the stadium could be finished on time. In
fact, the work which was being done was of such poor quality
that an entire side of the foundations folded in. But the
event had to take place, so all, or most, of the construction
workers of Moscow were pulled off their regular jobs building houses, so desperately needed, and sent to work on the
stadium. Needless to say, the stadium was finished on time.
Construction of houses was delayed.)

Foreign experts and sports writers were invited. The Spartakiada, when it came off at one this afternoon, was a kodachrome dream. Thousands of participants, dressed in different, loud and impressive colors and costumes, swarmed the
large field in fine acrobatic displays. Asians with dark skins
and slanting eyes marched impressively across the track which
skirts the green playing field. Tall, fair-haired Germanic
peoples from the Baltic recalled another chapter of Russian
and Soviet history. Proud, dark-skinned Georgians defied
every Slav in the arena with their precision marching and
courageous pose. The leaders of the Soviet Union stood in
a small booth in the center of one side of the stadium, which
was decked with a huge red banner proclaiming "Long Live
the Communist Party of the Soviet Union."

Possibly the only consistent fun I got out of the entire event
was a young girl named Rita, who looked like a cross between
a Russian and an Uzbek. She had arrived in Moscow from
the Crimea, hardy, rugged and dark. She spoke a little English and practically no French. I met her in front of the
Moskva Hotel, where she had latched on to an American

woman tourist who was on her way to the stadium. Rita was a swimmer, not good enough for the Spartakiada, but anxious to see the event. She had come all the way from the Crimea at her own expense. We started out speaking English, but soon discovered that we got along much better in Russian. She explained that she did not have a ticket to the stadium but she wanted desperately to see the display. I told her, not knowing at all how, that I would see to it that she got in, even if I had to give her my ticket. She suddenly grew bold, and said she would come along with us in a bus reserved for American tourists, with the Intourist guide, a young man who did not seem to mind in the least.

As we approached the stadium, the traffic grew thicker, the bus moved slower, and Rita got more sober. "How can I possibly get in without a ticket?" I thought I had a solution, based on over six months of Moscow experience. I told Rita that she could pretend to be our Intourist guide, that we would be a delegation of American educators who do not know a word of Russian. "What a wonderful idea! It's much better these days as a foreigner than a Russian, especially as a part of a delegation." Encouraged by the boldness of the scheme, she took all of our tickets—there were about seven of us in the crowd, including the Intourist guide who decided to go along with the American scheme to outwit the ticket holders at the gates. Of course, we were one ticket short, but Rita held all of our tickets, proudly led her little delegation up to the ticket-taker and handed him all the tickets. He counted them very quickly, never noticed that there was one ticket less, and Rita took the tickets back, smiled at me, and turned to the ticket-taker and announced that we were a group of American scholars, an "important delegation," she added.

"Please, please, this way," the man said obsequiously.

"God, how wonderful to be a foreigner in Moscow these days!"

August 7 : Isaiah Berlin, one of the West's most thoroughly competent people, arrived in town yesterday. Lunch at the *Druzhba* (Friendship) outdoor cafe (set up after the Geneva Conference) was an enlightening experience. One of the most amusing stories he told concerned a recent statement by Nasser regarding the Suez Canal seizure. He was ripping into the "Western imperialists," and then he said that 200,000 Egyptians had been killed during the time of the French construction of the canal. This, he added, must be avenged. Berlin said the Egyptian historians, not always known for their accuracy, must have got confused in their research. 200,-000 Egyptians were indeed killed, but in an earlier and disastrous Egyptian endeavor to build the canal! It was because of these deaths that the Egyptians later allowed the French to build the canal.

A late dinner at the outdoor seventh floor restaurant at the Moskva Hotel, with an adequate band and lots of flowers, can be fun—once you are upstairs. To get upstairs though is sometimes rough. This evening, an American tourist with whom I had dinner decided to get a pack of cigarettes in the middle of his meal. This necessitated his going down to the third floor of the hotel, then taking a different elevator back up to the eighth floor where his hotel room was located, get the cigarettes, go back to the third floor, and then take the elevator up again to the seventh, where the restaurant is located. The only trouble was that my friend could not get a ride up to the seventh floor. The elevator operator refused to take him up. She said she could only go to the 15th floor, but not to the seventh.

"But why!" my friend shouted. "Please take me upstairs, my food is getting cold."

"No, I won't."

"Please."

"No."

"Dammit," he shouted. "Take me up there. I am an American tourist. I have never heard anything so foolish in my whole life. Why can you go to the fifteenth but not to the seventh?"

"Listen," she answered, "don't threaten me. We Russians have a bomb too."

August 12 : A Norwegian jazz band, invited to Russia on a "concert" tour, to a country which frowns upon jazz as a decadent art form, performed this evening at the American House, possibly the only refuge of real Americana in the Soviet Union. It is a three-piece group, loaded with rhythm, with a fine, keen ear for the down beat. The club was packed, and the dancing lasted until 5 a.m. Sunday morning. An amazing hodge-podge of nationalities lost their identities in old-fashioned dizzy jazz. Everyone was delighted. It was like a reprieve from a musically-inclined god.

At 5 a.m., it is a difficult job getting a taxi, but we managed to hail one after an hour. The four girls piled into the back seat. I sat up front with the driver, who looked very severe. He turned around, saw four bodies huddled in the back seat, and said: "I can not take five passengers. Four is all that is permitted. Three in back, one in front. That is the law." I pleaded with him to please take us up to Tchaikovsky Avenue, that we had waited an hour to get a taxi, that we were very tired. He sympathized, but he did not yield an inch. "A law is a law," and a law in this law-abiding country must not be broken.

"Please, just take us up to the American Embassy," I pleaded in final desperation.

"Oh, you are Americans! Why didn't you say so. Of course, I'll take you there." And he set off briskly up the *Sadovaya*, smiling, his entire disposition changed. "I love Americans. We all do, I think. We read a lot of nonsense about you, but we remember what you did for us during the war. We don't want any war, and we know who our friends are. Americans are a cultured people, a very cultured people. We are . . . we are just not right. Something is lacking here. We are just not right, but Americans—they are a cultured people. I like them." The evening of jazz couldn't have been climaxed any better.

August 13 : North of Moscow on the Leningrad road, about thirty minutes by car out of the capital, is Khimki river port. Boats run along the Moscow River, from this port, all the way down to the Caspian Sea, by way of the Volga. The river system of Russia is not as vital today as it was 800 years ago, even 200 years ago, but it still performs an important economic function. Today, on a bitterly cold August morning, a group of Americans took a boat to a place called Sunny Fields. It is about three hours out of Moscow. Reinforced by a hearty supply of orange juice and vodka, we braved the winds, the rains, and the cold on the deck of this small river boat, which chugged its way from one peasant village to another, picking up passengers, dropping others off, with the lazy dispatch characteristic of Russia on most occasions. The ride to Sunny Fields was pleasant but uninspiring, especially since few of us had had more than three or four hours sleep after the jazz at American House. Sunny Fields itself was hardly sunny this rainy day, but it was pleasant. We had a sandwich lunch, cookies, and wine. Entertainment was supplied by an amateur group of performers for a group of chauffeurs who had the day off and were spending it up at the Fields, as we were. One comedian was excellent. He wore a false mustache and walked like Charlie Chaplin.

The weather chased us back on an earlier boat. We sat down on the top deck, and we were followed unintentionally by a large contingent of this chauffeur "delegation." Soon the inevitable conversation started, and so too started one of the frankest displays of a totalitarian system at work I had ever seen. All of the people on deck were simple, ordinary, nice Russians. They had had a lot to drink, and they were feeling good. One woman stood out from the mass. She wore a kerchief. She looked sort of nervous. She obviously did not like the idea of her "charges" so close to a group of foreigners. She was openly uncomfortable in our presence. Three or four men came up very close to me and asked if we had enjoyed our stay at Sunny Fields. We told them that we had, that the weather had not dampened our enthusiasm too drastically.

These were middle-aged Russians and by the look of their faces and hands, they worked very hard.

"Where are you from?"

"America," I answered calmly.

The usual gasp followed, and the kerchiefed woman immediately looked very perturbed. She smiled and gently insisted that the men move away, that they were obviously disturbing us. I told her that they were in no way disturbing us, that we wanted to talk with them. One of the older men said: "Yes, we wish to talk, now it is all right to talk. We want peace and friendship. We are a peaceful people, and we want peace with all peoples." He was spouting the line, but he spouted it sincerely. The woman immediately agreed, since this is indeed the current line, and it is a popular one. Many more Russians started jamming around us, but I noticed that the woman did a thorough job of keeping all of the younger Russians away from the conversation. She wanted the older ones to leave as well, but they seemed adamant, and indeed after her own line about friendship and peace, she was not in a position to enforce her decision too openly.

We started to exchange cigarettes. They took Kools and Pall Malls. We took "Northern" cigarettes. I volunteered my lighter, but one Russian, dark-skinned, healthy, cast-eyed, and with terribly bad teeth, insisted that we use his lighter. It was indeed a fine lighter, which got a flame started faster than my wind-proof Ronson. He displayed it to the entire group very proudly, claimed it was a Russian lighter, which is better than our Ronsons. I asked him if I could see it. He gave it to me hesitatingly. Under the lighter were the words in German "Made in Austria." The bad-toothed one was very close to me. I merely pointed to the Austrian sign and mumbled "Russian?" He looked me in the eye, and we understood one another. There was a look of shame, false glory, a vacant pride. The woman asked if she could see his lighter too. He shoved it into his pocket, said, "Not important. What is important is that we want peace. Anyone, anyone at all who fools with us will be killed. We are very powerful. We want to be left alone. We don't care about who pushed us around. If anyone tries, they will regret what they did. We will cut off the hand that tries to strike us." (This is almost exactly what Bulganin and Cyrankiewicz said right after Poznan. His memory was good. The woman seemed momentarily satisfied.)

The next inevitable subject was automobiles. We dis-

cussed the prices of American cars. Finally, one man volunteered that his plant still uses all the parts which they copied
from American cars which they received during the war. He
seemed very hostile (and this pleased our "Red" woman) as
he asked why Americans do not invest in capital repairs. He
seemed terribly smug. I told him that it takes less money generally to get a new car than to invest in capital repairs. His
hostility changed to docile acquiescence. The woman started
to get angry. My statement had struck home the fact that
Russia is very poorly equipped with consumer and luxury
goods. She moved all of the young people away again—those
who had come over during the last five minutes. She then
started on the older men—the hard core of five men who had
been around me from the start—but they refused to move at
all. They wanted to talk. They asked me what a dozen eggs
cost. I told them honestly that I hadn't the vaguest idea. My
mother, I said, had spoiled me, for I had never shopped for
eggs in my life. The men nodded understandingly. The
women laughed. The kerchiefed woman forced a weak grin,
but she was very unhappy. She wanted the conversation to
end. She began to lose control over the younger people who
kept coming back for more of the discussion.

The oldest man, who thought he knew how to satisfy the
woman's desire to keep the conversation "clean," so to speak,
told me in a great conspiratorial tone that everyone knew that
it was impossible for an average working man to live well in
America, "under capitalist oppression." He leaned over very
close to my face as he said this. He seemed terribly content
with his observation. The woman beamed at his "alertness."
I decided to launch my father on a personal campaign of enlightenment against Russian Communist propaganda. I spoke
to the Russian in just as conspiratorial a tone of voice, leaning even closer to him (the effect this had was of tightening

the group around our two heads, one poised against the other), as follows:

"My father is a proletarian worker. He is an ordinary American working man, who has labored with his hands all his life. He is an American proletarian (throwing in their terminology). Shall I tell you what he has under 'capitalist oppression?' He has a house in a fine New York suburb, which he has completely paid for. He has a car which is his, and this car is a convertible. He has put me through two universities, and my brother through one. My mother does not work, because she doesn't have to work. My father goes to his dacha in the country for two weeks every year. He gave my sister a large and beautiful wedding. He is a respected member of his community. He has some money in the bank for a rainy day. For all of these reasons, he loves the United States. That," I concluded, "is what an ordinary American worker has."

My words tumbled upon these people like a pile of bricks. They were dumbfounded. They *knew* I spoke the truth, and they believed me. Their cockiness had been reduced to a pitiful beaten expression.

Our woman, at this, had had enough. She merely told them all to get back to their seats, which they all did, slowly, meekly. The terrible pressure of truth and the terrible reality of their position both had a depressing effect. There was no more singing, no more laughter. They sat by meekly at her "request." I had never seen Soviet democracy work so effectively before. It was a stunning experience. Soon a young group of men and women, not a part of this group and therefore not under our woman's direct control, approached us, asked us to sing American songs, which we did the rest of the way into Moscow. The chauffeurs sat by and only listened. Their outing was over. They looked like puppies with their tails between their legs. The boat docked finally, and we had returned to Moscow. When I left, I waved at the chauffeurs. They did not wave back. They merely sat on deck until we had left. When we got on land, one of the young men of this group who had been pushed off to the side, rushed over to me, shook my hand, and raced off, saying, "Thank you, thank you very much."

August 13 : I met a young Russian girl in the library today who told me (after a short discussion of America and nylon stockings) that she hates Soviet novels. "I read only Russian novels now. Russian novels of the 19th century. Those have no politics. They are pure art. We are all—me and my friends —sick and tired of politics in art. We want art again. Real art. Here, things are still far from good. They are just not right. We crave art, pure art." When I suggested that maybe the new trend in Soviet life might lead to greater freedom in the arts, may lead to works of art, with no politics, she answered: "Possibly, we will see. I have no faith, no confidence. I hope so. I hope so," and she forlornly left, promising to look for me in the library so we could discuss "pure art" once again.

August 15 : This afternoon, I wanted to take a street car to the end of the line. It didn't matter which one, or where it would end up. I wanted to go to the end of the line. I got on Tram 47, near Gorki Park, with a friend, and told the woman who sells tickets that I wanted two tickets to the end of the line. "That's ridiculous," she said. "Who just rides to the end of the line? Where are you going?" "I am going to the end of the line." Apparently disgusted with my inane request, she sold me two tickets and then made some crack about "nutty foreigners" to a friend seated nearby. The trolley rumbled loudly through a cobbled-stoned street, as it made its way slowly towards Lenin Hills and the University.

On one street, I caught the sight of the high, silver spires of the main church of the Dmitri Donskoi monastery, proudly reflecting the golden light of the sun. I leaned my old Retina out of the window and snapped a picture of the church. The ticket-taker lady leaned over, her eyes afire, her face suddenly alive: "That is our very famous monastery, Dmitri Donskoi. The big church—oh, how beautiful it is. I remember years ago I used to go to services there. Now, it is a museum." At the word "museum," her voice, her face, her entire disposition frowned. "What sort of people are they? How good can they be if they make a church—such a beautiful church—a museum (frown)? There is a little church nearby where one can still pray, but now the big church is closed. What kind of people can they be—if they make a church into a museum?" Her face was heavy. Tears came into her gray eyes. She took the blue shawl from her head and wiped her eyes. "What kind of people can they be?" Then, she grabbed my arm, and asked: "Are there many churches in America? Do young people like you go to church?" I assured her that there were many churches in America and that many young people go to church. "Then, you do believe, don't you?" "Yes, I believe." She crossed herself, twice, and said: "Thank God, thank God for America."

The trolley rolled into the outskirts of the city. New construction projects were going up on all sides. The buildings, no longer very tall, stood about eight stories high, at the most. Stalin's successors feel that tall buildings are wasteful. The sun beamed down on the high spire of the University building. I didn't like the building. It was too large, too big, too garish.

A woman, about thirty-five, a severe Soviet type, got on the trolley at one stop. Our ticket-taker couldn't restrain her excitement. "Here is an American, a young man from America," she said, pointing towards me. "I am very pleased," the other woman said, very coldly. She sat down near me. "How do you like our city?"

"I like it fine."

"Are you now convinced that we do not want war?" I told her that I felt that the *narod* (the mass of the people) did not want war, but I stressed the *narod* part of my reply. Her question set me on my guard immediately, since only those with a strong Party upbringing make so direct and rapid a pitch. My reference to the *narod* made her aware of the fact that I did not feel the same way about the Communist elite, which are never referred to as part of the *narod*. My friend, the ticket-taker, fell into a heated discussion with the woman, extolling America, Americans who speak Russian, American help during the war. The woman countered, extolling Russia, saying that everything that America has, Russia has, only more of. My friend disagreed. Soon, the woman got off the tram. She seemed in a terrible huff. She didn't even say goodbye. My friend immediately became very conspiratorial. She leaned over, glancing around to check the empty trolley, and said: "She is one who is no good. You can see that. She is like so many of them. They are all no good. And there are so many like that in our country. So many. At night, I am afraid to walk home from the terminal. I hug my money to my breast. I fear some hooligan or bandit will take it from me. Yesterday, one tried, hit me, but he didn't get my money. There are more hooligans now than ever before. They don't want to work. They are enrolled in institutes, but they don't study seriously. They are just enrolled. Oh, my God, there are so many of them. We are just not a cultured people, like the

Americans. We have so little. Even these new buildings are not like yours. Yours are nicer." I told her that possibly Russia might have many good things too in years to come. She answered: "No, I don't think so. Here we don't know what's happening now. Everything is peculiar. Things are just not good." The trolley moved into the final stop. My American friend and I left. She shook hands with us, thanked us, and then blessed us and crossed herself. She smiled, warmly, tenderly. She looked like a wonderful woman.

August 21 : A chartered plane left Vnukovo airport this afternoon at 3 p.m. and set a course due east. The plane was chartered by the press department of the Ministry of Foreign Affairs. Its passengers were representatives of the foreign press corps. They had been invited to spend seven days (three days might be added on later in the trip) of sightseeing in the virgin lands.

The virgin lands are located in northern Kazakhstan and southern Siberia. Three years ago, faced with the tremendous problem of feeding a rising population with an inadequate food supply, Khrushchev decided to embark on a brave, bold new scheme. The untouched lands of western Siberia and northern Kazakhstan were to be put to the plough. In 1954, the virgin lands boasted a splendid crop, far outdistancing the Ukraine, traditionally the breadbasket of Russia. Khrushchev's political career seemed more and more secure. His scheme had worked; Russia had its new food base. Last year, though, the virgin lands produced very little. Russia was again saved by the dependable Ukraine. She had enough to eat, but not too much. This year, the summer has been cold around Moscow and parts of northern Ukraine, but the virgin lands were in fine shape, and they produced a bumper crop. So has the Ukraine. The new food base and the old food base, working together, seem to have solidified Khrushchev's political position even more than did the Twentieth Congress. He is apparently so pleased that he has invited the foreign press colony to take a trip and see for themselves how productive indeed are the new virgin lands.

August 22 : For the last four or five months, I have been doing most of my research on Uvarov at the Historical Library. I decided this evening that I would try once again to get into the archives of the Lenin Library. I brought my passport along as identification and had no trouble obtaining an entrance card into the Main Reading Room of the Library. I looked through the card catalogue and found very little information on Uvarov with which I was not already familiar.

I walked over to the Head Librarian—an old, heavy-set woman with a wispy moustache. I explained my purpose and told her I would appreciate the opportunity of seeing Uvarov's personal letters. Her moustache twitched nervously. She asked me if I wouldn't mind waiting, and left for a few minutes. When she returned, she told me that I would have to get special permission. She outlined a procedure that would have taken at least two years to complete. I realized that there would be no point in arguing, thanked her, and left.

August 23 : I noticed that the librarian with the moustache only works on alternate nights. A young lady assistant works on the other nights. I had a pleasant, five-minute chat with the younger librarian, during which she asked me about the cost of a woman's suit in the United States. I told her I hadn't the slightest idea. I then asked her why it was that I couldn't get into the Manuscript Room where Uvarov's letters are kept. She said she knew of no regulation that prevented me from applying for permission. I told her I knew all about applications for permission, but that procedure would take too long. She said she would try to help me.

This evening I was seated at a Library table, reading a French secondary source on Uvarov, when the young librarian came over and said she would like to talk to me. She led me to her desk and told me that I could go straight to the Manuscript Room and get to work on Uvarov's letters. Another librarian guided me through a maze of dark corridors, from the newer part of the Lenin Library, to the older part, and finally she escorted me into the Manuscript Room. An old, distinguished woman stated with great pride that I could have any material on Uvarov I wanted.

Before me was a stack of personal letters, faded with age, written by Uvarov over one hundred years ago. I couldn't believe my eyes. It made almost no sense. After innumerable personal pleas, after official Embassy letters, after months of frustration, I found myself in the Manuscript Room, simply because I made friends with the right librarian. It was a great moment in my search for Uvarov and Russia.

II · JOURNEY TO CENTRAL ASIA

August 24 : There is a deep sense of excitement and challenge prior to leaving for Central Asia. I have a diplomatic passport and assurances that things have changed, and yet I can not shake a slight feeling of the jitters. Tashkent, Bukhara, Samarkand—these are names only from history. I feel almost as though I were intruding on the dream of a million kids, barging into their cloudland of minarets and Tamarlane, of fierce and wild Mongols, of a relentless sun and a cruel desert. Perhaps like so many places in the world and so many dreams, they had best remain tucked away in the privacy of your imagination. Tomorrow Tashkent will be real, Tashkent, 1956. I am almost sorry that this is true. Right now, the entire area is the battleground Harold Lamb described many years ago in his biography of Timur, the Lame. Right now, in my mind, it still is Tashkent, mid-fourteenth century.

August 25 : Departure times for Soviet aircraft are calculated to drive any normal man mad. Rarely does a schedule call for a respectable hour of departure. This morning it was 2:15 a.m. when my plane—a two-engined, twenty-seater—pulled away from a cool Moscow, with temperatures dropping to about 8 or 9 degrees centigrade and set a southeast course. I was on my way to Central Asia.

First stop some four hours later was Uralsk, situated in the extreme northwest tip of Kazakhstan, the second largest republic in the Soviet Union. The airport was very primitive. There were no hangars, only a series of low-flung huts. The temperature was higher, and the sun seemed warmer. Great expanses of sandy wastes seemed to run off the field in every direction.

Two and one-half hours later and further east was the good-sized north Kazakhstan city of Aktyubinsk, a major rail and plane depot. The modern Soviet air terminal was a good indication of the city's importance. It was flooded in a hot blaze of desert sun, which felt good after the cold and dampness of Moscow's summer. Scores of young Slavic children ran barefoot in front of the terminal, carrying flowers. Many rode new bicycles, in strange contrast to their otherwise shabby appearance. The young man who met me at the plane and walked with me to the restaurant said that we were near the virgin lands, which, he explained, pointing to the vast East, are right over there.

The ride over the Aral Sea to the town of Dzhusaly was very rocky, and for a while all the plane's passengers were sick. A ragged batch of travelers limped from the plane onto a dust-swept airfield, without runways, hangars, or other planes. We were right in the middle of the Kazakh Desert, along the old Syr Darya River. The sun was suddenly merciless, and the dust was sharp and snappy. Pictures of Stalin were strangely out of place in the middle of the grass air strip, but he was there. An old Russian, with a large handle-bar moustache, told me, pointing to some small trees planted along the path, that they had been planted there four years ago and watered from an old water hole found nearby. The trees looked shabby, and he said that the water was found to be saline after a while, a complaint, he added, which he has heard repeated many times about all the water which is tapped in this region. He looked plaintively at me. "Water to us is like gold to you," he explained.

Our final lap was most exciting. After a few hours, a large city loomed off in the distance . . . Tashkent.

Tashkent is probably the largest city in Central Asia. The plane seemed to fly on and on over low-lying huts, each with its own little garden. This sight was almost pleasant after such a long journey. The plane taxied into Tashkent well beyond four in the afternoon, after a fourteen-hour trip. There is a three-hour time difference between Moscow and Tashkent, so that by the time we made our way to the Hotel Tashkent, located on *Pravda Vostoka* Avenue, it was almost 7:45 p.m.

As soon as I put my bag in my hotel room, I set off for a quick walk around town. I walked down *Pravda Vostoka* Avenue, which seems like one of the major streets in the city. It led to Gorki Park. (There is a Gorki Park in every Soviet city, it seems.) I bought my admission ticket (required in almost every park in Soviet Russia). The park had everything —games, movies, dancing and a free concert. A young Uzbek boy told me that Gorki Park was the only place in Tashkent where one could have a good time. After he had volunteered this information, he melted into the crowd. A lottery was being held in one part of the park, the winner of which was to receive 300 roubles. One young lady dissuaded her friend from buying an admission ticket. "It's all fixed," she explained.

I walked slowly back towards the hotel. The best restaurant in town is located in this hotel—at least, so Intourist claimed. But if this is the best restaurant in town, then Tashkent did not make its reputation on its catering. An odor of ammonia filled the entire dining hall. The waitresses, all fat and unattractive, wore dirty uniforms, and the clientele seemed to match the waitresses, blotch for blotch. Finally, the food was unappealing. No ice cream, but lots of grease.

My dinner companion was a young Russian, born in Tashkent, in his fourth year at a textile institute. He explained that Tashkent has a large needle trade, and one could always make a living in Tashkent if one knew about the needle trade. He was alone before I joined him. He had apparently been drinking heavily, but quietly. "There is nothing else to do in Tashkent. I go to the park, but one can tire soon of the park. There is nothing of interest here. There is nothing to do. Here, everything is dull. Things just are not right." He stopped talking, had a stiff shot of vodka, which seemed to brace him considerably, for he decided that he had talked enough. He did not say another word the rest of the meal, nor even acknowledge my goodbye, after I had finished my meal. He merely sat quietly eating and drinking all alone. Like so many other young people, he seemed without orientation or purpose.

August 26 : I awoke early this Sunday morning, full of a deep resolve to see as much of Tashkent as I could possibly shoehorn into one day. After breakfast, I left the hotel and started my search for the "old city," that part of Tashkent which the Soviets have not yet succeeded in destroying. The "old city" is called the "old city" by everyone but Intourist, which would prefer to forget its existence and is annoyed at your insistence upon recalling it. The first person I asked was an old Uzbek woman, who was dressed in a black loose-fitting dress which hung to her toes, which were not covered by shoes. A multicolored rectangular kind of big veil hung over her face, and she wore a long white head shawl. "No. 4 car to end . . . you see it," she said, pointing up the street. I saw a trolley rumbling towards the street corner stop, and I ran towards it, jumping over a rut with water which ran down the length of the block. In the corner of my eye, I noticed a small dark-skinned boy urinating in this rut of water.

The trolley ride cost only 30 kopecks, and it is the longest ride through time one can take so cheaply. The hotel was located in a fairly decent part of town, dressed up with Soviet buildings and stores. As the trolley noisily made its way through Tashkent, the streets became narrower, dustier and dirtier. Cars became less frequent, and camels more frequent. The sun even seemed stronger, and the people seemed poorer and different. Their dress was old, possibly the same as their forefathers wore five hundred years ago. Their *khalats* and skull-caps were dusty and dirty. Their skin was dark and their eyes were slanted. Their cheek bones stood high on their broad faces. The buildings now were clay and brick with rectangular holes for windows. The camels, worn down by centuries of sand, dust and the sun, walked droopily, unhappily, on the streets, along with dark-skinned Uzbeks, whose gait seemed just a touch snappier. Life here seemed very slow, out of step with the 20th century.

The end of the line faces on the ruins of a large mosque, which is now being restored. There were MVD troops who stood around on street corners, but comparatively few. I have seen many more in Moscow. I walked along Komsomol Square, down a wide avenue to the oldest part of town, the great market place of Tashkent, which was quite extraordinary. The narrow streets of this section of the old city were swarming with people, masses and masses of people, who wished to sell anything from a piece of thread to a fur coat. The sellers lined up against the wall, holding their merchandise in their hands. The purchasers simply walked back and forth, finally spotting something, then haggling long and

hard over the price—all this in this country of the single, socialist price and economy. Every single kopeck counts to these
people, and I have heard one old man argue with the seller of
a hat over twenty kopecks for half an hour, desperately, passionately. Haggling seemed second nature to these people.
They wouldn't know what a single-priced store would be.

Along these old streets, many women still wore the traditional Moslem veil, which covers their head, face and breast.
These are the thoroughly unassimilated Uzbeks—those who
gave birth to the *Bashmachi* of the twenties, those Central
Asians who refused to bow down to the Soviets. I got the feeling walking these streets that Tashkent in the sun is lazy; in
the shade, little business deals were constantly taking place.
Beggars walked the streets openly, asking for alms. An old
man stopped his camel in the middle of the street, and he and
the camel stooped over and took a long drink from the rut
which ran along the street. I suddenly felt sick. I wanted to
tell him and his camel about the little boy I had seen a few
hours earlier, but I realized that this would not have done
any good. His world was different from mine. He wanted to
drink, and he drank the water closest at hand. A woman was
nursing her child, as she walked through these crowded
streets, being jostled at every step. One young man pushed
her hard against the wall, and she turned around, cursing.
"Look where you're going," she shouted after him.

I walked slowly back from the market place to the center
of town, a distance of three or four miles. The sun pounded
down on the pavement, where there was pavement, softening
it to the imprint of my shoes, until I felt I was picking up
part of the street with each step. The low-slung huts of brown
clay and brick, which filled every hot little alleyway in the
old city, thinned out as I approached the more Soviet part of
town. Here, the streets were all paved, and native dress was

less in evidence. The musical quality of the Asian Uzbek and Tadzhik languages took on a harsher Slavic tune.

The buildings here were partially pre-Revolutionary, partially post-Revolutionary in origin. The huge opera and ballet house, imposingly constructed in the middle of a large square called Theater Square, shouted out the wonders of Communism and the pleasures of Russian culture at the backward, resisting culture of the Uzbeks, many of whom stood in front of the theater as I passed, speaking in Uzbek and gesticulating furiously, pointing to the colonnaded front. I recalled Harrison Salisbury's comment about Tashkent being "Russia's Number 1 advertisement in Asia."

Right in the middle of the Central Asian desert, the sixth largest city in the Soviet Union, with over a million in population, Tashkent is possibly the most striking indication of the multinational character of the Soviet Union—that Russia is more than European, that Russia is also partially Asian. The cliche that Russia is a Eurasian power loses its cliche quality after only one day in Central Asia, for the truth of the matter is that Russia is and has been for many hundreds of years a geographical hybrid of East and West, whose human offspring have always had to fight the psychological battle of drifting further East or resisting the tide and turning towards the West. These two poles are fixed points of orientation in a Russian mind.

In between the old city and ballet theater is Stalin Square, which fronts on Stalin Park, whose entrance is adorned with busts and pictures of Stalin. I rested there before continuing my walk. I wanted to see some of the old churches or mosques of Tashkent, and I asked a young Russian, seated on the same bench, if he could please tell me where they are located. He glanced nervously about him, before answering; then, he said cynically: "We are non-believers. Such questions are of no interest." He looked about him again, then turned to me and said, wearily: "Here, those of us who wish to pray go to the old graveyards. There, there are many crosses!" I set off on a crusade to find old graveyards but had no success. No one would tell me where they were. A young Uzbek, who told me afterwards that he was a true Tashkentite, born and bred, who never fought in the war, never has left Tashkent, regarded me most sympathetically after I had asked him for the location of a mosque. "I really can't help you," he said unconvincingly. "I don't know where mosques are." An older Uzbek, whose ancestors probably rode with Batu through Russia 600 years ago, told me that there are many mosques in the old city but he did not know one which functioned. As I watched him ride off down the street on his small donkey, I realized how ironic history can be. Six hundred years ago, he dictated terms to the Russians. Now, he obeys them.

As I continued my hike back to the hotel, I thought about what a peculiar city Tashkent really is. It seems devoid of a definite character. It is neither Asian, nor Russian, completely. Its mood is different, vastly different from Moscow, Leningrad, or Kiev, and its psychology is almost as confusing as its architecture. Here, I was called a "stilyag" (a Russian dandy) rather than a "foreigner." People in Central Asia are not used to foreigners. Here, Stalin remains at least a visual god. His statues far outnumber those of Lenin, and most of the major streets and thoroughfares still bear his name. Here, a major park is still Stalin Park. Here, the Museum of Art, set in the "Russian" part of town, has two favorites. One is Peter the Great, whose picture is on every wall, in every gallery, devoted to any time period; the other is Joseph Stalin. Here, alongside an old Uzbek woman wearing the traditional veil, I saw a young Russian girl walking quickly through the street carrying a tennis racket. Here, beside the Uzbek riding his little, skinny donkey, I saw a young Russian riding a new bicycle. And he was in pajamas.

Here, at the Tashkent Hotel, I have a small wash basin in my room. The ordinary street in Tashkent is fortunate to have one hand water pump, which supplies water to the ruts alongside every street in Tashkent. This water is used for cooking, drinking and washing, and I recalled the little boy early this morning. Here, the text devoted to "Overcoming the Personality Cult of Stalin and Its Consequences" first hit the news stands this afternoon. This is old news in Moscow, Kiev, or Leningrad.

Tonight I met an FAO delegation, which is touring Central Asia to inspect irrigation works. It stopped nights on collective farms, slept under the stars with the peasants, walked for miles through the desert. Finally, it hit Tashkent and is staying at the Tashkent Hotel, taking day-long trips to nearby institutions. Members of this delegation were of the opinion that the Russians are approaching the problem of licking the irrigation issue in Central Asia with the precision and order of a battle division facing a tough, known enemy. They thought that inside of three, four years, the Russians will have made very excellent progress. Through the FAO, the Russians invited representatives of eleven under-developed countries to see how the Russians are tackling this problem and simultaneously to learn from Western representatives some of our advanced methods.

The FAO group went off to the theater, but I returned to Gorki Park. If this Park, as I had been told, was the only place to have fun in Tashkent, then I wanted to have fun in Gorki Park myself. Gorki Park, Tashkent, is no Gorki Park, Moscow, but for all the Tashkentites, it is Central Park, Luna Park and Coney Island all rolled into one. Most interesting, I thought, was the dance area, a large, fenced-in area, with a small stage, a loud four-piece orchestra, over-crowded with hundreds of young men and women, Russians, Uzbeks, Jews, thrown together in a huge, active bubble of life. The *stilyags* danced fast, and confidently. The unsteady, shy type moved slowly, poorly. Some girls dressed well and danced very close to their dance partners. Others danced a foot removed from their partners and would not relinquish an inch of breathing space. Most of the men were unsophisticated in their approach. They simply approached a girl, a question in their eyes, the answer in their arms within a moment. The girl had no choice.

An MVD officer who was standing nearby decided that as the band struck up "Stompin' at the Savoy" (much to my surprise) that the time had come for a lecture on jazz and fast dancing. "All of this energy could be invested in building a hydro-electric power station, rather than wasted here on a dance floor. This is nothing more than a polite form of hooliganism." Everyone nodded. After he left, they laughed.

August 27 : It will take a long time before the essence of all the recent talk about more initiative on the lower levels of governmental administration, if sincere, filters through the administration to the little fellows who run things in, say, Tashkent. I think that a good case in point took place this morning inside the Intourist office. Every foreigner living in Russia is obligated by Soviet law to inform the Ministry of Foreign Affairs if he wishes to travel more than 40 kilometers from Moscow. (A similar restriction has since been imposed upon Russian diplomatic personnel living in Washington.) Two weeks before I left on this trip, I had a note delivered to the Ministry of Foreign Affairs, informing it of my whereabouts day by day, stating what means of transportation I would use to go from one area to another, when I would go, etc. The regulation is that these notes must be delivered within forty-eight hours of your anticipated departure. I sent mine in early because I was going to Central Asia, an area which only recently has been opened up to foreigners, and I anticipated some difficulty. The Ministry in Moscow said nothing, however. I was jubilant until someone in the Embassy informed me that the difficulties would arise not in Moscow but in Central Asia, where I would discover that tickets to a certain area would simply be unavailable.

This morning I entered the Intourist office to arrange the rest of my week's stay in Central Asia. My original plan had been to spend a few days in Samarkand, followed by a couple of days in Bukhara, and then go on to Baku. There are two ways of going to Baku from Bukhara. You could take a train from Bukhara to Chardzhoi, in order to pick up the Tashkent-Chardzhoi-Ashkhabad-Baku flight, or else you could return all the way to Tashkent, which is a kind of focal point for travel in Central Asia, from where you could take the exact same Tashkent-Chardzhoi-Ashkhabad-Baku flight. From every viewpoint, it makes a good deal more sense to follow the former course. First, it is considerably cheaper. Second, it is simply more logical than having to retrace an old path. This, in fact, was the plan which Intourist and I agreed upon this morning. Intourist said it was more sensible. I was told to return at 4 p.m. this afternoon with roubles and I would get the tickets.

Promptly at 4, I returned, roubles in hand. Mr. Barnakhadzhaev (who is the Uzbek nominal head of the office in Tashkent but who showed little authority and always had to check with a Russian next door), had apparently received his instructions that a far more logical plan would be to doubleback to Tashkent in order to pick up the flight at the outset of the journey—this, they explained, in order to avoid any difficulties. They said that Chardzhoi would be too uncomfortable for me even in transit. I suggested that this latest switch made very little sense, but poor Mr. Barnakhadzhaev seemed so nervous (his legs bounced crazily under his desk) that I finally surrendered. There really was little I could do. I had to submit to the will from next door, though it ended up costing me an additional 450 roubles. Experiences such as these make traveling in Russia "with understanding" a difficult thing.

As I sat there in the office awaiting the final dash of illogical reasoning from next door, an old woman entered the office, said she wanted to buy a ticket to Moscow and thence to Israel. She had just received her passport and visa and had just arrived in Tashkent from somewhere further east. She had to deal with Intourist to get her tickets. My Intourist officials, who tried to retain their patience with me, grew very hostile towards her, told her to return in several days and then they would see about a ticket to Moscow. They scolded her soundly for not knowing the rules of foreign travel. They told her to leave the office. She did, quietly.

I decided right then and there to get as far away from things and people Soviet as possible. I took a trolley in the direction of the old city, for it seemed somehow the most honest part of town. Beggar after beggar came onto the trolley. Each stop brought on a few and discharged some others, and I was amazed that the ordinary Uzbek was in no sense annoyed or distressed at this procession of beggars. Indeed, rarely was one refused in this land whose religion encourages alms-giving.

One of the favorite games which the youth of Tashkent play with the passing trolleys is to ride for miles and pay nothing. For example, a young Uzbek, barefooted, bare-chested, wearing an old pair of trousers, lurks behind a tree, waiting for a trolley to roll by He never jumps on the trolley when it is stationary. He waits until it has pulled away from the stop. Then, he races out from behind the tree, runs along-side the trolley, and then in a graceful leap jumps on to the running board, hanging on from the window. When the trolley comes to a stop, he jumps off just as gracefully and does not jump on again until it is in motion. This afternoon, I had the very distinct impression that there were more per-sons hanging from the windows of the trolley outside than were inside. And the conductors rarely seem to get upset at this constant "violation of trolley discipline."

One of the main streets in the old part of town is called "Beg-Agash." The only reason I could read the sign was that the Uzbek language is now written in the Cyrillic script, the same script as the Russian. In 1920, or thereabouts, the Uz-bek language was written in Arabic script, as were all the other Arabic languages. In the middle of the twenties, though, when the Turks adopted a Roman script, the central Asians also changed their script to Roman. The Russians, though, were unhappy. They did not want their Central Asian charges to have so much in common with their lingual brothers across the border, so they imposed their own script on the Uzbeks, who since the late twenties have written their language in the Cyrillic alphabet.

What made this street special for me was that despite the filth, dirt, heat, dust, general misery of the street, an old lady, who did not wear a veil, rode down the street on a little, old donkey, with the most regal bearing. In another setting, one might have taken her for a queen. She was the proudest old lady I have ever seen in the Soviet Union. Further down this street, I noticed a small window, set in a clay building just off this main street, with a horrible caricature of Stalin.

The next square featured a large statue of Stalin. Here, he looked like a massive Greek god.

In the old city itself, I stopped along one of the streets to snap a picture of an Uzbek in a small cart pulled by a donkey. He stopped his cart and said, "Good shot?"

"I hope so," I countered.

"You from Moscow?" he asked.

"Well, I am from Moscow, but I am not a Russian. I am an American." He seemed incredulous, then said, "I guess things are better, like they say, if one can meet an American in Tashkent these days."

I told him that I was very much interested in the history of Central Asia, that I was especially interested in seeing some of the old mosques. "There are no mosques here. Only our homes are our mosques." He told me afterwards that he too like the Uzbek I met yesterday, had not served during the war in the Soviet army. He told me that many national minority groups were not trusted to fight. He did not seem resentful at not being able to fight for the Soviet Union. He did not even seem resentful when he spoke about the absence of mosques. He merely seemed to accept the status quo as a fact of life which must be recognized, not fought or opposed. Certainly, Russian nationality policy has been no raving success, but, at the same time, it has not produced a seething kind of discontent. I saw no evidence of this at all. Nationality policy has been somewhat of a failure with regard to language. Tadzhiks and Uzbeks speak only their native language on the street. Their parents speak to them in that language, and it is the language they speak among themselves. Many Russians also speak these native languages rather than Russian on the street. The average Tashkentite, native or Russian, seemed to be more at home with native languages than with Russian.

After dinner, I sat down on a bench and listened to the sounds of Tashkent. Next to me two young Russians were in a heated and somewhat secretive discussion. One was telling the other that he knows a painter, an Uzbek, who paints "in a western style." (The style was not defined, but the listener seemed to know exactly what he meant.) This painter was going to hold a private showing of his works in his apartment for friends very shortly. Before he said when or where, he motioned to his friend to leave.

I left, too. As I entered the hotel, I noticed that a plaque outside the door identified the hotel as the headquarters in 1920 for Khuibyshev and his Russian troops. I shall go to sleep soon. In my mind, I keep thinking that tomorrow I travel the last part of my long, private road to Samarkand. Tashkent has been somewhat of a disappointment to me. I had expected more. I feel once again, as I did before I left Moscow, that possibly Samarkand too, like Tashkent, had better remain a part of my imagination than a part of my experience.

August 28 : I don't know whether it was the disagreement with Intourist yesterday, or the tightness of my room, or the stuffiness of the air, or the general heat and irritability of Central Asia, but I could not shake the feeling all night long of being watched. It was the first time I have had this uncomfortable feeling since I arrived in the Soviet Union exactly seven months ago. The walls seemed to have sprouted ears and eyes, and every crack in the floor was a lurking agent. It was a long, tough night. When I left my hotel room in the morning, I noticed a man in a dark suit sitting not five feet from the door. He hadn't been there before. Downstairs in the lobby, two militia men awaited my arrival. They said nothing, but they watched closely as I paid my hotel bill, picked up my luggage and walked slowly towards a taxi, which was waiting outside and which I had ordered last night.

At the airport, a young English-speaking hostess sat me down in a chair in a corner of the waiting room, told me: "Don't go anywhere without me." Three dark-suited and suspicious looking types stood a few feet away from me. None of them took his eyes off me. I couldn't help but obey the hostess' suggestion. I felt myself one step short of complete arrest, which was a new feeling for me. I caressed my diplomatic passport, sighed deeply, and even smiled. Soon, the plane would leave Tashkent, and I would be delighted to leave.

Five minutes later, our plane zoomed into the quiet, blue sky of morning. There were only about five other passengers. All six of us were barging in on Samarkand. I prayed silently that Samarkand would be wonderful. Our two-engined plane droned over the Central Asian desert, spotted every now and then with a collective farm oasis. The sand looked amazingly white. In the distance, a row of low-slung mountains guarded the approaches of Samarkand. The plane gained altitude, flew over these high hills. In the distance was the jewel of the East, Tamarlane's ancient capital, the seat of medieval Asian culture. In the distance was Samarkand. At first glance, I knew I would not be disappointed. And, when the plane landed, I knew that the Soviets too have a high regard for Samarkand, for to one side of the airfield stood 24 sleek, modern jet fighters.

A *Zim* waited to take me to town. The road from the airport to the hotel passes through the location of the ancient city of Samarkand, runs past the famous observatory of Ulug Bek, a grandson of Tamarlane, literally cuts through low mountains, which are scarred and ripped open by excavations

and underground homes, still inhabited by old descendants
of the Mongol invaders, who ride by on their small donkeys,
seemingly oblivious to the 20th-century *Zim* which honks
and hoots its way past the slow-moving donkeys and riders,
missing them only by inches. Old, beautiful ruins dot the
landscape more and more frequently as the car approaches
the outskirts of old Samarkand, where the market place is
located, where the true Asian still lives, runs through old
Samarkand until it once again arrives in the 20th century
and the usual Russian and Soviet architecture. The difference
between new Samarkand and new Tashkent is that the former
is pretty. The latter is heavy, unattractive. The former is like
a white picket fence. The hotel is clean, and the chamber
maids pleasant, as are the waitresses. I had a short bite, set
my watch back one hour (Samarkand time is only two hours
different from Moscow), and set off to see the ruins of old
Samarkand with a trained Intourist guide, who happened to
be an archeologist.

We drove back through the old city, beyond town, to the
famous observatory of Ulug Bek. It sits on top of a small hill
and only recently, thanks to the fine archeological work of
the Soviet Academy of Sciences was the area excavated. Only
the base of the observatory survived the centuries. The bottom third of a huge ring, instrumental in Ulug Bek's reading of the stars, still remains in the base of the observatory,
a tremendous monument to a great scientific establishment.
A recent memorial to Ulug Bek stands in front of the observatory.

Down the hill a little ways, along the road, is a fancy (by
Central Asian standards) *chaiana,* or tea house. I insisted
upon going immediately to the next ruin rather than have
tea as my guide suggested. It is located on the Street of Kings,
where all or most of the beautiful mausoleums, built during

the time of Timur, are still located. In the sun, their blue, white and green mosaics glitter brightly, and sometimes it was hard to realize how old these tombs really are.

Deep in the recesses of one tomb, built high on top of a hill, a Moslem service was going on. Ten people sat, cross-legged, in an empty room, speaking to a spirit, which is said to live in the bottom of a deep well, set behind a stone wall on one side of the room. A mullah welcomed me in. We spent ten minutes observing their quiet devotion, then walked out of the tomb, back to modernity.

Aside from some walls, which were falling in with age, the only tell-tale sign of old age here was a thrust of hay which grew, oddly, from the cupolas of most of the turrets of the tombs. Apparently, the clay with which they were made many centuries ago contained soil and possibly a seed or two.

A block or two away is the fabulous Registan, an architectural complex built in the latter part of the 14th, early 15th centuries, which served for Ulug Bek as a Moslem higher school of spiritual learning. Blue mosaics grace the tall spires and wide flat front. Inside, the courtyard was filled with visitors from nearby cities. In the 16th century school building, restoration work was being undertaken, and, unlike Vladimir's "restoration" of Rublev's ikons, it appeared that they were doing a good job.

Over lunch, I glanced through a history text on Central Asia and found this quote from a famous Arab traveler who visited Samarkand in the middle of the 14th century. He was Ibu Batuta, and he wrote: "It is one of the greatest, the fairest and the most magnificent of cities. It stands on the bank of a river called 'Potters' River,' covered with water mills and canals that water the gardens. At this river, the people gather after the late afternoon prayer, to amuse themselves and walk about. Here there are balconies and sitting places, and stalls, where fruit is sold. There are also large palaces and monuments that bear witness to the high spirit of the inhabitants. The greater part are ruined and a portion of the city is also devastated. It has no walls or gates and there are no gardens outside the city itself."

Life appears to have changed considerably, but the old ruins have retained their fascinating beauty. They captivate me, much as they must have captivated Ibu Batuta.

Deeper in the old city of Samarkand stand the graceful, blue mosaic walls of Tamarlane's tomb. The great warrior died on a campaign against China, and his body was brought back to the city of his birth, called "Green City." There he was buried with the pomp due a great warrior and leader. His grandson, though, the far-sighted Ulug Bek, who built the observatory, the Registan, and many of the tombs on the Street of Kings, thought it more fitting that Timur be buried in Samarkand, the city he made his capital, the capital of a world empire. A tomb was built. There, Ulug Bek himself is buried, together with Timur, Timur's son, father and, I believe, first and favorite wife. On his tomb in old Arabic is enscribed: "This is the resting place of the illustrious and merciful monarch, the most great sultan, the most mighty warrior, Lord Timur, conqueror of the earth." His casket was opened about 15 years ago, and it was discovered that Timur was a very tall man and had indeed a lame foot. The blue dome of the tomb reflects a soft light, which is at once majestic and striking. Around the tomb are sprawled little huts where Uzbeks live almost oblivious to Timur's grave. It is said that not long ago a vicious breed of Uzbek lived around the tomb, who threatened passersby and had a notorious reputation for theft.

The restaurant in the Samarkand hotel is noted amongst Western travelers for its hospitality, its relatively good food, its fine silverware (for distinguished foreigners, of which every foreigner is one) and the complete isolation in which you eat. The head waitress has a system down to perfection. She forces you to eat alone by simply not serving anyone who approaches the table and asks to sit down. This evening, though, a young Armenian joined me at the dinner table, refused to leave when told to do so, and ordered a bottle of vodka. He started telling me that he doesn't care about what happens to him. He claimed that he had no job and very little money, but he would not tell me why or how he got into this fix. He asked me whether I liked the music the band played. I told him that it wasn't bad. He looked at me incredulously, screwed up his face, and said: "There is an old Russian saying, 'If you don't have meat, eat fish.' Like everything else in this country," he said, "it is second rate."

I visited the marketplace this afternoon. It is much different from the one in Tashkent. Here, the marketplace is in a large, wide square, not along narrow alleys. Here, the peasants from neighboring villages bring their fruits, which are now in season. Big watermelons, cantelopes and grapes. The peasants sit for hours, days, even weeks, before their wares, waiting for a customer. Many Uzbeks sell *tibiteiki,* those little native Uzbek hats, which every male in Central Asia seems to wear, for purposes of decoration and protection. One *tibiteika* costs 150 roubles, but it was handmade. One Uzbek tried to sell me a snuff box, but I could not make him understand that I simply had no use for one. At last I was told that he understood no Russian. Many of the Uzbeks who wore especially loud and colorful native garb are usually from the smaller villages. The natives of Samarkand have toned down their dress considerably, removed much of the color. Interestingly, the village Uzbeks seemed to stick together, not to mix with the city Uzbeks.

Later this afternoon, I visited the Samarkand Historical Museum, which is probably one of the best museums—if not the best—in Central Asia. I was particularly impressed by the extent of restoration work. Soviet archeological efforts are top-flight. Expert teams are constantly at work at many of the old cites, restoring some works (as they now are the Registan), reclaiming others, laying the groundwork for the restoration of entire old cities, the only remains of which are the old foundations of houses and mosques. Some of their work is on display at the museum, which by the way supplied a special corps of guides for me, one specialist for each period and topic. The history of the Uzbek people is traced in this museum, as well. The old robes or *khalats* are beautiful, as are the trays, plates and lacquered boxes.

The last five or six rooms in the museum are reserved for the history of Soviet Uzbekistan. As soon as I saw the rooms, I felt sorry for my guide. Stalin was all over—in every picture, every painting, every wall statement. Yet, throughout the entire explanation, never once did he mention Stalin's name. It was as though the guide constantly missed the obvious. In trying to explain the superiority of Soviet Uzbekistan to pre-revolutionary Uzbekistan, the guide completely undercut his strength. He pointed to a hack design on one *khalat*. "This design took Soviet Uzbeks five minutes to make by machine." Pointing then to a beautiful, delicate masterpiece of intricate, careful designing, done three hundred years ago, he exclaimed: "That took one man a lifetime. Is there really that much difference?" The difference, in fact, was striking. No better testimony could have been offered to describe an attempt to destroy native culture than to witness the drop in creative mastery between Uzbek workmanship and the finished Soviet product. This point was hammered home time and time again, as he proudly displayed one trite Soviet object after another and contrasted each with a native Uzbek object. For a moment, I thought he was mad to make the difference so obvious,—so clearly superior was the Uzbek workmanship, but he was unaware of my reaction, for he continued, proudly showing one Soviet monstrosity after another.

A small group of Uzbeks were following the guide and me through these various rooms. In one room, there was a painting of Russians killing natives.

"Who are the Uzbeks?" I asked.

The guide turned to me and whispered: "They are the *Bashmachi* . . . rascals who raised trouble during the early twenties."

He didn't want the Uzbeks to hear his description so he whispered even lower, as he continued his explanation: "They are counter-revolutionaries who had to be wiped out. They were regressive forces. They held up the imposition of Soviet authority, which is an advanced form of government. In opposing the Soviets, they became regressive, anti-Soviet and hence anti-revolutionary."

I was especially interested that he no longer regarded them simply as "nomadic bandits." My guide also began to whisper when he came to a picture which portrayed the Russians storming a Samarkand fortress in 1888 and killing many Uzbeks. Why the Soviets insist upon retaining these reminders of Russian brutality in Central Asia on every wall in the Soviet part of the museum is beyond me. The guide did not want the Uzbeks to hear, though they could see everything.

August 29 : Today, the proud blue domes of the ancient monuments provided only the background for an excursion into three major aspects of Soviet Samarkand. I visited the

Pushkin Library, the Uzbek State University and the Frederick Engels Cotton Collective Farm.

The Pushkin Library in Samarkand is located in a brownstone, one-storied building, the former home of a Russian colonizer in central Asia. The reading room is large. To the right of it are two smaller rooms, filled with dusty books. To the left are two other smaller rooms and a door to the back yard. The director of the library and her crew of assistants are in one of these rooms. Repeating an old pattern in Central Asia, the director was Russian. The assistants were Uzbeks or Tadzhiks. The other room was loaded with musty books. The back yard was settled by about twenty middle-aged Uzbeks and Tadzhiks who were stretched out on their traditional rugs, catching forty winks. The sun had not yet reached the center of the sky but the heat was already heavy and commanding. Many of them slept peacefully in the shade of a large tree. The few who were awake were reading. One young man was tickling a girl's feet, as she pretended to continue sleeping. I was approached by the director, who had been informed by Intourist of my arrival, and she asked if there were anything special I was interested in. I told her I was interested in source materials relating to the times of Timur. She said she would see what she could find. As I waited, I found myself slowly, quietly, surrounded by all of the Uzbek and Tadzhik girls. They are small, thin, petite, and very pretty. They wear long, thin dark braids, which trail well down their backs. Their smiles are ingenuous and sweet, their eyes soft and charged with curiosity. They wore their national dress of bright-colored skirts and blouses and kerchiefs on their heads. They were full of questions, and they were all so pleasant that I would have been thoroughly delighted to go on with the conversation for many more hours. But the director returned, handed me three books—two were

post-revolutionary reference works on Central Asia, the other
a late nineteenth-century account of the Russian march into
Central Asia—and told me quite apologetically that Samarkand possessed no other historical books which bore a direct
reference to Timur. I glanced through these briefly, but they
were not what I had expected. I asked the director where, if
not in Samarkand, can you get source material and archeological research reports on Samarkand.

"These days, one finds out all about Central Asia in Moscow. Work in the Lenin Library. There, there are many
books on Timur and all reports."

I asked her if it were not somewhat strange that Samarkand's principal library contained no other works on its foremost citizen of the past.

"No, all research, all information on Central Asia's past
is in Moscow. Years ago, all of this material was removed
from Samarkand. One best studies Uzbek history in Moscow."

I thanked her and walked out into the back yard, where I
found my Uzbek and Tadzhik girl friends. They continued
their interrogation, prompted by a strong curiosity about
every aspect of American life, with the exception of the Negro question. We took pictures together, and one little girl
turned toward me and said:

"If you send me a copy of this picture, I shall treasure it
all my life. I don't know why, but I love Americans."

I promised her a number of copies. I was already a half-
hour late for an appointment to visit the State University
and a chance to speak with the Rector of the University, so
I excused myself and started to walk towards the door.

"Do you know where the University is?" one of them called
after me.

"No, but I'll find it."

"No, I shall escort you there. May I?"

I said, "Please," and we set off down the street, both of us very proudly—I for having found some genuinely sincere and nice people, she for having the "honor" (as she said) of escorting me to the university as a sign of hospitality. On the way, a "short-cut" she said, we passed an old, fenced-in, tall brown stone building. I recognized it instantly as the fortress where the Russians killed so many Uzbeks back in 1888. It was the same fortress as the fortress in the painting which hangs in the museum. Today it trains MVD troops. Then it housed Russian soldiers. There wasn't much difference.

"I know the history of the building," I could not help but comment very softly.

"We all know the history of that building," she answered, even more softly.

The Uzbek State University is located on Maxim Gorki Boulevard, a wide, heavily-greened avenue, which is very attractive. The University is large, and looks older than its 28 years. One of the Intourist guides was waiting in front of the Rector's building, set to the left of the main building. He was all smiles, as he announced that the Rector had taken time out of his busy registration-week schedule to see me. I insisted that was too much of an imposition—that I would just as soon walk about, see the buildings, meet the students. This, however, was precisely what Intourist did not want me to do. I was asked, somewhat more forcefully, to go ahead with the Intourist plan, rather than my own. I complied. Our meeting with the Rector took place in his red plush office, one wall of which was occupied by a large picture of Lenin and an equally large picture of Stalin. Within minutes his secretary brought in a large tray with tea, cookies and candies. I saw immediately that everything was going to be very proper. Our Intourist guide parked himself on the couch with me; the Rector, dressed in a neat, white tunic and trousers, sat alone on a hard-backed chair.

The picture of the university I got is somewhat as follows: 4,000 students attend full-time, and about 3,000 part-time, either in the evening or in specialized programs. All courses are taught in the Uzbek language, though the knowledge and study of the Russian language is absolutely mandatory, just as is the study and mastery of dialectical materialism and Communist ideology. Uzbek history is taught as part of the total complex of Soviet history, pre- and post-revolutionary vintage, and not as an integral, independent discipline. Uzbek culture and literature are also taught as part of the total complex of Soviet culture and literature, and the progressive influence of the Russian culture is hammered home time and time again. I got the impression of an educational attempt to smother the dignity of independent Uzbek studies and to mold—at the risk of rewriting—Uzbek history into the totality of Soviet history, regarding everything pre-revolutionary as regressive in a Marxist sense and everything post-revolutionary as progressive, in this same sense—thereby inflicting upon every student the impression that he is involved in the wave of the future, having freed himself absolutely from the shackles of the past. To a certain extent the success of this attempt will determine the success of Sovietization in Central Asia.

As our discussion continued I noticed that the Rector spoke with a very distinct accent, stopping every now and then to check the Russian word with the Intourist guide, who of course spoke fluent Russian, though he was an Uzbek. Our meeting was conducted in Russian. Therefore I could not resist bringing up the subject of the Tashkent Conference, which had just concluded, on the problem of how better to teach the Russian language in non-Russian schools. The topic was a sore point, and the Rector tried with a distinguished lack of grace to steer the subject to biology, which is his specialty. But I insisted; and he said the Conference merely demonstrated the "indissoluble bonds" which tie Uzbekistan and the other Central Asian republics to Russia, that the Conference merely pointed up such problems as pronunciation, (which is difficult for Uzbeks and Tadzhiks, because Russian sounds do not exist in the nationality languages) and not the problem which I had raised—that the difficulty might be the result of a desire on the part of the local population to retain their native languages and simultaneously to resist the imposition of the Russian language and the Russian culture. My reasoning was brushed aside as so much hog-wash.

I asked what changes had been made in the curriculum as a result of the Twentieth Party Congress which, indeed, had called for certain definite changes to play down the personality cult, increase the role of the popular masses, and accelerate the study of technical courses to the detriment of academic courses. The rector answered that no changes had taken place in the schedule or curriculum since last year, despite the injunctions of the Congress.

At this point, the head of the Humanities Department entered our little confab, a bright, enthusiastic Russian (the Rector was Uzbek) who immediately started talking too much for the liking of the Intourist guide. The guide promptly whispered something to him in Uzbek which had the effect of stopping his tongue. He had been talking, very rapidly, about severe shortcomings in the humanities, the absence of a range of study and a depth of penetration, the hope of overcoming these difficulties under the new situation, with Stalin gone and Leninism resurrected. He said philosophy would once again be stressed, that Locke and Montesquieu would be read, and John Dewey too. It was at this point that he was impolitely asked to shut up, which he did.

The Intourist guide seemed upset, and he switched the subject to the American Presidential elections, asked for the differences between Stevenson and Eisenhower; and the tone of his voice suggested that he wished once again to bring up the old Communist argument that in effect there is no difference between the Democrats and the Republicans, that both parties are the tools of a small fistful of capitalists from Wall Street, who dictate all policy through their representatives in Congress. I answered his questions by drifting back, much to Intourist's disappointment and the humanities head's glee, to Locke and Montesquieu, explaining that the American system of government is based on the system of checks and balances expounded in *The Spirit of Laws,* and on free elections with a legitimate choice. It rests upon the free expression of the people, since the people, not the system, according to Locke, were the governors of society and not the tissue out of which leaders make a society. The humanities man smiled, slightly, while the Intourist man and the Rector squirmed uncomfortably. I saw that the interview was over, but I was happy in having said what I had and in seeing the functioning of a nationality university.

In the afternoon, I picked up another Intourist guide and set off on a thirty-minute ride to the Engels Cotton Collective Farm of the Samarkand *Oblast* of the Uzbek Republic. It was 2:30 p.m., and the sun was high in the sky and mercilessly, brutally hot. The streets of Samarkand were almost deserted, except for an occasional straggling donkey or horse, ridden by an Uzbek peasant from a nearby farm. The air was dusty, and I wondered why Timur hadn't chosen a better climate for his capital, until I once again thought about Moscow, the other extreme in winter or summer.

Our driver, an Armenian, was curious about Armenians in America and whether they lived well. I told him that a college friend was Armenian and he lived very well and that I guessed all Armenians lived as well, generally speaking, as all Americans. He said that he thought they did not, because he had read so in *Pravda*. When I suggested, as diplomatically as I could, that possibly everything in *Pravda* is not the truth, he looked at me with an air of great surprise, as though I had just opened an entirely new world of speculation. I felt almost sorry for him.

We soon turned off what might be called the main dirt road on to a subsidiary dirt road, where we raised a veritable dust storm behind the churning wheels of the big *Zim*. On either side of the car, as far as I could see, were fields and fields of cotton, which the Intourist man explained were still ten days shy of harvest time and full maturity. We drove on for miles past exactly the same scene of flat fields planted with cotton, until we came to a lone building, with posters emphasizing the debt of Uzbekistan to the Soviet Union for so many billion *poods* or *hectares* of cotton.

"This," the Intourist man called Peter exclaimed, "is the center of activity of the collective farm." Not a soul budged as we walked towards the building. No noise was heard except the barking of some stray dogs. Our only witness seemed to be the sun, full-faced in the almost chalk-white sky, as we walked towards the building. The fields were empty. No one worked. No one was even seen. Finally, a heavyset Uzbek walked out of the building, raised his right hand to his heart as a sign of welcome, and introduced himself as the farm's bookkeeper. When I explained that I should like to see the farmers at work, he said that would be possible but that first it might be a better idea to take a look at the fields of cotton, to which I agreed. We walked along one dirt path, away from the "hub"

towards the horizon. On either side of the road was a ditch,
dry, supposed to carry irrigation water. All land in Central
Asia is irrigated. "For us, water is gold," the man explained.
The cotton buds were very small and were not clean white in
color. They stood as tall as my knee. Some drooped under the
hot sun.

Further along the road, a small conclave of low clay huts
were grouped together. Dogs barked, loudly, as we approached. The bookkeeper went ahead to warn of our arrival
and to lock up the dogs, which he explained were very vicious
with strangers. After a few minutes, under the open sun, which
made my head spin, we were waved on. The Uzbek peasants
were sitting in the shade under a tree near their little hut
homes. Children ran about barefooted and bare-chested.
Their hair was crew-cut. This conclave was one brigade, of
many brigades, into which the entire farm was broken down.
The head of the brigade is an important man in the system,
one of the ten or twenty important men in a collective farm
of two thousand workers. Each brigade leader was responsible
to the collective farm chairman, deputy chairman and bookkeeper who, I was told, were elected by a full meeting of all
the members of the farm. Whether each ran unopposed, or
led a vigorous campaign, I could not find out.

Anyhow, the homes of each of these families seemed
roughly identical. I saw one. It consisted of two rooms, one
of which was furnished in Uzbek style with one bed and
many carpets, both on the floor and on the wall. The other
room was bare, except for a small hammock. The peasant
smiled, seemed very flattered, that we were seeing her home
and asked us to join her in a cup of "green tea" and grapes,
the traditional signs of hospitality in Central Asia. We apologized that we hadn't the time and left. Before we did, though,
I asked the woman if I might take her picture in front of her

house. She said this was not necessary. Peter, the guide, didn't think so either, and I did not press my point.

From her house we drove to the collective farm's culture point, agitation point, library, amusement center—all rolled into one in a small clay hut, surrounded by orchards of fruit and a small open area, heavily wooded. A number of rugs were brought out, spread on the ground. We sat down in the cool shade, grateful for a respite from the sun and the dust. Soon, two women brought out plates and plates full of beautiful black and yellow grapes, the largest I had ever seen in my life, flat Asian bread which was delicious, and many pots full of green tea. The four of us were joined by the head of the agitpoint, where propaganda is disseminated, and we drank tea, ate grapes and bread, then figs and watermelon, and we talked, believe it or not, about the vast glories of America. We discussed the many cars, models, and, what astonished them, the fact that there were so many cars all coming out with new models every year. We talked about seven different channels functioning on television in one city at one time. We spoke about express highways. We spoke about jazz music, which Peter was very fond of, recalling his days in Moscow when all the students at the institute listened to Munich or Tangier Voice of America music programs every night and danced till all hours of the morning. We talked about the Empire State Building and skyscrapers, the word for which in Russian is "skiskraiprz." We talked about having five suits and being an ordinary workman. We talked about ten dresses and being a wife of an ordinary workman. And we spoke about the destruction of Russia during the war, that ordinary people want no war ("the ordinary people of Russia hate war") and that peace is best of all. We drank green tea in toast of these sentiments. Then the driver turned to the Intourist man and said: "Isn't this better than hating

Americans? Why can't we just get along like this always? Why must we always be told of inevitable war?" Peter shrugged his shoulders. He didn't want the Armenian driver to destroy the pleasant sensation of warmth and friendship which we had all worked hard to establish there in the orchard of the Engels Collective Farm in Samarkand. He obviously liked the friendship, too, much more than the violent anti-Americanism of Soviet officialdom. And I liked it too.

It was 6:30 when we left the farm, and though the farmers were supposed to work from 6-1 and from 4-7, I did not see a single peasant in the field. The landscape was as undisturbed as when we first arrived three hours earlier, only just a little cooler. I had had a wonderful time, and driving back I almost had the feeling that I had known these two men—one an Uzbek, one an Armenian—all my life. They were good people, who would much sooner get along with me than carry the torch of enmity, as the Tashkent Intourist people seemed inclined to do.

In the evening, I took a walk to Samarkand's Gorki Park. I paid my rouble for admission and entered a fairly clean park, which was crowded with young people strolling along arm-in-arm, under huge banner posters extolling the 6th five year plan. I sat down on a bench, was soon joined by two young Uzbeks and within minutes we were chatting. One was astonished to find I was a visitor from America. "We really have come a long way in two years, if you are here." The other Uzbek was the silent type, but his friend kept up a steady chatter. Both worked on a silk *artel* on a nearby collective farm. He said he loved to travel but has never had the opportunity to do so. "Now, we can. Now we can do many things we couldn't do before. Oh, things are much better now. Things are much better," he repeated, as though to soothe himself, to convince himself.

I asked him how he knew that things would continue to grow better. "They must. We can't go back again. There have been too many going-backs. Now, we must go forward, to better things. The 'Pope' is dead (Stalin was the 'Pope'), and now things have to be better." His last words sounded like a plea, a kind of hope. "Don't you think so?" he asked plaintively.

"I hope so," I answered.

"Oh, God, I hope so."

On this note, my friends went to the movies, and I went to bed, hoping as they hoped that their dream would come true.

August 30 : Bukhara is located west of Samarkand only on the map. In every other way, it is east. Bukhara is almost wholly an Asian city. The imprint of the Russian bear or Communist Red is, at least superficially, reflected only in the posters and banners urging the fulfilment of the 6th five year plan and more cotton production, and even here the red of the banners has faded to pink. Bukhara is a backwater town. It probably has not changed considerably—if at all—since Peter the Great tried occupying the Khanate of Bukhara in 1717. (Russia finally succeeded in subduing proud, if backward, Bukhara and Samarkand 151 years later under General Kaufman.)

The airport is located an hour's *Zim* drive from the heart of the city, and the road is paved only with pointed rocks. The airport has no runways, only flat paths in the fields. In a quick comparison with Samarkand, I got the impression that the Communists would just as soon forget about Bukhara and concentrate on Kogan, a rail junction further south.

Bukhara is a series of low clay huts, which seem to simmer

in the hot Asian sun. Dirt roads run around and between them without any kind of consistent pattern. Dirty, dark children play in the streets. Men ride the paths on tired-looking donkeys, prodded on by a wooden stick which the driver cracks against the sides of their necks. Women walk slowly through the street, heavily bundled against the cruel power of the sun. The men wear heavy white turbans, wrapped loosely around their heads. Dust rises at every step. The general impression of poverty, filth, dust and heat is oppressive. In one quick ride through town, I saw monuments to the degradation human beings can endure, to the backwardness and squalor in which they can live, to the colossal difference between Asia and the West, for Bukhara is Asia, and Bukhara is under Russian control, and once again I was struck by the fact that Russia is indeed a Eurasian power, astride the vast Eurasian continent like a mammoth state goliath.

The hotel in Bukhara is the rough equivalent of a large outhouse. It is two-storied, one of the few two-storied buildings in town, dark, and though clean, gives the impression of dirt for some reason. My room looked out over the main street in town, which, of course, is called Lenin Street. It is probably the only paved street in Bukhara. Down from the hotel is the central square of town, where the principal park is located. Right in the center of this square is an old mosque, which has been converted into a pool room with three tables. The adjacent building, which once housed the Moslem religious students, now houses the directors of the Bukhara political indoctrination center. Opposite the old mosque is a religious school—that is, opposite the mosque was a religious school. Now it is a kind of ragged apartment house, the apartments of which are in rigorous demand because of its "Fifth Avenue location." The streets are constantly mobbed, with poor and shabby people shuffling back and forth, hidden under their turbans and shawls, all carrying some kind of bundle, all going somewhere and yet seemingly nowhere. Donkeys, occasional cars and trucks, and horses are the means of transportation.

Bukhara is a city of ruins. There is little new in Bukhara. Old mosques now have only a modern use, either as a warehouse or a Communist culture center. The principal landmarks of the city are three round, hollow stone structures. They are the old trading centers. Made of stone and covered as protection against the sun, they look like large walnut shells, placed upside down many years ago at three points in the city convenient for marketing and trading. They have not lost their utility, are still used as a marketplace, and are swarming with Asian peddlers, who live and function in a spirit and environment completely different from what Communism envisages.

In the center of this marketplace, somewhat set aside, but striking, almost arresting, in its beauty and strangeness, is the blue-bordered Minaret of Kalyan, built in 1120. The guide was quick to point out that the minaret was more than a "tower of death," which it is usually called. It was also an observation tower against foreign invaders, dust storms and oncoming trade caravans. But he did admit that many thousands of people have had to walk this vertical gang-plank, only to be thrown off the top onto a stone square, where some people then made their living pilfering the dead, smashed figures and selling the bodies. Today it stands as a towering symbol of a dead culture. Not far from the tower, which can be seen from every vantage point, is another Registan, not as beautiful as the one in Samarkand, but, according to the guide, also due for an architectural face-lifting. Like its Samarkand brother, the Bukhara Registan was also built by Ulug Bek, one of three which the astronomer-king built. The roofs of the inside rooms are frescoed and carved with intricate, beautiful patterns. Students studied in the Registan for eight years. It was a kind of religious boarding school, where the students ate, studied and lived in the same quarters. About 45 students lived in the Bukhara Registan at one time. The guide insisted that some young Uzbeks are still studying Mohammedanism "somewhere in Bukhara." He also claimed four students from Bukhara are now studying their religion in Cairo. The back of the Registan is used as a basketball court, and some of its buildings are used as warehouses for grain.

I had heard about the rug-weavers of Bukhara and the old Jewish community which still exists in this Asian city. I went out looking for both. I had no luck with the rug-weavers, but I did find the old Jewish synagogue, located about two blocks from the hotel, off Lenin Street. There were no distinguishing marks on the outside of the building, which looked like any other building on the street, clay, brown, dirty; but a group of children pointed out the building and I entered it. The Bukhara synagogue, known throughout the world as one of the oldest Jewish communities in Asia, consists of three small rooms, separated by a small courtyard, with the Star of David carved into the wall. The walls are covered with ancient Hebrew scripture. The congregation reads from the pages on the wall, for I was told that there are only three prayer books. I was told that only very old people attend the synagogue, that young people under 40 rarely do; that these Jews do not know Yiddish but speak Hebrew, Tadzhik, Uzbek and a little Russian; that the Rabbi fears the eventual extinction of the Bukhara Jews because the youth never attend services. I asked if there were other Jews in Bukhara who speak Yiddish, Jews who had come to this central Asian city more recently than 1300 years ago. I was told that there were, those who fled Hitler during the war and ended up here, where they thought themselves safe from future persecution. One old Jew, who took pictures on the street for a living (this seemed to be a thriving business in Bukhara—many people had their cameras in the street taking pictures) told me that Jews in Bukhara are now able to leave the Soviet Union if they have a relative in Israel who wishes to take them out of Russia and pay their expenses to Israel. Even if a visa is finally granted, this man said, there are many difficulties which the Russians still impose to make their departure as difficult as possible. One old lady, whose son is in Israel, received her visa one year ago and is still awaiting transportation out of this city. The Western Jews who live in Bukhara are very, very unhappy with their lot. The Bukhara Jews, thoroughly Eastern through 1300 years of indoctrination to the weather and the food, complain only of the falling enthusiasm of the youth for Judaism.

At night, I saw a tremendous amount of drunkenness and hooliganism. Gangs of young men marched down the streets in the evenings, all of them high as a kite, picking on people as they passed. Emotions ran high, as fights broke out in the main square of town. Militiamen watched the brawls, as disinterested in the outcome as the people who passed by and over the struggling bodies. Individual drunks staggered down the street. Men fondled women openly on park benches in the central square. Others sang and cursed loudly in the street. One man of about 35 made love to a woman of about 50 on a park bench. The woman laughed and cried, screamed and whispered. A Russian, next to whom I was sitting, was the only one who seemed disturbed at the lovemaking. He went over and told the man that a foreigner was sitting nearby. "So what?" he answered. "I am a foreigner here too." He continued, oblivious to the benches to his left and right, which were packed with people who were just as oblivious to him as he was to them. An enormous emotional spontaneity reigned in the street, and the militiamen stood by, watching, chatting, eating ice cream, putting in their time. No one seems to have anything to do.

Bukhara is a fantastic racial hodgepodge. Uzbeks, Tadzhiks, Jews, Germans, Russians, Ukrainians, Armenians and Azerbaijani all mingle in this ancient city. With only a day left in Central Asia, before departing for the Caucasus, I feel as though I should have permitted Central Asia to remain a part of my historical fancy, never to have barged in on the reality of misery and unhappiness, of forced social and economic transformation, which is Central Asia today. By the look of Bukhara, the Russians have either decided to abandon the city to the sand and the sun or have lost their battle to Russify it. I have a feeling it is the former. For they have succeeded to a sizeable extent in whipping Samarkand and Tashkent into a Slavic mold. Both those cities have parts which look like sections of Moscow or Leningrad. Bukhara has only itself.

August 31 : I got up early this morning for a last-ditch effort to see the Bukhara bazaar and the Bukhara rug weavers. The hotel, whose director was very concerned about my whereabouts, supplied a guide for my walk to the market place, which is located about twenty minutes walking time from the hotel. We took a bus. When we arrived I noticed immediately that this bazaar was far more disorganized than the Samarkand bazaar. Here peasants sat haphazardly, unhurried in their lackadaisical quest to sell a watermelon or some grapes. In fact, they seemed just to sit there to give themselves something to do, not necessarily to embark on any great business ventures. Yet the market place was packed. The peasants wore exciting native costumes, and I decided to take some pictures. No sooner had I taken one picture than a militia man approached me and asked who I was. I told him I was an American, and I continued to take pictures. He tapped me gently on the shoulder and requested that I go with him to his station. I told him that I did not have the time. He strongly suggested that I go with him. I just as strongly suggested that I would not. Within seconds I was surrounded by about ten militia men. I decided that possibly I should go with him. Suddenly, I realized that I was being arrested. I asked the sergeant why I was being arrested. He told me I was not being arrested, that I was merely being detained until he verified who I was. I suggested that while he call the hotel I could continue taking pictures. He declined the suggestion. A huge crowd had gathered around the militia men and me. My guide conveniently vanished. The sergeant called his immediate superior, informed him that a foreigner was taking pictures of the market place and asked for instructions. The chief told him to detain me.

When he told me the chief's decision, I realized that this bit of stupidity might make me miss my plane. I told him that I was a representative of the American government, that there are international laws on the treatment of diplomatic personnel, that he was acting in violation of these laws (whether he really was, I am not sure). My outburst had the effect of making the sergeant very nervous and upset. I suggested again that he call the hotel, check there on my passport, and call his chief back after my identity had been verified. I told him that if he declined my suggestion, I would make a severe complaint in Moscow against the treatment accorded me in Bukhara. I started to walk off at this point, but he grabbed my arm. I shook loose, and told him angrily that he had better not do that again. The crowd had grown to mammoth proportions about us. He had to save face, and so he screamed that I was in the Soviet Union and would have to abide by Soviet laws. I told him my detention was proof enough of my being in the Soviet Union, that this sort of incident would never have occurred in the United States. Some members of the crowd snickered. He decided to call the hotel, and he discovered that I really was checked in, and that he was not involved in any great discovery. He called his superior, told him of my identity, and then he turned to me, his entire demeanor changed—sugar and cream—and said that he was very sorry, and he saluted. I told him that I wanted his name, which he gave me. His lower lip was trembling, as he saluted again. I felt sorry for him and walked off without pursuing his humiliation any further, but I could not resist the desire to continue taking pictures, which I did, much to the amazement of the populace. In their eyes, the dreaded MVD had been challenged and made to back down by a foreigner.

When my guide saw me taking pictures again, and not in the MVD jail house, he suddenly reappeared and told me that due to the shortage of time we would not be able to walk to the rug weavers, who were further down the road in the wrong direction. A glance at my watch told me that I had wasted 40 minutes with that MVD sergeant and that indeed I would just barely make the plane in any case. We hurried through the streets towards the hotel, where I got my bags, got into a taxi, and sped away from Bukhara, still cursing the militia man for preventing me from having enough time to see the legendary fabulous rug weavers of Bukhara. On the other hand, I was delighted to get away from Bukhara and boarded the plane for Tashkent with a definite feeling of relief.

The ride from Bukhara to Tashkent takes about three hours, with one stop at Samarkand. I was greeted at the Tash-

kent airport by the most disagreeable of the three disagreeable Tashkent Intourist guides. I had not asked him to meet
me, but he did anyway. I decided that rather than check into
a hotel, I would leave my bag with the airport personnel, go
into Tashkent, have lunch, see a play, and then return to the
airport in time to catch my plane to Baku. Intourist did not
approve of my plan; the guide wanted me to check into a
hotel. I told him that I would not check into a hotel, that I
fully intended to carry out my plan. Further, I informed him
that I had not asked him to meet me with a car, to which he
had to agree. I told him that if he wished, he could drive me
into town, but I had no intention of paying him 86 roubles.
He agreed, but he was very upset. I noticed that he, like the
militia man, had an uncontrollable lower lip.

I walked over to Theater Square, sat down next to a non-
Slavic, non-Uzbek-looking man of about forty. He told me
that he was a German, that he had been a Volga German, deported to Central Asia during the early stages of the war, and
first now able to move away from the small town (he did not
tell me the name, though I asked) close to the Chinese border
where he had lived in a kind of exile for 15 years. He told me
that he still could not leave Central Asia, but that at least he
could live in Tashkent. Though his family has lived in Russia
since the time of Catherine the Great, this Volga German said
that he would gladly leave the Soviet Union and go to Germany. He volunteered that to his mind 60% of the Volga
Germans living in Central Asia would emigrate if given the
chance. He said he loved the Russians, that he thought them a
good people, that he disagreed with German racists that the
Russians were *Untermenschen*, but that despite his love for
the people he hated the government. He said this feeling was
shared by many other Germans he knew. He said the only
other people he knew who would leave the Soviet Union in

similar proportions were the Jews. Later in the afternoon another incident confirmed my German friend's impression of
the discontent of the Jewish population in Central Asia. I
stopped at a small shoe-repair booth—this seems to be a thriving business in Tashkent, like photography in Bukhara—
before going to the theater, to have my soles repaired. The
repair man turned out to be an old Jew from Kiev, who has
been living in Tashkent since 1942. He told me after a while
that not 60% but 80% of the Central Asian European Jews
would gladly leave the Soviet Union if given the opportunity.
"Here in Tashkent, we all envy the baker. At least, he's got
his loaf of bread." He looked up at me, after this remark, a
warm smile in his eyes, happy with his unhappy joke; and,
shaking my hand, said: "Don't ever forget us."

The play was a Russian translation of the French *Sixth
Floor,* a light, gay play, which the Uzbek theater people did
very well. What interested me more than the play, though,
was the fact that the manager of the theater had been informed of my coming, had met me at the door and personally
escorted me to my seat, spoke nonsense with me at every intermission, and again personally escorted me from the theater
to the waiting taxi, which sped me off from Tashkent back
towards the airport. He made certain that I did not have the
opportunity of speaking with anyone else.

In the airport restaurant while waiting for my 1:35 a.m.
plane to depart, I was joined by a young Korean, who was
taking the same plane to Tbilisi, where he worked as a school
teacher. He taught history, and when he discovered that I had
an interest in history, he thought that he had at last found a
Westerner able to speak the truth, without the bias of an
alien discipline. "We historians share one thing: we both
speak the truth. We both seek the truth." I told him that I
had every intention of speaking only the truth. We spoke first

about the Negro problem. He asked me if I thought that one day the Negroes in America would have the same rights as the whites. I told him that a Supreme Court decision two years ago declaring segregation in state schools unconstitutional had removed the last barrier between complete legal equality among Negro and white. He knew nothing about the Supreme Court decision. I told him that the issue of race prejudice was a live issue only in some southern states and that I thought in time the issue would lose its significance even in those states.

He then asked me whether I thought true freedom, class freedom, really existed in the Soviet Union. I told him that I definitely thought that true freedom, under whatever name, did not exist in the Soviet Union. I told him that since the revolution Communism as a vital ideology had lost its essence, had in fact become a bloodless doctrine. "But we have elections, free and secret, just as you do. How then can you say that we do not have freedom, at least equal to yours?" he protested. I told him that where no true choice exists, no true freedom exists. "I thought you would say that," he rejoined, "and I cannot help but agree with you. Our freedom is a paper freedom." He had been very nervous since the start of our talk, and once he had permitted himself to make this statement he became so nervous that he abruptly asked to be excused. He moved to another table, carrying his tea and cookies, and finished his meal there.

A half hour later the Baku plane was ready to depart. The hour was late. I was very tired, yet at the same time thoroughly excited about the prospect of visiting Baku and then traveling northwestward through the beautiful, poetic Caucasus to the Soviet aristocrats' paradise, Sochi. Mixed with the feeling of excitement was a deep-sigh kind of feeling of relief. Central Asia had been interesting—on occasion it had been fascinating. But I was delighted to leave.

September 1 : The plane to Baku made its usual stops at Charzhoi (which I slept right through), and Ashkabad (on the Persian border, a city which foreigners can use only in transit), before the sun rose to brighten the final leg of our trip from Central Asia to the Caucasus. The Caspian Sea looked like a white mirror in the early morning sunlight. It reflected every measure of the sun's intensity. The rays of the sun seemed to bounce right up off its surface into my eyes. In the distance the shore with hundreds and hundreds of oil wells suddenly loomed. We flew for what seemed like hours over fields of oil wells, many drilled right into the water, until we arrived at the airport. The second I stepped off the plane I knew that I was in a totally different area, for the climate was not only bristling hot; it was also terribly humid. My clothes stuck to my back in a matter of seconds. For all the heat of Central Asia, there had been no humidity. Here, on the shores of the Caspian Sea, just around the corner from Iraq and Persia, the heat had a murderous companion.

The ride from the airport to the Intourist hotel (which was complete luxury in comparison with accommodations in Central Asia) was more revealing than picturesque: we drove for seventy minutes before we hit Baku; and we drove through one oil field after another. The pumps on these wells slowly rose and fell in a terrible monotony—the resultant product, black gold, so crucial to the Soviet system. The sight of the lazy, rusty pumps belied oil's great importance to the Soviet system and made the Germans' frantic, but unsuccessful, push towards Baku seem a little foolish.

The Russian drive towards this area started back in the

early 18th century, when Peter the Great had schemes of expansion envisaging the old Azerbaijan fortress of Baku as a stepping stone to Persia. One of Peter's lieutenants is reputed to have stated: "The hopes of His Majesty were not concerned with Persia alone. If he had been lucky in Persia and still living, he would of course have attempted to reach India or even China. This I heard from His Majesty himself." In 1723, the Russians took this entire region from Persia; and though after Peter's death in 1725 they renounced their claims to the region, they formally annexed it in 1806. They never did seem to leave Baku; and one hundred years later, as a result of foreign investments, the Baku oil industry began to be developed. By 1860 Russia had pumped about 160,000 tons of oil out of Baku and, by 1913, 9,000,000 tons. The figures have risen steadily, until now Baku ranks as one of the most productive oil regions in the world. Little wonder, I thought, as I sped towards town through the oil fields, that this town was until recently completely off limits for foreigners.

Sections of Baku are still off limits, as I discovered when I requested an Intourist guide to take me all over the city and he took me to only a limited part. "The rest," he said, "is uninteresting." "Uninteresting" is one of those fine Soviet words which generally means "off-limits." Baku was until recently one of the centers of the Mohammedan faith in the northern tier of the middle East. When Zinoviev, who was later purged by Stalin during the big trials of the thirties, made a violently atheistic speech in Baku during a 1920 congress of Eastern peoples, the Bakuians rose in direct revolt against the imposition of Russian and Communist theories. The revolt was suppressed, but it is said that the memory of this Communist anti-Mohammedanism has never been erased from the minds of the Baku citizens. I had the very distinct feeling while walking the streets I was permitted to walk, or visiting the museums and parks I was permitted to visit, that it is more than the strategic significance of Baku which compels the Communist overlords to be cautious and forbidding guides.

Aesthetically, the city has little to sell itself on except its harbor, which is wide and handsome. It is shaped like a huge horseshoe of dry land surrounding the still salty water. For a moment I thought that this harbor resembled Plymouth Bay harbor in Massachusetts even though the one fronted on a large sea in the middle of the Eurasian continent while the other faced the Atlantic Ocean. My sightseeing tour through Baku was so restricted that it bordered on being thoroughly uninteresting. The only area that had a certain element of fascination was the old city, which is situated very close to the Intourist Hotel, a block from the wide boulevard which runs the length of the shoreline through town. The old city is set on a relatively high hill overlooking the harbor, one of the many hills which make up the total landscape of Baku. The houses are old and the streets between them look more like cobblestoned alleyways. An old mosque, which served as a part-time fortress many hundreds of years ago, probably against the first Russian soldiers who marched into the region under Peter's expansionist steam, is the only part of the old city I was taken to see. Old, with great blocks of stone, it looks out on the sea like a haunting relic of the past. In the back yard is an old underground bath, discovered quite by accident in 1941 when the protective covering of earth fell in and revealed the remains of an old, cool Moslem bathing house.

Later, I walked over to the Baku Historical Museum, which is located in a very beautiful building, the former residence of a Persian oil millionaire whose son I understand is now living in the States, but which is far from the show the Samarkand Museum is. The history of the Azerbaijan people was traced back to the stone and bronze age, moved slowly through to the 17th or 18th centuries, and then made the rapid and not quite comprehensible leap into the 20th century, when the museum once again depicted the Azerbaijan people—helped by such good Azerbaijani as the Georgian, Stalin—struggling to liberate themselves from capitalist terror. Every cliche was repeated both by my guide and by the full and uninspired propaganda paintings, which depicted starving workers up in arms against fat millionaires. The Soviet period was devoted to the gifts which Baku has received from foreign emissaries, including Nehru. Nothing else existed in this museum, except the beauty of the museum itself, which has nothing to do with Communism or its architectural taste.

The heat of Baku and the humidity seemed to grow with each hour of the day, and I could not wait until evening time, when the sun went down, the lights went on; and, walking through the park which stretches the length of the harbor, I realized Baku looked pretty. The darkness hid the ugly spots, and the electric lights shone upon the thousands and thousands of Baku citizens who walked back and forth along this park. They too undoubtedly have nothing else to do. Hundreds were jammed around a parachute jump, watching one young daredevil leap from the balcony in his parachute to the ground about 50 feet below. The exhibit thrilled everyone, but no one tried to follow the young fellow's example, though I waited for his successor for half an hour. Afterward, I took a boatride on the "Druzhba" (Friendship), one of two old tubs—the other is called "Mir" (Peace)—which, loaded with breeze-hungry and bored Baku citizens, move out into the bay for twenty minutes, then return to the dock. Along this dock, by the way, is a yacht club, possibly the only one in the Soviet Union. It's private and guarded, but I saw small yachts there.

Just before the boat docked, I met an Armenian who spoke excellent English. He insisted upon speaking English, because, he said, he wanted to practice. We walked through the park, found a rather secluded park bench, sat down with two ice cream cones apiece, and he started to tell me about his life. He was born in Palestine, lived there until 1948, when "I made the greatest mistake of my life." He decided to return to the land of his ancestors. "All Armenians love Armenia. Once, we were a great people. I think we still are. I thought that the Communists had given us a chance to build an Armenian life once again. I found out in one year that I was wrong, that such a life under Soviet rule was impossible. Since then I have been trying to get out. But this I now know I cannot do. I am hopelessly their prisoner, here so close to my own home."

He spoke quietly, calmly. He spoke as though he had no emotion left within him. He did not seem to wish to impress me. He simply wanted to talk English with someone from the free world. "Baku is a crazy kind of city. There are many nationalities here. Armenians, Jews, Georgians, Russians, Ukrainians. But the Russians are a minority only in number. They run Baku. They call the Azerbaijani zvery (wild animals) and the Azerbaijani call the Russians "onionheads." But there is no open opposition, no hostility on the surface. During the day, they smile. At night they hate." A three-man detachment of Russian sailors marched by, one behind the other, a sort of Slavic MP, and my friend turned his head away, into the bushes behind the benches. "It is not good to be seen with foreigners. Actually, I don't care. But still it is not good." I asked him if he had detected any changes since Stalin had been downgraded. "Yes, this cannot be denied. Things have eased up considerably. Now, people will not be arrested as much in the middle of the night, and people talk a little more, but only amongst their best friends. In the presence of some who are not trusted, no one says anything but 'the weather is hot' and 'when will it cool off.' The Communists are like sheep. If the top says boo, they jump underneath. They do not think independently, and why should they? They have it so good here now." My friend had apparently decided that either he had talked too much, or it really was getting late, but he apologized, said he had to get up early in the morning to go to work. "I only make 500 roubles a month working in a plant, but my wife makes 300, and we get along. I must go, but thank you for listening to me. I feel like a person again." With these words, he picked himself up, shook hands rather limply, and walked off.

As I saw his stooped figure shuffle down the pathway, I wondered whether he had any blood in him at all. He seemed so completely without spirit, so lifeless, so corpse-like.

September 2 : The heat this morning was terrible, but I had a date with Nina, and Nina is an impressive woman, with a splendid tradition. I could not stand her up. As I shaved, I couldn't resist the temptation to chuckle. Imagine Intourist arranging this date! Nina is 55 years old. These days, she is not very talkative. In fact, she hasn't opened her mouth in the last fifty years. Some people say she spoke enough in the first five years of her existence to last a lifetime. Despite her known reticence, I was anxious to meet her. I had read about her, and I had read her work, and now I wanted to meet her in person. She lives in a small, one-story clay house on Parallel Avenue, house No. 102. The house is located in one of the many slum areas of Baku. I drove there in an Intourist car, so that I would not be late for the appointment. Moreover, Intourist, sort of as a middleman in this date, wanted to see that I did not wander astray on my way there. I was taken to the door, met there by three strong young men, who wear the uniform of the MVD, and a middle-aged man, who knows a great deal about Nina's doings. I entered a small room to the left of the entrance way, which was covered with portraits of those young men who dated Nina first. Men like Lenin, Stalin (whom Nina does not seem to like these days, because her guardian did not mention one word about him though his face was everywhere to be seen) and Lado Ketskhoveli, Nina's chief suitor until the end of 1902, when the Tsar's men had him arrested and killed.

"Where's Nina?" I asked her guardian. "In a moment," he said, "in a moment." The room to the right of the entrance way is also very small, a kind of sitting room, which is used today by Nina's guardian and his family. Behind this room is a small room, which used to be inhabited by a Georgian family, when Nina was young and active.

"Where's Nina?" I asked again, more impatient than ever to meet this elusive beauty. "In a moment," the guardian said. Finally, he took me into the last room in the small house, a tiny kitchen, with an open stove and some cabinets. I didn't see Nina, and I was beginning to get annoyed. "I came here to see Nina." I protested. "This moment," the guardian said, and pulling what seemed like a window curtain back, I looked down into a cellar-like room, well underground, lit only by one electric light. In the middle of this small, dark, underground room, without any apparent means of entering or exiting, stood Nina, clean, proud and very dignified.

Nina is an underground printing press. "Nina began to function in 1901," her guardian started to explain. "She played a very major role in the Revolutionary movement, not only here in the Caucasus, but throughout the Russian Empire. In September 1901, she began to roll off *Iskra*, the best illegal Marxist newspaper inside Russia. She also published *Borba,* which some consider the second best Marxist illegal newspaper. *Iskra* means the *spark,* and on the banner, we always ran the Pushkin saying, 'From the spark will come the flame.' Pushkin made this reference with the Decembrists in mind. The early Russian Marxists thought *Iskra* would be the spark out of which a Russian Revolution would flame. They were right, for the Revolution did flame up in 1917, after numerous sparks like *Iskra.* Work must have been very difficult for Lado, the chief editor. There was very poor circulation in this small room, and work proceeded in candle light, which ate as much oxygen as the people who worked here breathed. Its best advantage was that it was well hidden. Let me show you how they entered this room."

We walked back into the room in which the Georgian family had lived. He opened the door to one closet. I looked in. There was no entrance way. Just a plain closet. Then, he pulled a small string, concealed under a board, and the entire floor fell away, revealing a small, narrow flight of stairs leading down to Nina. It was obvious that here was a neat operation.

"How about the noise that the machine made?" I asked. "Certainly, someone might have heard the noise and given the entire show away?" He agreed with me. "The person most likely to hear this noise was the man who lived next door to Nina, the owner of this house, the man from whom the house was rented. Fortunately, he was drunk most of the time, and only thought that he imagined a noise. After a while, though, our luck ran out. His horses, which used to stay in the little shed alongside Nina, did not drink like him and they made noise and stomped their feet at the mysterious, steady monotonous sound. The old rentier heard his horses make noise, investigated and found that Nina was living there too. The

Georgian, though, decided to pay for Nina's rent; this shut
the rentier up, and he never told the police, though his
rent for Nina rose every week and was a terrible burden for
the editors and reporters on Nina. But, these people had a
mission. They did not like tyranny. They knew that to overcome tyranny they had to endure great suffering, which they
did. But they worked and worked hard for their cause, which
they considered right."

I considered my date with Nina a great success.

But I couldn't fight Intourist's greatest ally, the heat, and I
decided to take a train to Tbilisi, capital of the Georgian Republic, early this afternoon. The train from Baku to Tbilisi
runs south in Azerbaijan for about four hours, just about the
time it starts to get dark, and then swings westward, into the
mountains of the fabulous Caucasus, towards Tbilisi. The
terrain is like parts of western America, sandy, dusty and hot.
The sun set behind a mountain that looked a little taller than
the one we had just passed and a little shorter than the one
we were approaching.

I shared a compartment with a dark-skinned, chubby,
young Azerbaijani girl. She was going to Tbilisi for a week.
When I asked why, she told me that she was a teacher, with
a post in a small town in southern Azerbaijan. She had
taught French in this school for one year, and now she
thought that she needed a change. She was tired of a small
town. "There is no fun there. What is a young girl to do?
After work, I like fun, but there is none. In Tbilisi, there is
lots of fun, much more even than in Baku, where I was born.
I love Baku, but I must admit that it is not Tbilisi. Even in
Baku, there is little to do. In Tbilisi, the people are different.
They somehow always have much to do."

I shared peanut butter and jelly sandwiches with her, but
she told me that she thought peanut butter was a terrible

tasting food and then quickly apologized for her bad manners. At one point, she burst out laughing: "No one at home will ever believe this. Me, having dinner with an American. Two years ago, I think this would never have happened. It's better this way." She stared out of the window, her black eyes fixed against the setting sun. "Much better," she mused. "Have you ever heard about Mtskheta?" she asked. When I told her that I had, she beamed and said that I must not miss seeing Mtskheta, the ancient capital of Georgia, which she considered one of the most beautiful sights in the world. "You must also visit the graveyard, high on the hill, overlooking Tbilisi, where Griboedov is buried. There is a beautiful inscription on his tombstone, written by his wife." "What is it?" I asked. She blushed, and said, "You read it, and maybe if we meet again, you will tell me whether you like it." The softness of her dark eyes made me think it concerned love, for she leaned back and almost swooned as she thought of it.

After a while, I asked her if she had gone out to the virgin lands to work on the harvest. She winced, and answered that she did not especially enjoy physical work. Her father, who had died recently, was an important doctor, and the family always had the necessities of life and then some. Her mother, even to this day, does not work, and her sister is a student at Baku University. She confessed to me that she had been asked to go to the virgin lands after she had finished the pedagogical institute but had used "pull" to duck the responsibility. The man who exercised this "pull" for her was the same man, a friend of her father's, who was now trying to get her job changed from this small Azerbaijani town to the Georgian capital. I asked her if she did not have guilt feelings about having resorted to this means to seek a transfer. She answered with no sign of shame or guilt that if she did not use pull, she would get nowhere. In fact, she added, "If I didn't use pull, someone else would. Pull is the best way of getting anything in Russia. I think it is the only way." She told me that corruption in the university is rampant, that some students gain admission over others simply because of the social and political position of their father or mother, while other, much more deserving, students are forced to seek employment and never get into a university. "Many of our young people are this way. I admit this. I am not ashamed. I have no conscience. I do not believe in God. In our family, we do what is good for us. That is the way it is here."

She spoke such heresy in a matter-of-fact tone. She did not seem in the least afraid. Our compartment door was open, and it is quite possible that she might have been overheard, but this possibility did not seem to upset her at all. "When I get to Tbilisi, I am going to have lots of fun and try my best to get a transfer from my little town. I know that someone must live and teach in such small towns, but it doesn't have to be me." As the train continued to rumble through the night, climbing higher and higher into the mountains, we spoke about jazz (which she loves very much), poetry (she prefers love poetry and is crazy about Akhmatova), and baseball (which she thinks is "infinitely inferior to soccer. Soccer is for men. Baseball is for boys.") It was almost 2 a.m. and both of us were fighting sleep. "Would you mind leaving the compartment for a moment. I would like to change." As I waited outside, I thought about how different this girl was from the "girl back home"—and in so many ways. She was a peculiar combination of the bitter and the sweet, the tough and the soft, a confirmed opportunist who "was crazy" about love poetry, a hard product of the Soviet system, who had to ask me to leave the compartment so she could undress and get into bed.

September 3 : The beautiful sunset of last night seemed to presage a lovely day, but this morning was gray. Heavy dark clouds hid the tops of the high mountains as the train chugged its way slowly towards Tbilisi. Everyone seemed very gray and unhappy. "Tbilisi looks especially beautiful in the sun. This is a city which needs sun," my companion arose to tell me. She was unhappy about the clouds, but I was tickled pink. For the first time in well over a week, the temperature dropped to a liveable 28 centigrade, and the cool air which zipped through the compartment perked me up considerably. "This is not a day made for kodachrome, but it's bearable," I mused.

At 9:30 a.m., the train slowly entered Tbilisi, and, despite the gray clouds, the setting of the city was picture-postcard beautiful. Tbilisi is located around a portion of the Kura River which flows through one of the many valleys in the Caucasus. It sits in this valley, and parts of the city, on either side of the river, seem to be climbing up the mountains. Higher into the mountains, one gets the distinct feeling that many of the small houses are chiseled and carved right into the mountain side. They are small, graceful houses which appear undecided between the valley and the lofty peaks and at night the stars above. Numerous bridges criss-cross the Kura. As we drove from the station to the Intourist hotel, which is located right opposite the Council of Ministers building, I noticed that the people themselves looked different. Georgians are much taller than Russians or Ukrainians. They are a dark, straight, confident people. The men almost all wear moustaches, and the women are very handsome. They seem better dressed, and Tbilisi does not look haggard, like so many other cities of the Soviet Union. Like a beautiful woman who is her own best judge, Tbilisi seems to know she looks good. Tbilisi is like Kiev, with mountains. Trolley cars run up and down the rising and falling streets, and the private cars, unlike their Moscow counterparts, intimidated into silent movement, blare and scream their unfrightened warning.

I was ushered into a huge suite at the hotel, which cost sixty roubles a day (without food), 15 dollars, and promptly called up the only American at the hotel. Intourist told me he was there. He was a California photographer, traveling through the Soviet Union "just to see what it was like." Max, the tourist's name, had scheduled a trip to Mtskheta, the ancient capital of Georgia, and I joined his onesome party. Mtskheta is located about 30 minutes from Tbilisi along a narrow mountain road.

Small farmhouses freckled the landscape, and if there were collective farms in the area, I didn't see any. Fat, healthy cows mooed as our *Zim* splashed through the wet road. Even the rain, which had just started to fall, did not ruin the picture. If anything, it added a new dimension. Our guide, a fine, young, handsome Georgian, pointed to the old fortress of Mtskheta, which was located at the very top of the highest mountain in the region, as we approached the ancient capital. Clouds hugged its steeples and surrounded it with mist which made the entire setting seem almost unreal. Its walls did not appear to be built on any foundation. Rather, it rose straight out of the mountain top. It was so beautiful that I knew immediately why Lermontov had written so inspiringly about it.

A large, noble church raised its cross high into the sky. Around the church were small houses, each with a little garden, which sat on narrow, winding, cobble-stoned streets. Mtskheta was the capital of Georgia for three centuries, until, some time in the sixth century, the rulers of Georgia, pressed on all sides by a constant stream of invaders, decided to move to an area with better defenses and Tbilisi was founded. In 329, Christianity was introduced into Georgia, some 650 years before it occurred to Vladimir to Christianize the Russians, settled at that time around the Dneiper in Kiev. The large church in Mtskheta is one of the largest I have ever seen in the Soviet Union. I am told that services are still held there on occasional Sundays and on the large holidays. It was built some time during the 13th century, but within the church itself is a smaller church, which is said to date back to the 5th century. Inside this smaller church is an ikon of Christ, which Georgian pilgrims brought back from Palestine on a fifth century visit. Another unusual ikon also hangs on the bare walls of this church. The eyes of Christ seem to follow your eyes, whatever your position or angle. There is a stone wall about 15 feet high which surrounds the church, and at the four corners are turrets. In ancient days, the church also served as a fortress against heathen tribes which attacked the ancient capital. A number of families still live inside the wall of the church. Another church we visited is cared for by Georgian equivalents of nuns, old women, dressed completely in black, who have dedicated their lives to soliciting to the needs of the Georgian faithful and caring for the church proper. It, like the other, is very beautiful, and the ikons which adorn the walls are different from the Russian ikons, in the sense that they are older and far more sophisticated in their facial portrayals than anything the Russians were capable of producing until Andrei Rublev came along in the 15th century. The city itself is very small, very quiet, and though we wanted simply to walk around (we could not have spoken to the natives, since I am told they speak only Georgian, not Russian), we couldn't.

After a lunch of Georgian wine and Georgian shashlik, we

set off for an afternoon in the Chavchavadze ten-year school. Chavchavadze is almost as big a name in Georgia these days as Stalin, and a large picture of the old nobleman hung alongside one of Stalin in the principal's office. I understand that the Chavchavadze home, located outside the city limits of Tbilisi, has been converted into a state museum.

The educational structure of this *decyatiletki* (ten-year school) is much the same as that of other ten-year schools in the Soviet Union. It is the public school and high school of the Soviet Union. Children generally enter these schools at seven or eight years of age, study there for ten years, and then move on to either institutes or universities, or simply enter the hard world of industry or agriculture.

Approximately 1,000 students attend classes in this school, and each year about 250 are graduated. Last year, half of this figure went on to a higher education, while the other half embarked upon a life of labor, not specialized educational training. It is interesting that of those who continued their educational training, only the smallest minority entered higher educational establishments located outside Georgia, which would seem to indicate a desire to remain in Georgia. Children in the 1-4 classes study about 28 hours per week (they work a six-day week), and the children in the higher classes have an additional 7-hour-a-week study schedule. This schedule, by the way, is conducted exclusively in the Georgian language, although Russian is mandatory and is taught about 8 hours per week.

One of the interesting questions which was raised during our meeting with the principal, an attractive Georgian woman of about 50, who spoke Russian with a distinct accent, was the effect of the Twentieth Party Congress injunction on greater emphasis on technical subjects upon the educational curriculum in this Georgian school. The principal explained that this new emphasis in no way lowered academic standards in the humanities. But it was somewhat difficult to accept this conclusion. These students go to school about 35 hours a week. The principal admitted that half of those hours were devoted to technical courses and the other half to the humanities. I know that Soviet students are required to take the Russian language for eight hours a week. That means that roughly ten hours a week are allotted to the humanities—not a great deal, really, to develop a strong attachment to the liberal arts.

The principal, though, was in no apologetic mood as she explained the emphasis placed upon technical courses. "This is part of our desire to raise the technical proficiency of our youth," she explained. When one considers that this emphasis is applied throughout the Soviet Union, one understands the great number of engineers and physicists which the Soviet educational system is grinding out these days and one can appreciate the greater need for a concomitant encouragement in this direction on the part of our educational system.

The principal then took us on a tour of the classrooms, which were all well-furnished and clean. The teachers were mostly Georgians, though we did notice some Slavic teachers amongst them. There was a picture of Stalin in about every room we visited. De-Stalinization has certainly not affected this school. Joe is all over, looking handsomer, more impressive in every reproduction. In fact, the library pinned a copy of the latest school newspaper, which the students publish every week, on the wall. Prominently placed on the front page is a huge portrait of Stalin, beneath which is a poem which Stalin wrote while a young student in Tbilisi. It is a poem about freedom and the beauty of the Georgian landscape, about the fact that Georgia can not live under foreign despotism. I found it a most revealing insight into the young Stalin, and it might add to our understanding of why young Georgians today hold him aloft as an object of worship and respect. I had the feeling that the overt picture of Tbilisi is probably the same as might have greeted a visitor in the days of Stalin's rule. His face is there, everywhere, for people to see.

As we walked out of the library, classes broke, and the young Georgian students walked in orderly fashion from one room to another, all dressed in their little uniforms. The second shift was in class this afternoon. The first shift, mostly of younger pupils, ends at 1 p.m.

When we returned to the principal's office, I asked her if this school were destined to be converted into a boarding school. She said that she had received no immediate word of such a conversion, that in fact at this stage such a move would not be possible simply because of the lack of space. She did say, however, that she believed that within ten years all young Soviet school children would be studying and living in these boarding schools.

Boarding schools are new to Soviet Russia, and 285 of them were opened this September throughout the country. Admission is voluntary at this stage, but the government is moving in the direction of boarding schools being the dominant and eventually the only form of secondary education in the Soviet Union. Behind the move, which is described as a matter of the "greatest state urgency," is the desire to keep the children away from their parents so that the principles and aims of the system can be better instilled in them and the training received at home be minimized as much as possible. She told me that by 1960 the state expects about 1,000,000 students to be enrolled in boarding schools, and soon after all students. Somehow, this all seemed like a frightening testimony to what a modern totalitarian state can do to indoctrinate the youth with the ideals or lack of them of the state system. Because of the limited number of schools, and because of the desire of at least a minority of parents to "get rid" of their children, it is expected that the 285 boarding schools will be filled. Certainly, it will be a question of the greatest importance to follow the progress or difficulties of these new educational institutions. We thanked the principal, told her that we were happy to see so many Georgian traditions upheld so well.

In the evening, Max and I took a short walk. We walked only about five blocks up Rastrelli Avenue (Rastrelli is the great 12th century Georgian poet, who is about the third most omnipresent figure in Tbilisi), but we were followed by mobs of Georgians who wished to know our impressions of Tbilisi. I told one group that I thought Tbilisi was beautiful and certainly as interesting as Kiev, which did not quite satisfy them. When again surrounded by Georgians, I told this group I thought Tbilisi the most beautiful city in the Soviet Union (mostly to see their reaction). This is what they wanted to hear. "It certainly is the most beautiful city in the Soviet Union. What other city could compare with it? Moscow? Leningrad? Tbilisi, Georgia, this is the most beautiful," one middle-aged man said. After the crowd had dispersed somewhat, I asked him where he has traveled in the Soviet Union. "Nowhere else, where else is there to go?" he answered, with confidence, completely unaware of the illogical element of his presentation. But the point was, he needed no logic. Tbilisi to so many Georgians is the most beautiful, the most interesting, and the most thrilling of all cities, and I guess this takes in New York, Washington, Boston, Paris, London, Prague, and Hongkong, though they've never been to any of these, it's a safe bet. There is a pride here in Tbilisi, a powerful feeling of patriotism for Georgia, a strong confidence in Georgia

—quite apart from its relationship to the Soviet Union—which I have found nowhere else in the Soviet Union.

September 4 : My guide suggested that we visit the Georgian State Museum, just down the street from the hotel. The museum is located in the same building which once housed a Georgian seminary about 100 years ago, right through in fact until the institution of Communist power in Georgia. This fact alone has little significance, but it just so happens that this particular seminary was the one in which Stalin was a young student about 70 years ago. At that time, he was an up-and-coming young student of the Georgian faith. His mother, a hard-working Georgian who was stuck with a drunk and a tyrant for a husband, had always wanted her young son to become a priest, and she succeeded in enrolling him in this seminary, where he did well but encouraged the enmity of his tutors by his sympathy for the rising revolutionary currents which zipped through the Russian empire in those days. Soon, he was expelled for his revolutionary activity, after which he embarked full-time upon his activities which eventually led him to the throne of the Russian empire. (Stalin was born in the small mountain town of Gory, where I am told his birthplace, a hut ("same as your Abraham Lincoln," my guide explained), is now enshrined in Grecian columns for all the faithful to pay homage to.)

I was taken down to the basement of the museum, past two MVD guards; we came to a locked door. An old man, whose life has undoubtedly been dedicated to the art behind this locked door, opened it and we entered a large room covered with old ikons. A younger student of this ikon art escorted us around, and, because he had great difficulty speaking Russian, I relied upon a Georgian-to-Russian translation by my guide to see me through his explanations. No sooner had I seen the first gallery of ikons than I realized that I was visiting no ordinary museum, for here are the finest, most sensitive, most beautiful ikons I have seen anywhere in the Soviet Union. Ikons which date back to the seventh, eighth, through to the twelfth centuries were so dignified, so magnificent, so refined and sensitive that I knew I was seeing what might be one of the finest collections of ancient church art in the world. They were graphic evidence of an artistically-flourishing ancient civilization. The guide told me that Ambassador Bohlen, on a trip to Tbilisi three years ago, had identified part of one ikon as the sister part of an ikon which is now located in the United States. What was especially interesting, I thought, from the viewpoint of cultural change and dynamics was that the artistic level of these ikons dropped drastically in the thirteenth and fourteenth centuries, with the Mongols' incursions, and has never again reached its once brilliant levels. It experienced a further obvious drop in beauty from 1801 to the present day. In 1801, the guide did not say, Georgia fell under the control of the Russian throne. He did mention, however, that Georgian art students are once again beginning to devote themselves to the study of this ancient art form in the hope of recapturing the greatness of the past modified in the image of the present, a Georgian present. To Georgians, this represents a movement back to their renaissance, which they peg to the tenth and eleventh centuries. Proudly, they mention that this preceded the Italian renaissance by 200 years.

I dismissed my guide after we left the museum and set off alone for a short walk around town.

Soon, I met a young Georgian, who introduced himself as a student at the Pedagogical Institute with a special interest in America. He said that he had heard that an American tourist was in town and had lain in wait for me to leave the hotel alone. We talked about many facets of American life, in which he was especially interested, and after a while, when his natural suspicion had been abated, he started to tell me about the student uprising, which had rocked Georgia this past spring. His description of the events coincided almost exactly with what I have already reported in these pages, only his casualty figure was placed at 150, rather than 100, which I had been told.

I asked him if he thought that the students were still up in arms over the denunciation of Stalin. "We feel this very deeply," he answered. "You are an American. You might not understand our feelings. But we are a proud people and a good people. When Stalin ruled Russia, we felt secure. Now, our security has been removed. We have never liked Russian rule. We don't like it now. Only we are small, we are few in numbers. Will the Russians listen to us? They are so many. They don't have to. But of one thing I can assure you. They will not be able to treat us the way they treat the others. We wouldn't allow it." He spoke without fear. He walked alongside me, and his bearing was, like his description of his people, proud.

After a while, he told me that great changes were taking place in Georgia, and, he thought, throughout Russia. He was not quite certain of what they were, "but we all feel that a change is taking place, a definite change. How far it will go, where it will lead—we don't know. I don't think that even Khrushchev does." We sat down on a bench in the park, and we were silent for a while, as we watched the people walk past us. "You have some very beautiful women in Georgia. They certainly are more attractive than Russian girls," I remarked. "Yes, they are more beautiful. When I marry, I shall marry only a Georgian girl, only a Georgian girl. They make good,

reliable wives. But I do enjoy going out with Russian girls,"
he added with a gay twinkle in his eye. "They are so much
more understanding."

After dinner, I set off for the streets once again, gracefully
avoiding the Intourist guide once again. (At dinner, I noticed
an interesting thing. The maitre d'hotel who had served me
the evening before showed up in the restaurant to check on
how things were going—in the uniform of a Red Army colonel!) In the lobby, I met a group of Czech tourists, and I
joined them in an after-dinner walk around town. They spoke
to me very frankly. I certainly did not have the impression I
was speaking with people from the Communist bloc. They
were more outspoken in their criticism of what they saw than
I, and they spoke with amazing frankness about the Czech
situation back home. Most of them spoke English and French.
They told me that they had to travel in groups. Individual
travel was strictly forbidden. They said they did not need any
passports, and they did not know anything about the Russian
law that Russian citizens must carry internal passports.

"We are shocked, though, at the poverty, the misery, the
unhappiness we see here." They thought Tbilisi to be shabby,
though I regard it as one of the least shabby of Soviet cities.
"In comparison to Czechoslovakia, the Soviet Union is a very
poor country." They told me the conditions in Czechoslovakia had improved 100-fold in the last two years. "Look, we
are here now. This we could not do two years ago. Now, we
want to travel west. We want to go to Paris or London. We
want Prague to be a part of Europe again. Now, we have the
feeling it is a part of the East and not the West, and Prague
is the West." They regard their government as an "Eastern
imposition," certainly not Western and definitely not Czech.
"Let us pray," they mentioned in parting, "that times will get
still better and we can even travel to America. We all still

know what Wilson did for us, and we never forget the kindness of America." After I left them, I still could not believe that I really had heard such words from Czech citizens.

I stopped for a moment in a small park before I returned to the hotel and sleep. On the bench beside me was an old woman. She looked at me for a while, then asked: "You are a Russian *stilyag?*" I smiled and answered: "No, I am an American." "Good," she shot back, thoroughly delighted. "We don't like Russians here, and we certainly don't like those two fat fools." Proud of her bravery, she picked herself up, said goodnight and walked off quickly. "Those two fat fools" is what she had said. Those two fat fools.

September 5 : I was determined that my last day in Tbilisi would be a full one, and I made an appointment to meet my guide at 8 a.m. I wanted to ride the vehicular trolley car, which runs up the face of a sixty-degree cliff to a large restaurant and park, some 650 feet high. It was a wonderful vantage point, and I had intended to take a great many pictures. My guide informed me, though, that cameras could be carried up to the top of the mountain but that pictures could not be taken. For this reason, it appeared that I was not permitted to ride this vehicular trolley alone. I was not trusted.

Eight sharp, my guide and I met in the lobby of the hotel, and we set off for the highest point overlooking Tbilisi. The clouds still hung very low around the city. Everything was still quite gray. I was told that this trolley has been operating for about 50 years, that it is the longest one of its type in the world and that it was the oldest. Half way, we passed a famous old white church, which is all alone on the mountain side. My guide promised me that we would see it on the way down, for Stalin's mother is buried there, as well as the Russian poet

Griboedov. When we finally reached the top of the mountain side, where the restaurant and Stalin Park are located ("in the evening, many young people come here. It is so dark and so quiet and so beautiful, that we lose track of the time, me and my girl friend," my guide said), I quickly put my camera in my pocket, for there were many militiamen standing near-by, and they had all been looking at me and my camera.

The view was very beautiful, even in the grayness of the day. The Kura River twisted and turned through the city. Little stone bridges leaped from one bank to the other. The old section of town, which consisted of small huts carved right into the mountain, was very obvious and clear. The newer part of the town, where the hotel was located, was also clear but much less attractive. The cars looked like peculiar beetles from this height and the people like ants. In the distance, some clouds were breaking, and the skies brightened. "This is a very pretty city," I mentioned to the guide. "This is a city of legends," he answered. "There is a legend about the origin of Tbilisi. There is a legend about this church (pointing to the church which sat so lonely on the side of the mountain). There is a legend about mountain water and eye sicknesses. This is a city of legends."

"Tell me one of them."

"Well, about the origin of Tbilisi. I'll tell you about what the old women say about the origin of Tbilisi. At least, this is what my grandmother says. A long time ago, maybe in the fifth century, the king of Georgia, who lived in Mtskheta, went hunting. When he came into this region, he spotted a stag. He drew his bow, aimed carefully and shot an arrow right into the stag's chest. Blood started to run from the wound. The stag rubbed up against a tree and managed to get the arrow out of his chest. The stag then ran towards one of the many warm springs which surround Tbilisi, and jumped in. The waters of the spring did not even turn red. Within minutes, the stag leaped out of the spring and raced off into the woods, no sign of a scar, no sign of blood on his chest. The young king was amazed, and later on when he sought a better place for the Georgian capital, one with better defenses, he recalled the area not far from Mtskheta where springs cure wounds and the mountains were high. He called it the city of warm springs. Tbilisi. To this day, the city of warm springs is still the city of warm springs. The Russians couldn't pronounce Tbilisi too well, so they changed it to Tiflis in 1801, when they took over, but now it is once again Tbilisi, 'the city of warm springs.' "

When he had finished, he bade me walk over to a small trickle of water, which came out of the rocks, high on this mountain top. "There is even a legend about this trickle of water. It is said that deep in the night, people still come to find small trickles of water from the rocks and mountains about Tbilisi so that they can cure ailments in their eyes. They fall before this trickle and let the water drip into sick eyes or eyes which have lost their ability to see. But I could go on forever with legends, for this is a city of legends and the Georgian people are a simple people who believe in legends and superstitions. Not so much here in the city," he was quick to add, "but in the countryside."

I looked around, and a huge statue of Stalin caught my eye. In the restaurant, there were many portraits of Stalin. All over Georgia, there are portraits of Stalin, and, when Stalin ruled Russia, all over Russia, there were portraits and statues of him. And the mausoleum, too, there was a perfect monument to superstition and the primitive quest for a material symbol for a dead god, a kind of concrete totem pole commemorating a dead chieftain. No doubt, it was here, right here, in the tiny nooks and corners of the Georgian mountains, where superstitions and legends still abound, where Stalin was born, here was the womb in which the personality cult was conceived.

As we walked down from the restaurant to the church—along a steep and somewhat dangerous path—I could not resist at least a picture of the church. I took out my camera, focused it, and was about to shoot, when the guide came over and strongly cautioned me against taking the shot. I pleaded with him, until finally my protestations that this church was gorgeous, that I wanted a remembrance of my Tbilisi visit, won him over momentarily, and he agreed that I could take a shot of the church but to be quite certain that I got none of the background of the city into the shot. He knew and I knew that this was impossible. Some of the background would inevitably get into the picture, but I took the picture and then continued the descent. The church itself is not beautiful, but its location is exquisite. Deep in the base of this church, which goes back to the twelfth or thirteenth century, is a small private graveyard. Side by side are two romantic tombstones—one to the poet Griboedov, the other to his beautiful Caucasian wife, a young princess whom he married when she was sixteen and he about 35. The poet died in Persia during an uprising there, but his body was brought back by his young bride, buried here. On top of his coffin is the figure of a young girl leaning against a large cross, tears in her eyes, a figure of great sadness. It is on one knee. On the coffin is the inscription the young bride herself wrote:

"*Um i dela tvoi bezcmertny v pamyati russkoi*
"*Ho dlya chevo perezhila tebya lyubov' maya!*"

A rough translation of this could be:

"Your works and deeds are immortal in the memory of Russia
then why has my love outlived you!"

The outraged cry of a woman, deeply in love, young and beautiful, the prospect of a lonely life ahead, alone with a memory shared by every Russian. Some of the Chavchavadze family are buried here too, as well as Stalin's mother, whose gravestone is simple, made of black marble. A huge crowd gathered around this gravestone. A young Georgian related the early sadness of this woman's life and her later glory, living in the shadow of her great son. She died in the early thirties and was buried here in this famous, small graveyard, reserved for the elite of Georgia.

We walked down the remainder of the mountainside, past small huts inhabited by gypsies, towards the hotel. I then dismissed the guide. I walked to the old part of town and by accident stumbled upon an old Georgian Jewish synagogue. These Jews were preparing for the first night of Rosh Hashanah, the Jewish New Year. In the courtyard, a man stood in front of a long line of women and men, each carrying one or two chickens. He wore an apron which was covered with blood. He was killing the chickens in a special way, by slitting their throats and then permitting the blood to drain completely out of their bodies. This presumably made the chickens kosher, for, according to ancient writ, Jews can not eat dead chickens which might be diseased and unhealthy, only chickens slaughtered in this way. A little boy carried buckets of chicken blood out of the courtyard every few minutes and then returned with empty buckets. Inside the synagogue, four old women were busy scrubbing the floor. An old man, who stood in front of the gate, showed me inside the temple and then left me to return to his vigil. Inside, the temple was impressive and the ceilings were in an Eastern style. When I once again entered the yard, I was approached by several men and an old woman. The men asked me several questions, about where I was from, but they left me a mo-

ment after the man at the gate screamed at them in Russian
to go back to their benches and to leave me alone. The old
lady did not leave me. She said she wanted to talk to me.
"Don't tell him anything bad," the man screamed again, but
she started to talk to me about the life of the Jews in Tbilisi.
The man picked himself up, walked over to her, grabbed
her by the back of the neck, and threw her to the ground. "I
told you to shut up. I told you to shut up." I helped the old
lady to her feet. She said "Thank you" and limped off to the
bench where she had been seated. I wanted to grab this man
and throw him down the same way he had thrown her down,
but I couldn't, because it might have caused a diplomatic
incident. I walked out of the yard, shaking with anger.

One young man followed me, told me that there was another synagogue in Tbilisi, if I wished to see it. He took me
to it, down back alleys until finally we came across a small
building. This, I was told, was the temple of the European
Jews, those who settled in Tbilisi when Catherine the Great
had instituted the pale of Jewish settlement and forbade
Jews to live elsewhere. Some sneaked off to Tbilisi, which
was then not under Russian control, and they still live there,
but they feel themselves completely different from the Georgian Jews, who date back to the fifth century. These Jews, like
those in Bukhara, speak no Yiddish, only Georgian and Russian and a little Hebrew. In the small Tbilisi ghetto, the
Georgian Jews have been entrusted to keep the European
Jews in line. The latter are distrusted. The former are not
as suspect, if they are suspect at all. An old Jewish lady at this
second temple asked me if I were a Communist. I told her
I was opposed to Communism. "How can you travel here
then?" she asked, puzzled. I told her I worked in Moscow
and that the Foreign Ministry had given me permission. "It

still is very strange. One can never tell what's going to happen here next!"

I walked down the street to the river. The sun was beginning to break through the clouds, and I noticed the remains
of an old fortress on top of the hill, overlooking the city. A
man took time out from selling watermelon to explain that
this was the fortress built in the sixth century to ward off
attacks of heathen bands which roamed the mountains. "Now
people live there. The quarters are poor, but it is as good
a place as any. I live there, and it is not really too bad. I've
lived there for years. Now, I am getting older and it is harder
for me to climb up the mountain, but I still like it there.
I like it anywhere here. I am a Georgian."

I took a cab to the University. The Tbilisi State University,
where all the trouble erupted last spring, is a beautiful University, set on a tree-lined street. I entered the University.
Classes were already in session. Girls and boys walked up the
pathway to the entrance. The girls usually walked together
and the boys together, the boys looking the girls over, the
girls pretending to ignore their glances. The Georgian men
almost all wore mustaches. They looked tall and strong. The
only language I heard was Georgian, interspersed with an
occasional Russian word. I sat down on a bench. I was alone
on the bench, but on the benches to my left and right there
were crowds of Georgian students, many of them awaiting
their next class, some I guess cutting a class then in session.
I sat there listening, watching, waiting, for about one hour.
Finally, one young man, apparently on a bet that I was not a
Georgian, asked me a question in Georgian. I shrugged my
shoulders. He shot back at his friend something in Georgian,
which must have been "I told you so." A crowd quickly gathered around me, and the inevitable questioning started. I
hadn't planned on what followed, else I would have brought

along sandwiches, for the question period lasted for five hours. The questioning ran from baseball, to Stalin, to Marx, to housing, to clothing, to Negroes, to Jews, to Eisenhower and Stevenson, to soccer and the Olympics.

In the course of a rapid give-and-take, I found out some differences between the Georgians and the Russians in a similar situation. First off, the Georgians, who are so nationalistic, are very hurt and quickly grow offensive when you honestly state that something displeases you; in their opinion, nothing in Georgia could offend anyone, for everything in Georgia is just about the best anywhere in the world. A Russian in a similar situation very frequently encourages you to rip the system apart, stating that through politeness you are not telling him the truth about his country. The Russian seems more alert to shortcomings and much more eager to discuss them —to the point just short of where they begin to tear into the essential fabric of the system. Secondly, with Stalin, you touch on sacred ground. With a Russian, Stalin is all the things *Pravda* says he is, generally speaking. With these students, he is nothing short of a god. Finally, these students seem much more cocky than the Russian students around Moscow University. They give you the impression they hold their future in their hands. With the Kremlin across the street from the University, one rarely gets this impression in Moscow.

I spent one hour on a nearby lot explaining in horribly fractured Russian the essentials of baseball, which they were very much interested in. "We think baseball is the game of the future." I did my best to convert as many of them as possible into Yankee fans.

I then was called upon to give a forty-minute lecture on the Negro problem in the United States. *Pravda*, which I did not read today, apparently had a story about some riots

in Clinton, Tennessee, and I had to explain our policy on the
Negro question. I told them about the 1954 Supreme Court
decision, which they did not know about. I even went back
to the Civil War, Lincoln, and the carpet-baggers, and I concluded that this is a problem which is being solved but that
it will take many years yet before the issue heals. My frankness in this discussion disarmed them, and I felt that afterwards they were quite sympathetic and in no sense hostile.

Our next topic was finger-printing, which I explained as
a law, much the same as the law on an internal passport in
the Soviet Union. This device for checking on a population
was not employed, in the United States, that it offends me as
much as finger-printing offends the Russians these days. But,
I added, I want to come here and see for myself what is going
on. If a Russian really wanted to visit the United States to
understand us better, he would not permit the finger-printing
issue to stand in his way. I was surprised that many of the
students agreed with me.

"Tell me," one student called out from the rear of the
crowd, "tell me, what do Americans think of Stalin?" I
couldn't hedge too well on this question, and I answered
frankly that we were in disagreement with many of his policies. The students seemed almost shocked.

"Certainly, you all regard him as a great and noble person,"
he states.

"We think that when the history books of the twentieth
century are written, Stalin will undoubtedly play a major
role, but we do not think that he was a noble person, nor
that he was a good person." I saw the looks of horror come
over many faces, and I added: "You asked me and I have
answered you truthfully. I knew that you would not want me
to lie." They agreed that this was a better policy.

The same student, who might have studied political economy, came back with another question in this field: "What do Americans think of Marx." I couldn't help but laugh at this question. "To tell you the complete truth," I answered, "we don't even think about Marx!" All the students started to laugh, and they laughed heartily, healthily, with delight. "We think Marx was a major political theoretician of the nineteenth century, but we believe that his system has been disproved time and again by the facts of history," I added. "I personally do not agree with his program—in fact, I am very much in opposition to Communism—but he undoubtedly exercised a major influence on the course of world history in the last hundred years." The students all agreed that his influence was paramount, but they believed that Stalin was responsible for revitalizing Marxism. "One must admit, if you are a capitalist or not," one student interjected, "that Stalin made many, many creative additions to Marxism and Leninism." There was no arguing the question of Stalin, I decided, and I tried my best to steer the discussion on to other questions, but I was unsuccessful. Time and again, they brought the subject up. "You must admit that reading Stalin on linguistics is a fascinating experience! He was so brilliant. He could write on anything. He knew everything." I almost choked over the "fascination" of reading Stalin on linguistics, or for that matter, Stalin on anything, for to my mind Stalin was one of the dullest, most plodding of writers. "He certainly was interesting," I commented, almost in self-defence.

Just at that moment, Kupradze, the Rector of the University and also the Chairman of the Council of Ministers of Georgia, walked out of the University building, down the runway, and into a waiting car. "That's our Kupradze," one student remarked. "He's a big man," I remarked, "holding two very big positions."

"Yes, he's big," a student agreed, "but he's not that big!" Some of the students laughed.

"Kupradze speaks about the personality cult almost as much as any Russian," I remarked.

"Many people speak about the personality cult, and they can speak about it as much as they like. We don't believe it anyway."

"Some people," another student chimed in, "even say that pictures of Stalin are being removed throughout the Soviet Union, that they are going to remove him from the mausoleum. These things they can not do. These things they are not doing."

When I objected that I myself had seen his pictures being removed (I recalled one instance in the Lenin Museum), the students replied that they did not believe this. And, when I concurred that indeed a rumor was circulating in Moscow that Stalin's body might be removed from the mausoleum, the students maintained their resistance.

"This is not true," one student said.

Another added: "You simply can't remove Stalin without removing Lenin. Both were inseparable in life, and Stalin was faithful to Lenin. In many ways, he was even better than Lenin. After all, he built the Soviet Union, not Lenin. A Georgian, not a Russian. No, this is quite impossible." I thought I might pursue the subject a little further.

I said: "But Russians are once again the rulers of the Soviet Union, and they are returning to Lenin and Leninism. Even here in your own *Zarya Vostoka* (the Georgian newspaper), they write about the harm of the personality cult."

"Those who write about the harm of the personality cult are toadies, who keep thinking that our fate is always tied in with Russia," a student said. "The Russians came here in 1801. Since then, nothing creative has taken place here. Now, it is my opinion that we are starting to think again. Even in art." He mentioned that ikon history is being studied again and that young Georgian art students are once again beginning to study ancient art forms and adopting them to modern times. Then, he concluded with a mournful air: "We have a lot of catching up to do."

After my conversation with the Georgian students I had just about enough time to return to the hotel and race off to the train station. The train left Tbilisi for Sochi about 9:20 in the evening. As soon as I entered my compartment, I knew that I probably would not get much sleep. As things turned out, I was quite right. My companion turned out to be the assistant economic planner of the Georgian Republic. He was traveling to Sochi to pick up his wife and child, who had been staying at a summer *dacha* on the shore of the Black Sea for the last two months. He planned to spend one day in Sochi, help his wife pack, and then return tomorrow evening to Tbilisi.

He was not a party-man, though he spouted the party line as well as any *Pravda* editorial. He picked on me from the moment he discovered that I was an American. He brought up every issue he could think of, and for a while I was not sure whether I was listening to a human being or a record of the last series of *Pravda* and *Izvestiya* editorials. He discussed the "persecution" of Paul Robeson, the "murder" of Negroes, the "hounding" of Jews, the "growing impoverishment of the workers," the "forced imposition" of cars and homes upon the Ford Motor Company workers, who were then faced with the prospects of having to live on credit and at the mercy of "overseeing capitalists," whom he compared with the ancient warlords in China, the inability of young Americans to get a higher education, because they had to pay for it, the urge of America to launch a war to prevent their "failing" economy from falling completely to pieces, imposing on peace-loving people soldiers "who rape women in the streets and chew gum."

When I discovered what sort of person he was, I suggested politely that possibly it would be best if we went to bed. He wouldn't hear of it, and he ordered two glasses of tea and cookies. He wanted to talk. He continued his tirade against the United States. When I could no longer listen to his senseless chatter, I said: "I think that I am listening to *Pravda*, not a human being, when I listen to you."

He answered: "There is no need for such sharp words." He seemed not in the least antagonistic on the surface, but he continued to speak in the same derogatory terms, until finally I cut loose upon him and the Soviet system.

After I had finished, he said: "True, we have made mistakes, but now we are correcting them"—a remark that might have appeared in any official Communist publication, fitting in with the new line of open admission of errors, as though admission were the cure-all for the mistakes. He told me he was firmly convinced that Communism is the wave of the future, that errors notwithstanding, Communism would triumph all over the world, including the United States. I told him this would never happen, and he laughed, condescendingly, almost as though he pitied me for my failure to see his "wave of the future." The hours dragged on. One o'clock, two, three, four, until finally at 4:30 a.m., thoroughly exhausted, absolutely beat, I appealed to him for us to try to get at least four hours sleep before we arrived in Sochi. I had fallen asleep twice during his tirades, but he had awakened me. At last he seemed to take pity on me, for he agreed that possibly a few hours sleep would be just the thing.

What amazed me was his complete sincerity, his total lack of bitterness or rancor, his dedication to the system, and his abysmal ignorance of America and the "American way of life," for lack of a better phrase. He seemed almost like a man with a faith—which indeed he was despite the fact that he is not a party man—who knows the answers, because he has read the answers and believes the authors no matter what changes take place, no matter what violence and suddenness attack the current party line, no matter the pace. The future was his, to his mind, and the zigs and zags of today were justifiable in anticipation of tomorrow. The contrast between his position and the position of the street worker who barely makes enough to feed and clothe himself had no effect upon him, for this fact was part of a changing today and tomorrow all would be fine.

September 6 : I awoke to find the Georgian commissar just as eager to continue his verbal assault upon the United States, but I shoved him off just as he was about to start. "Tell me about Sochi," I asked. "Tell me what I should see when I get to Sochi."

"Don't you wish to continue our little discussion of last night?" he asked almost plaintively.

"No, I'd just as soon talk about Sochi, baseball, or literature, but not politics. There's no common ground in our thinking. There is just a big gap, and every time you spout the Communist line straight out of *Pravda*, the gap grows wider and wider."

"I really don't understand you," he said in desperation. "You defend a system which is dying, you justify race terrorism, and you deny that Communism will conquer throughout the world."

I couldn't go on. I hadn't even had a cup of coffee or tea, and he was raring to start this early in the morning. "Please forgive me, but I can't argue with you. Let's us just sit here quietly. We only have two more hours to go, and we will be in Sochi." To my great surprise, he agreed, and for the next two hours, he spoke about the scenery, the Black Sea, and the beautiful Caucasus. The train started to run alongside the shore-line, as the sun rose higher and higher into the sky, which was almost white. The Black Sea glistened brightly below the merciless stare of the sun. On the other side of the train, the Caucasus rose abruptly out of the landscape and shot towards the sky. The scenery was certainly the most beautiful that I have ever seen in the Soviet Union. As we approached Sochi, and as the enchanting loveliness of the countryside lulled me into a quiet restfulness, I began to realize why Stalin had selected this region for his summer hide-out and why Bulganin and Khrushchev also spend lots of time here. Like their Tsarist predecessors, the present leaders of the Soviet Union also frequent the Crimea for relaxation, warmth and beauty. We passed little fishing villages along the way. On the beach, I saw people stretched out, taking in the sun. Some were in the sea, splashing one another. The closer to Sochi we got, the more sanitoriums I saw. This is the area of sanitoriums. Each industry, each branch of the service, each large concern has its own sanitorium, where all workers are theoretically permitted to rest during their vacations. Of course, there were not enough sanitoriums to care for all the workers, but I do believe that if the applications to the rest homes are handled above board, that many thousands—though hardly millions—of Russians do in fact spend their vacations there. The Red Army Sanitorium has perhaps the most impressive-looking building, built right into the mountainside and overlooking the blue Black Sea.

At about 10:30 a.m., we pulled into the railroad station in Sochi. Oddly, no Intourist man was there to meet me, which was very pleasant but shocked me. I got into a cab, asked to go to the Intourist Hotel (foreigners can not register in just any hotel), and settled back for a thirty-minute ride through town. Sochi is a lovely little town. It gives the impression in the bright, hot sun of being all white. Semi-tropical trees grow in large back yards. There is no sign of want in Sochi. The stores look full of customers and merchandise. The streets are clean, and the people are bronzed almost black. The avenues are tree-lined, and there are many parks, heavily planted with red and black and yellow flowers. We turned towards the sea, and approached the *Primorskaya* Hotel, which is large and white and very attractive, set on a high hill, overlooking a crowded beach.

After a light breakfast, armed with my camera, I walked down to the beach. It was not quite as large as Coney Island, but it was just as packed. What really amazed me, though, was the bathing suits, which almost aren't. The Slavic women —most of the people looked Slavic—are heavily endowed, and they fell out of their suits every other moment and were not in the least disturbed, as they made the necessary adjustments in full view of the entire beach. The men also wore a kind of bikini suit. Actually, they have two suits. One is this bikini affair which they swim in. The other is more like ours. This they sunbathe in.

The beach itself is very uncomfortable. Every inch is crowded with rocks and pebbles, and I suppose that I was more than a little jealous of these heavy Russian women who had so much natural protection against the nasty rocks. This public beach, however, is not the only beach. There are also private beaches—private, in the sense that only people from a particular club or sanitorium are able to use them. They were less crowded and they seemed much more comfortable. In fact, the first impression one gets of the beach and Sochi is that this is in strong contrast to the misery and squalor in the rest of the Soviet Union. Sochi in the old days was for Stalin and his immediate associates. Stalin is no longer with us, but his successors still use this area for their relaxation. Sochi exists for the Soviet aristocracy, the new blue-bloods of Russia. These are the people who grew up with the system, made it tick, gave and give it its life's force. These are the newly entrenched, those who would stand to lose the most in the event of another 1917.

I had lunch with a group of touring Americans and a girl from the Embassy. It was wonderful simply being with them, speaking English, sharing American impressions and American humor. After the meal, I took a long swim in the Black Sea, just as the sun was setting. The water was warm and fun.

We shared our dinner table with two young Soviet students, a very attractive girl from Khuibyshev and a young sportsman from Rostov. Both were in Sochi for a two-week vacation, before returning home for school. The young man studied economics, and he was not very talkative. The girl studied engineering, and when the American girl I was with expressed some concern that this was not the proper profession for a pretty young girl, the Russian answered that girls in this country undertake jobs just as men do. Two minutes later, she modified her statement: only fifteen percent of the students in the oil institute were girls, and most of these got desk jobs and rarely went out into the field on problems. The economist asked us to join him in toasts to friendship and peace, and he was not just giving us the line. He meant friendship and peace. "Yesterday, we ate here, too," he said, "and we met a young American, who told us that he thought that everything in the Soviet Union was very bad, that the women dressed badly, that the food was terrible, that everything was poor and cheap. We began to think that all Americans are like him. This is very bad. If he does not like us, why does he come here? Why doesn't he just go home? To us, this is the best, this is the finest country in the world. Granted, we have seen no other country, but we have this confidence. Maybe we are right; maybe we are wrong, but this is what most of us believe. He is a guest here. He should respect our feelings."

I had to agree with him, and I told him that I hoped he would have the chance to meet many more Americans. "There is no doubt that it is better this way. Of this, there is no doubt." (I remembered what an American diplomat mentioned back in Moscow in reference to the same problem. "Every American tourist is a kind of poster of American life and Americans. This year and next they ought to be handpicked." A joke, but with a good deal of sense).

September 8 : The sun today was bright and hot. I had breakfast, took a swim, and then hired a car to go to the highest observation point in this area of the Caucasus. All the adjectives which describe beauty could be applied to the sight which greets one on the highest point of the mountain. The mountainsides are rolling, bumpy and deep green, and the Black Sea looks blue near the shore and purple farther out. It is very easy to rest in this environment, and with the prospect of returning to Moscow the next day I decided to get back to a fine, comfortable horizontal position on the beach.

Near me on the beach was a young man of about 35, who introduced himself after much hesitation as a school teacher in Sochi. His specialty was the English language, and though he spoke poorly he was delighted at the chance of practicing his English. After a while, we started to speak about current events, and we drifted quite naturally into a discussion of the

Suez crisis. Almost immediately, I sensed that he was not a straight party man, for his discussion drifted further and further away from the Communist line until he started to talk outright political and ideological heresy. He said: "The way it seems to me, there are really two histories. One is ours, the kind we read in the papers. The second is yours, the kind we can not read. I think I like yours better." He then went into the *whys:* "Our history gives us only one path, one course. Yet, we know from the history only of our own country during the Soviet times that many things can happen in history and usually do."

September 9 : I joined the Soviet aristocracy this morning for a quick swim before breakfast, and boarded an 11:40 a.m. plane back to Moscow. By the time we hit Rostov-on-Don, the skies had clouded over. In Kharkov, it was raining. By 8:15 p.m., Moscow was rainy, dreary, and miserable. As I got off the plane, and pulled up my coat against the rain and the cold, I laughed aloud. This morning, I swam in the Black Sea. Tonight, I freeze in Moscow. The sharp change in climate, the reverse of what it had been when I flew off to Tashkent, once again testified to the hugeness of this country, which cannot be overemphasized. Because with all they have, they still want more.

III · A FAMILIAR CHILL

October 6 : While working on my old friend, Sergei Sem-
yonovitch Uvarov, this afternoon in the Manuscript Room
of the Lenin Library, I struck up a conversation with a young
Russian economist, who is associated with the Institute of
Economics. After the usual questioning as to why any Westerner would be interested in Uvarov, Sasha told me that after
he receives his degree from the Institute, he will be required
to spend three years working for the state, wherever and in
whatever capacity the state wishes. Many of his friends, he
said, end up going to the new lands in Siberia. When I asked
him whether he was especially pleased with this prospect,
he answered: "Listen, let's be frank. If I did not go to the
Institute, I would be drafted into the army for a few years.
This way, at least, I know that I will have a higher education
at government expense. Afterwards, if the government thinks
I should labor on the construction of Communism for three
years, I feel it is my duty to do so. I am not especially happy
about this prospect, but in a sense I feel that it is my duty.
My father took part in the Revolution; now, I have a small
role in another revolution. We are revolutionizing Siberia."
After a short pause during which he seemed to be collecting
his thoughts, Sasha, who is short, stocky, with a wild shock of
brown hair, concluded: "Those three years are going to be

very hard for me. I am not very strong, despite my build.
But if I can last out, I shall be sure of having a good job.
That is most important in this country. If a person has a good
job, he has enough money. If he has enough money," he finished with a Marxian dialectical flare, "he will live happily.
I don't know exactly how things are in the United States—
all I read is our publications—but I know that in Russia one
must be a materialist. Without money, you are nothing."

October 7 : October 8th is a big day in Zagorsk. Almost 650
years ago, its founder was born, and this afternoon at 3 p.m.
all the churches of the famous and fabulous Trinity Monastery were opened in honor of St. Sergius. Crowds of Russians,
young and old, came to Zagorsk, as we did, to participate in
the religious services on this high holy day on the Russian
Orthodox religious calendar. Outside the Troitsky Church,
built in the fourteenth century, was a long line of worshippers
waiting to enter so that they, like the thousands before them,
could pray, sing, and kiss the famous ikons. The huge Uspensky Cathedral, located in the center of this fortress monastery, served thousands today, and even the small, once
private, chapels, were opened. One of these, set off to the side
of the Uspensky Cathedral, had a small fountain. This fountain is said to dispense holy water which heals and cures.
Old, middle-aged, and young, men and women, stood for
what must have been hours to fill their small bottles or milk
cans with this water, which they carried with them during
services and after, when they left for home. Some women,
who did not have bottles or cans, soaked their handkerchiefs
in this water and wiped their faces with it. "It is good for the
skin. Try it yourself, and you will see," one woman told me.
Outside the small chapel, old women gathered around a small

fountain, which was fenced off from the crowd, reaching towards the water which rose up from a small spout. When the wind blew some of this water their way, they took their wet hands and rubbed their faces and necks. Some of them waited a long time, patiently, for the wind to perform its religious function.

The steps leading to all churches, as well as the benches all over the area, were crowded with people, who had brought food and drink. Many will undoubtedly wait until tomorrow, camping out on these very steps, so that they can participate in services on the anniversary of Sergius' death. Large groups of school children, in their grey uniforms, watched and waited with their teachers and their parents. Even the weather seemed in a festive mood, for the skies had opened and the sun shone upon this scene with a warmth most unusual for October in Russia. The church bells peeled a melodic tune, and the religious chant "God Bless Us," sung over and over again with a delicate and sensitive monotony, escaped from the over-crowded interiors of the churches, decorated with rich, golden ikons, into the sunlit air. Communism's atheism was a total failure this afternoon, as last Sunday morning, when I saw a group of young Russians baptized in a church not more than two blocks from the Kremlin. As one visiting American wondered: "Could this have been much different, fifty years ago, one hundred years ago, even two hundred years ago? I don't think so. There are certain constants in every society, which cannot be eliminated no matter how strenuous the effort."

We walked around town afterwards, through the N. S. Khrushchev Park of Rest and Culture, the Central Square, and the Zagorsk peasant market, where the apples were delicious, and then we had dinner at the *Otoykha* (Rest) restaurant. As we walked back to the car, preparatory to the two-hour return drive to Moscow, we passed one church after another which were not part of the total complex of the Trinity. If Zagorsk be any example, just Zagorsk, then religion is far from a dead matter in this land of atheism.

October 9 : A cow was led across the *Sadovaya Koltso* (the wide street on which the Embassy is located) this afternoon, very slowly, ploddingly, by a Moscow farmer—*a scene out of yesterday's Russia.* The sight of the cow and the peasant was in such sharp contrast to the large *Zims* which rolled past and the trucks which lumbered along that I was prompted to stare in amazement. The young student from Moscow University with whom I was speaking looked at this spectacle once, fleetingly, then he turned away and requested that I do the same. "What is there to see?" he asked. "A peasant (he used the old Russian word *muzhik,* which today is a term of derision) and a cow," he answered himself.

We walked up the block for a while, both of us in silence, until I could no longer resist asking him why he was so upset. "This is no place for farmers. We are not peasants here in Moscow." His remark was revealing. It was as though he were embarrassed at the sight of the peasant, the cow, and all the two symbols of rural life represented. His attitude was a good indication once again of the fantastic social revolution which this country has undergone in the past forty years, for certainly back in 1916 this sight was not that compelling a cause for displeasure. *Zims* did not zoom by, neither did trucks. The *Sadovaya* was considerably narrower and, more important, the migration of the rural population into the large cities, which was greatly accelerated in the late twenties and early thirties, had only just started, historically speaking; therefore, a peasant, five years removed from the farm, would not have been so upset at the sight of a cow, for there were probably many of them in and around Moscow.

I asked him if he was born in Moscow. "I was born in a small town outside of Khuibyshev, but," he hastened to add, "my family moved into Khuibyshev when I was very young, and when I was fifteen we moved to Moscow. We have been here ever since." I asked him if he has as yet served his term in the virgin lands, and he answered: "I was supposed to go this summer, but I got out of it."

October 10 : Valya is a twenty-seven year old Russian girl who works in a foreign embassy in Moscow. I know her because she works for a friend of mine. This afternoon, during a good Russian lunch she prepared—she is a fine cook—she told me that for the first time in her life, she was embarrassed into going to church last Sunday, and the instigator was her four-year-old son, Volodya. Valya and her husband both work; they have to, to make ends meet, and Volodya is brought up by Valya's mother, who is a devout Russian Orthodox. Valya and her husband do not believe in God. "We see no reason to," she explained; they do not, as a result, go to church. But Volodya has gone to church all his life with his grandmother, and in his young life, church and Sunday morning just seem to go together. Valya rarely gets out of bed until both the little Russian boy and his grandmother have returned home. Two weeks ago, her son asked her, finding her in her night-gown after he had returned from church: "Momma, why don't you go to church? Everyone I know does. And Granny goes, so why don't you and Poppa?" Valya said that she could not answer him that she does not believe, so she told him that she would go with him next Sunday. When next Sunday came, Valya got up early in the morning and escorted her son and mother to church. "And do you know, I enjoyed every moment of it. It was like when I was young all over again. I liked it, and I am going to go again. All thanks to my little Volodyushka." She beamed.

October 12 : The "thaw" may well have gone far enough. The "thaw" (the name is taken from a novel of Ehrenburg's) is the title given to the entire process of relaxation which has taken place in Russia this past year, a perfect example of which is the incongruous presence in Moscow these days of fifty American millionaires. If a number of unsubstantiated rumors are true, it's possible the Kremlin senses that destalinization has gone far enough, that freedom of speech and monolithic control over a population do not blend, and when they run up against one another, one must win. The two, to quote the Communists these days, cannot coexist.

These rumors run something like this:

(a) Molotov has been given a new job, which would tend to indicate that his star is on the ascendancy, the star of the hard policy, the anti-destalinization line. He is to head a new commission which is to set the cultural and ideological line for the new period of "freedom." In an era of great relaxation, it is quite possible and probable that theories on art could arise and be promulgated which run contrary to the aims of the party and what the party feels is good for the people.

(b) Two students have just been expelled from Moscow University for having voiced criticism, at a meeting called for this purpose, and have since disappeared.

(c) A third major letter on destalinization is now circulating through some of the major industrial enterprises in the Moscow region. The first two letters came out and were circulated (though never publicly) soon after the party congress. Those two called for open, ashamed criticism of the bureaucracy, short-comings, high-handedness in management, etc.—all of the hallmarks of the destalinization period. This one calls for a tightening up of the relaxation. Criticism is all right only if it is within limits.

(d) The word has been passed through these same enterprises that an old standard of Stalinism—spying on your neighbor for the state—has been reinstituted. Before the Party Congress in February, it is believed that one out of ten men in a plant was called upon to spy on the activities of the others and report any or all of their actions to the party cell chief. This system has apparently once again been instituted to curtail criticism, which has reached mammoth proportions.

(e) Finally, a vignette on what might be called unobtrusive totalitarianism. Recently, a factory worker was called upon to deliver criticism of the functioning of the plant's administration. In fact, a meeting was called specifically for this purpose. This worker got up and criticized the plant foreman.

The following week, he found that his work norm (all Soviet workers have norms which they must fulfill) had been tripled. Since he had already been working at peak capacity, he could produce only one-third of the new work norm, with the consequence that his salary, hardly adequate in the first place, has been reduced two-thirds. The net effect of this man's criticism has been that his salary, so reduced, puts him completely at the mercy of his plant's management, and undoubtedly he will either have to recant or leave his job with a bad recommendation, which would be bad for his future chances of employment.

Alone, each of these rumors and vignettes does not amount to much. Together, they paint a picture of a regime, about to call a halt to a process which it feels is getting somewhat out

of control. Freedom of speech, true criticism, cannot exist
side by side with the continued existence of a modern totalitarian state. If a halt is to be called to the process of relaxation at this stage, then the leadership is still in a position to
squelch any thoughts which might be antithetical to the
continued existence of a dictatorship.

October 18 : The librarian at one of the libraries I work at
could no longer resist. This evening she finally asked me the
inevitable question. "Why is it that anyone in the West is
interested in Uvarov?"

"To tell you the truth, I am not at all sure that many
people are interested in Uvarov, even in the West," I answered, "but I feel that he is a very interesting figure and one
who unfortunatly has been forgotten by many historians of
Russia, both here and in America."

"I can easily understand why people forget about Uvarov,"
she explained very confidently. "He was a reactionary. He
formulated a slogan, *Orthodoxy, Autocracy* and *Nationalism,*
which became a hallmark for the Russian reactionaries, who
wanted to oppress the people. There was nothing, absolutely
nothing progressive about him. Why should anyone write on
a figure who was not progressive?"

I asked her: "Don't you believe that it is important to understand both viewpoints?"

She answered: "Possibly, this is so, but history has more
than just an explanatory function. History must also instruct.
History must set an example. History must enlighten the
people."

"Is it enlightenment," I challenged, "to present only one
viewpoint? Moreover, if you wish to deal in Marxian terms,
then you must admit that Uvarov did in fact play a progres-

sive role, not a reactionary, regressive one, in Russian history. He had a great deal to do with the development of education in Russia in the beginning of the nineteenth century. He founded many universities, including Leningrad University. He left Russia a more advanced country than he found it, in his own way. I believe, therefore, that his role was progressive."

She stared at me for a while, playfully toying with a fat book which she kept opening and closing, until finally she said: "You are probably right. We have had only one viewpoint, for a very long time. But we are beginning to hear others." Then, she added, almost as a second thought: "You know, I think it really would be a good idea to read about people like Uvarov. After all, that is what history is for anyhow, isn't it?" This librarian, who is eminently intelligent, knows French and German and a little English, obviously was unaware that she had reversed fields within five minutes, and I got the very distinct impression that she did reverse fields not to be nice, or to avoid an argument. I believe she switched her viewpoint most sincerely, and, though it is possible, indeed likely, that she reswitched five minutes after I left this evening, she, like so many of the Soviet intelligentsia, is confronted with more doubts of a substantive character now, than possibly at any other time of her life. Whether these doubts are definitively resolved is at this point unimportant. What is now important—the doubts exist.

October 19 : It would appear to be quite likely that since the days of Catherine the Great no greater concentration of sex appeal has been deposited in the Russian Empire at any one time than right now. Last Sunday, a half dozen young and incredibly beautiful, well-dressed Italian actresses arrived at

Vnukovo Airport to open a festival week of Italian films in
the Soviet Union. In contrast to the drab, rather solid, tractor-
type female Russia boasts these days—these prototypes of fe-
maledom are like creatures from another world.

October 20 : For well over a thousand young Soviet people,
the news tonight from Poland was not distracting. They
were at the second monthly ball given by the Komsomol
(young Communist) chapter of the Lenin Library, in anticipation of the opening of the World Youth Festival next June
in Moscow. The scene was a wing of the new building of the
Lenin Library, *Korpus A*. The fifteen Union Republic flags
hung ostentatiously from the sides of an enormous stairwell
which led from a huge first floor to a huger second floor, with
marble floors, ceilings and walls. The marble was white and
very clean. The hall, large as it is, was swarming with young
men and women. Most of the men were students at nearby
military academies, and they were in uniform. The young
ladies, for the most part, all wore very tight, transparent
blouses, which are the rage with the young set these days.
Needless to say, these girls presented a rather pleasant contrast to the ordinary Russian woman seen on the streets of
Moscow. To either side of the large hall is a smaller hall.
In one, a lottery was taking place. The chief prize was won
by a young girl from Tashkent, and it was a toy doll. Each
chance cost one rouble. On the other side, a question and
answer game was in progress. A large, though hardly enthusiastic, crowd gathered about a young lady, who stood on a
podium in the middle of the room and read one hundred
questions from a sheet of paper she held in her chubby hand.
The first person who knew the answer shouted it out. If he
or she were accurate, he or she would receive a small token.

After the one hundred questions were read, the person with the most tokens received the major prize, which was a bar of chocolate. Secondary prizes consisted of a package of cigarettes or a box of matches or a small book of pictures from Moscow. The questions were varied, and, though they touched on more than politics, they seemed to be heavily weighted in favor of testing the knowledge of the youth on left-wing nineteenth century European thinkers and the writings of the major Communist leaders, past and present, plus a heavy dosage of Russian literature. For example: "Who wrote 'The Survival of the Fittest'?" "When did Lenin write his nationality pamphlets, for the most part?" "Where was Lenin in 1905 January?" This is the sort of question which was asked. When no one responded quickly to a question which concerned Marx or Lenin, the questioner politely scolded the youth for not knowing their bible. And when they did not know a line from Russian literature, she scolded them also, but not so politely. "We must know our writers, comrades. We must know our culture, our advanced Russian culture."

There were obviously members of other national groups there aside from the Russians, but they did not seem to take offense. In the main ballroom, a four-piece orchestra played the latest American jazz tunes, and the Russians danced poorly but happily and uninhibitedly to the quick and catchy tunes. The wall-flowers as usual stood alongside and watched. Girls generally bunched together, and it was not uncommon for the girls to dance together, though I never did see men dance together. After a while, games started in all four corners of the hall. I saw two of these. One was similar to our donkey's-tail game. A girl was blindfolded, spun around several times, pointed in the direction of a face which hung on the wall without a nose, and she was supposed to pin the nose in the picture's noseless face. The second game I saw reminded me too much of basic training for it to be enjoyable. Sides of nine were selected. Each member of each team wore an apron and a chef's cap. In front of each was a small sack of potatoes. The team which finished peeling all of the potatoes first won a dog doll. How they split the dog doll into nine pieces, or whether they did, I don't know.

I had been invited to this Komsomol dance by the deputy head of the Lenin Library Komsomol chapter, who works as a librarian there. Katya is a tall, very solidly-built girl, with a poor complexion and a beautiful smile. She must also be an efficient administrator, because she arranged—with a small corps of assistants—this ball and last month's, as she will next month's, and the month's after, straight through until the opening of the World Youth Festival. I met Katya at the library, and she asked me if I could come to the ball this evening. I told her that I wouldn't miss it for the world. When I arrived downstairs, no sooner had I stepped in than Katya was there to greet me. For the rest of the evening—I stayed only two hours—I was always, with one small exception which lasted only two minutes, if that, escorted either by Katya or one of her lieutenants. I am quite sure that their intentions were quite honorable, that their constant presence was only a measure of their concern that I have everything explained, and that I don't get lonely. On the whole, the evening was very pleasant, and I am quite sure that at least most of the boys and girls there had a "very good time." What struck me most was the militant way in which Katya had organized the evening and the incredible inferiority complex exhibited by one young man or woman after another. "Do you like our ball?" "Do you like the way we dance?" "Do we dance as you do in America?" "Is our clothing nicely tailored?" "Is the band all right?" "Does it play like your small bands?" "Is the vocalist good?" "Does he sing the Latin numbers as they do in America?" "Please be frank and tell us what you like and don't like."

October 22 : Poland is still the major topic in Russia today, but so far as the Russians know from *Pravda,* Gomulka has become a member of the Polish party again and Khrushchev took a trip there for a day to discuss "party affairs, which proceeded in an atmosphere of mutual understanding and comradely friendliness." The Russians do not even know that *Borba,* Yugoslavia's *Pravda,* praised Gomulka as the leader of the national Polish Communist movement, which is moving more and more towards a Yugoslav kind of national independence. Nor do they know that Gomulka today stated that Poznan was caused by the stupidity of the Communist Party leadership and policy. What they do know about the outside world they got today from the magazine *"Amerika,"* which hit the newsstands this morning at 7 a.m. and was all sold out at 8 a.m. I tried to buy a copy of the magazine at 9:30 a.m., but the newsdealer at the corner kiosk looked at me with a happy twinkle in his eye and said: "I only wish all my magazines and papers went as quickly as *'Amerika'* did this morning. Come back tomorrow morning. I shall have a few more copies. I'll try to save one for you, but you know the way things are. *'Amerika'* (using a play on words) is very popular."

October 24 : Hungary has just ripped a page out of Poland's recent history and stolen the headlines from Gomulka—though not completely. Apparently, Hungarian workers and students have risen against the Gero government and pleaded for the reinstatement of Nagy, whose name is associated with a higher standard of living.

Late this afternoon, Nagy became Prime Minister once again, and, promising a higher standard of living on the one hand, ordered Soviet forces into Budapest on the other to suppress what he described tonight as counter-revolutionary forces. Budapest Radio reported Soviet aircraft in action against insurgent mobs; it also apparently made a fervent appeal to all Hungarian wives to please implore their husbands to steer clear of the counter-revolutionaries and to occupy themselves with more pleasing pastimes at home.

Two mining towns located about 50 or 60 miles outside of Budapest have also caught the liberation bug, for they too have exploded in a warm passion of discontent and unhappiness. Hungarian students have called for "true national independence" and free elections with the participation of more than one party.

Nagy, meanwhile, appeals to the indulgence of the Hungarian people, in what appears to be a truly mass and spontaneous popular demonstration. He asks that the invading Soviet troops be received with "love and kindness." Obviously, he does not envisage that the Soviets will be received that warmly and kindly.

And, in Poland, where latest reports continue to ride the crest of sensationalism, Gomulka received a telephone call from Khrushchev in which the latter apologized for his outbursts last Saturday, when he said, pointing an angry finger at Ochab, that the "Americans and the Zionists" are again being permitted to dictate policy in Poland. He promised that the Soviet forces, still under the direct control of Rokossovsky, would be returned to their bases in Poland from the threatening positions around Warsaw which they have occupied the last few days. Cyrankiewicz, the Premier, today de-

clared further that from here on in, Rokossovsky will take
orders from the new Politburo, led by Gomulka, and that his
assistant will be Spikhalsky, who has spent most of the last
seven years in jail for "nationalist deviationism."

Speculation about the present was so rampant this afternoon that I decided to drift off into the past, to try to recapture the mood of an old, faded page of Russian history. I
took a trip with a British friend to Kolomenskoye, which is
a small village outside of Moscow, about 25 minutes by car.
The day was clear and sharp, and, though winter was in the
air, the fall was vibrant in a sort of last gasp. Kolomenskoye,
like many other small Russian villages, has its main street,
its small wooden homes, its garden plots, its chickens, ducks
and a pig here and there. Dogs ran and barked loudly on the
cobblestoned main street, and they chased one another down
unpaved muddy streets. Women walked slowly through the
alleys, some carrying bread, others wood. Some held two cans
of water which they pumped from the corner well.

Off to one side of town, high on an incline overlooking
a small and lazy-looking river, is a complex of churches.
There are three main churches. One, well off to the side, was
built in the early sixteenth century by Ivan the Terrible's
father. The same man, Basil III, built the central church in
1532, and it turned out to be one of Ivan the Terrible's favorite churches, as an old charwoman told us. Closer to the
main road, topped with blindingly blue onion domes which
stood proudly against a lighter blue sky, speckled with white
clouds, stands the Kazan church, built in the early seventeenth
century. Alongside it used to be a wooden castle where Alexis
Mikhailovich, the second of the Romanovs, lived for a while.
It was finally destroyed by Catherine the Great in the latter
part of the eighteenth century, when it was discovered that

most of the wood had decayed. No trace of it remains, though everyone there knows the story of its existence.

Opposite the church are two small wooden, log-cabin type structures. One is part of a bell tower or watch tower. The other is indeed a log cabin, built by Peter the Great in 1702 in Archangel, and transported to this location in 1934, as one old lady said, "in honor of the castle that his father (Alexis Mikhailovich) once lived in, almost to keep it in the family." The log cabin has a large sitting room, a bed room, a dining room, a work den, a quarterly's room and a storage room. We managed to get into the cabin—we had come too late—only because a contingent of school children, about 40 of them, between the ages of seven and ten, was to visit the log cabin too. The teacher explained the significance of Peter the Great to her young charges, "the future builders of Communism" (as the Soviet press calls them), as she pointed to the various objects in his work den, which is a fine large room with a big bookcase and two large models of schooners. "Peter the first worked hard. He labored strenuously, all for the glory of his Motherland. He read many books. He was very intelligent. He built a navy to fight off the enemy and to make the Motherland very strong, to make it glorious." The entire point of her lecture was to inculcate in her young pupils the image of a great and omnisciently wise ruler whose every effort was devoted to the glory and strength of the Motherland. Glory and respect for Russia achieved through hard work and conscientious study—this is the goal towards which the Soviet educational system is moving in its quest to re-educate and bring up the young generation. This almost Calvinist strictness and hard work—just reward psychology, all in the name of the Motherland, is the driving motivation of Soviet education. The teacher's insistence upon the theme pulled both of us back to the twentieth century and the enormous Russia which today is the hub of a huge wheel whose Polish and Hungarian spokes are splintering.

October 27 : *Kremlevskiye Kuranty* (which might be translated as *Kremlin Big Ben*) is a play written by the Soviet writer, Pogodin. The *mhat* staged it this evening, and for a Soviet play, it was not bad. The central character in this revised version of an original "Big Ben" piece that Pogodin did in 1934 is Lenin, and he is omniscient. He loves children; he has mastered all science; he is sharp; he is dedicated; he has a faith in the Russian people; he is absolutely wonderful. In fact, this play smacked of a Lenin personality cult, and my hunch was right. During one intermission, a Russian told me that he believes that when the play was written first in 1934, Stalin was the central figure. Stalin cannot be the central figure now, but Lenin can, and he is. A young Russian, who was sitting next to me, dressed in the finest Western fashion, including handsome horn-rimmed spectacles (so deceptively Western in appearance, in fact, that when he answered my question in flawless Russian, I was stunned), applauded wildly whenever Lenin appeared on the stage, or whenever a reference to Lenin's genius was made. "It's true," he asked me during an outbreak of applause, at the same time as he poked me in the ribs, "it's true, isn't it, that Lenin was the greatest man of the twentieth century?"

"I know a lot of people who think so, here," I answered.

He caught the significance of *here,* and he fired back angrily, "Even the most bigoted Westerner must admit Lenin's genius, for he was indeed the greatest man of the twentieth century."

Argument over Lenin was futile, but we found much to talk about which had, on the surface, nothing to do with

Lenin. My young Russian friend, who turned out to be one
of Russia's many *Kostyas,* a diminutive for Alexander, is a
student in his third year at one of Moscow's many art institutes. He is tall, literate, sophisticated and sensitive, and
he is keenly interested, "like all my friends," in the West,
especially America. "You know," he said, after we had picked
up our coats and walked out into a wet Moscow night, "there
is an expression amongst many of my friends, which might
interest you?"

"Really, what is that?"

"*Shtatny baron.*"

"Could you explain that?" We bundled up against the
wind.

"Well, you know that in Russian, the words "United States"
are *soedinyeoniye shtaty.* Well, we take the last word, *shtaty,*
and make it an adjective, *shtatny,* and tack it onto the old
Russian word *baron,* or baron. If we think a young fellow is
keen, quick and on the ball, a good guy, we call him a *shtatny
baron,* after the United States."

He had enjoyed a Viceroy cigarette during the intermission
between the second and third acts of *Kremlyebskiye Kuranty,*
and I offered him another. "Thanks very, very much. I do
love your cigarettes a great deal."

"Speaking about the popularity of America, how about the
popularity of *Amerika?* Have you been able to get a copy?"
I was making a reference to the release on Monday of the
50,000 copies of the new Russian-language State Department
magazine *Amerika.*

"How can I answer that?" He shrugged his shoulders and
raised his hands in a helpless gesture. "It was just impossible
to get a copy. I got to the newsstand near my house at 8:30
in the morning, and they were all sold out. I ran down to the
Metropole, but there were none left. Some reporters were

taking pictures, and they took a picture of me too. I waved
to convey my regards to the American people."

We continued our walk through a light drizzling, nasty
Moscow night, up Gorki Street, past the great statue of Yuri
Dolgoruki. Kostya was talking steadily, about one thing or
another, mostly about his experiences this past summer on a
collective farm in the virgin lands.

"I spent three months gathering in the harvest this summer.
Most of my friends did not wish to go to Siberia, but I did.
I have had an easy life. My father is a top-flight engineer and
he makes a lot of money. I have never been in need of anything. We have always had the two most important things in
Soviet Russia: money and connections. Anyway, the opportunity for some contribution arose and I grabbed it. Maybe
it is hard for you to understand what I mean by contributing.
You see, here we have a society which is based on fine, humanitarian principles, but which functions on base, narrow
principles. The entire administration stinks with bureaucracy. Fat bureaucrats with fat mugs and fatter rears sit
around for weeks, months, years, simply fulfilling plans." He
spat in disgust at the foot of the Pushkin statue, where he
had stopped for a moment to tie his shoelace. "All my life,
my father has brought such people into the house. Are they
interested in the principles of the Revolution? Are they interested in the people? No, they are interested only in themselves. They want more money and a second *dacha* and maybe
a second car. These are the people I have seen all my life, and
I must admit my father is the same way. I still believe in the
principles which I feel sure Lenin believed in. I want to see
our people happy. I want to see them live much better than
they do now. That is why I wanted to go to help in the virgin
lands. And this was not only a physical function out there. I
wanted to talk to the peasants, explain to them what is their

due, what they should expect from the system. Many of my friends did the same thing. We went to the people."

The rain had slackened a bit, and a cold wind snapped through the almost deserted streets. Occasionally, an old woman in a white apron would come out of a building, look about, and duck back in. Few cars were running. I saw no buses. "You know, Kostya," I said, "your statement about going to the people reminded me of the old *narodniki* movement of the seventies of the last century." I made reference to the period of Russian history when guilt-stricken young noblemen and members of the high intelligentsia "went to the people" to educate them, to cultivate them for the democracy they saw in the offing, only to be rejected viciously by the dark, suspicious peasant mass. Their idealism shattered, these young men switched tactics and became terrorists, out of whom the revolutionaries of Russia were born, out of whom Lenin was born.

"I had not thought of the parallel. Possibly, you are right. The way my friends and I view our country—Russia is still a peasant country. About 65% of the people are peasants. These are the people the government should be concerned about. Instead, they push them into collective farms, which they couldn't care less about. They want their little piece of land. They want to be masters of their fate and their harvest. They want to deliver grain to a person, a dealer, whom they know and can talk to. They are not interested in delivering grain to an impersonal agency. And, you know, this is the strangest thing. From birth, people in Russia are taught to think and act in collective ways. Yet, the farmers only want their plot of land. They couldn't care less about the collective land. In fact, they work most of the time on their own land, not the collective land."

Kostya was making reference here to the usual collective

farm situation, where a farmer has to work a certain number of days a year on the collective farm land, most of whose yield goes to the state, and the remainder of the time he may devote to his private plot, or garden plot, the produce of which he may sell on the free, open peasant market, where prices fluctuate roughly according to the laws of supply and demand.

"Our feeling," Kostya continued, fully inspired, "and I mean the feeling of the overwhelming majority of my friends at the Institute, is that the peasants, the ordinary people, must begin to get a fair portion of our national production and profit. This has not happened to date, and it is about time. The Soviet system has existed for 38 years—soon we will celebrate our 39th anniversary—and still there are enormous shortages. How many times can we be told to wait until tomorrow?"

"Well, Kostya, what is the answer to this problem?"

"I don't know, my friends don't know, and I am sure that Khrushchev, the *sorcerer's apprentice,* as we call him, doesn't know either, just as nobody in Russia these days has a real image of the future. Lenin had his image. His image was prosperity for all people, but his image has been distorted by Stalin and his friends like the present collective leadership. Recently the Komsomol group in our Institute had a meeting. Ivanov, who is a very sharp Communist and a group leader, was speaking about the new tasks which face us young people today and tomorrow and the day after. He recited the usual list of cliches, which we all know by heart, until one of the students, a man of 35 who received six wounds during the war, stood up and asked what he had fought for. Ivanov told him he had fought for Russia and the Soviet system. 'I fought only for Russia,' this man answered. 'I did not fight for the Soviet system.' The other students and I cheered his remark. Ivanov tried to regain control of the meeting by explaining that the reason things are not really so right in Russia today is that many mistakes had been made but that they are all now being corrected. 'It is the fault of the Stalin tragedy,' Ivanov capitulated. These days, he always uses the expression, 'Stalin tragedy,' no longer the Stalin personality cult, which has lost all meaning. 'That is no answer,' one student stood up and shouted. 'A Marxist explanation demands that the system itself is at fault.' All the students stood up, stamped their feet and shouted that Ivanov indeed had not given an answer to the question which was raised. The meeting then broke up, but a group of my friends and I went to a friend's house and there we continued the discussion. We ranged over the entire issue. Some called for inciting an uprising. Some called for assassination of the leaders and the convocation of a representative government. But others, and I am one of these, thought force and violence would get us nowhere, because if I thought that it would, I swear to God I would go to Red Square tonight with all my friends and stage an uprising, but it would yield no beneficial results. The Russian people are a frightfully inert mass. They do not move easily. And we can not do it alone. There must be a way, but so far we don't know the way. We have no image of tomorrow. All we want is a happy Russia where people get a fair share of a powerful industrial machine, but the bureaucracy stands in the way. What we all need now is leadership. We need another Lenin desperately. He could lead a revolution. Without leadership, we are nothing, and our dreams remain dreams."

Kostya lit another cigarette, and we walked along a deserted, dark street for well over a block, saying nothing, each of us wrapped in the power and emotional truth of Kostya's diatribe. We walked past one of the buildings of the Marx-Engels-Lenin Institute. Kostya spat against the building wall.

"You know," he said with a broad grin on his wide, handsome face, "we call this place the 'Institute for Black Magic.' Here anything can happen. My God, even Trotsky could be re-habilitated tomorrow morning. All history could be rewritten. This is a history which is like black magic. It can do any-thing."

Three young Russians walked past us. All were dressed in black or dark blue coats, with their caps pulled down low over their faces. As we passed, we heard one of them remark to the others: "*Stilyagy,*" and they all laughed, as we did too. "Kostya," I asked, "just what is a *stilyag?*"

"Well, the *stilyag* really means those Russians who are en-gaged in illegal selling and profiteering. Originally, it had nothing to do with being well dressed. Now, of course, there are many, many more *stilyagy* than before. And now, a *stilyag* is not necessarily one who is engaged in illegal sales. It has come to mean most any Russian youth who is well dressed—or at any rate dressed as a Westerner."

"In a sense, then," I interjected, "the resentment against the *stilyag* is a form of resentment against the West as a whole?"

"Possibly, this is so, but what is very true is that older people, or even younger people who are uneducated, who never went beyond the seven or ten year school, think of the *stilyag* movement, which is like a Russian teddy-boy move-ment, as a movement away from true Russian customs and manners. But I think that the *stilyagy* are those young Rus-sians who are moving on, who think of the present demands of life, not the past, who think about the future, who wish to enjoy their lives today, not dedicate it to something tomor-row, who wish to go out with sweet, lovely girls, not tractor drivers, who are simply interested in living a real, honest life now, today, not a dull humdrum life today in the hope their children will live better and dress better. Many of us have simply given up looking at the future and think only of to-day. Like today, I went to see a trial, which is open to the public, on Kropotkin Avenue, no. 35. Six Russians are on trial for selling Western clothing illegally. The prosecution, to bolster its case, brought as witnesses some of the buyers of Western clothing. But the tactic backfired. The first witness simply answered the prosecution: 'I was tired of dressing badly, living badly. I had a chance to buy a good suit, and I did, and I would do it again if I could.' What was funny was that all the people who bought this clothing were wealthy Russians who belong to our new aristocracy, just like my father."

"Was there any conviction?"

"No, the trial is still going on. You really should go there, because there you would see what I have been talking about. Things happen today which no one thought imaginable when Lenin lived. Most people with money have become just like the bourgeoisie of old. They want material comforts. I guess I myself am no different, for I too am a product of this system. The system breeds the people, and I am one of the people. The only people who have not become contaminated by the society are the peasants, because they stand above the so-ciety. They are pure."

"Are there any great leaders in your country today, Kostya, who stand for the rights and interests of the majority of the people? Aren't Khrushchev and Bulganin very able leaders? Many people in the West think so."

"Let me tell you what Khrushchev and Bulganin are good for. Khrushchev would make a fine district party leader, and Bulganin, good Mr. Bulganin (and Kostya used the English word *mister*), would be better off eating five meals a day, living in a suburban *dacha*, and reading Pushkin. They are

the kind of leaders who met the needs of the Stalin era well.
They kill, and sleep well afterwards. But these are not the
leaders to meet the challenge of the modern times. Now, they
rule sort of in between the old and the new, but they don't
realize that there is no going back to the old. There is no
retreat possible at this point. Only forward movement, only
change, and undoubtedly the people of Poland and Hungary
have realized this too, for they don't want us there any more,
and I don't blame them. Just recently, all the Polish students
at my Institute sent a letter to Gomulka expressing their complete solidarity with his actions. And my friend *Yanka,* a Pole
(Kostya used the Russian diminutive for Ivan), no longer per-
mits us to call him *Yanka;* he insists upon his Polish name
Yan. By the way, do you have any more recent news on the
events in Budapest?"

When I explained that the last BBC report I heard contained . . . , Kostya interrupted me: "We know all that. We
listen to the Voice of America and the BBC regularly. Is
there anything newer?" I told him that I really didn't know.

It was almost 2:30 a.m., and our coats were soaked from
the rain, which had now stopped. A strong cold wind whipped
through the empty streets. Kostya and I parted company at
the Metropole Hotel. I took a cab. He took the metro. "I
could afford a cab too, but I don't feel right spending money
foolishly, just to show off."

October 28 : For the fourth straight day, the Soviet press has
announced the end of the uprising in Hungary. One taxi
driver, with whom I rode today, seemed to hit the nail on
the head: "Whose side are the Hungarian troops on? If you
know anything about our revolution, you recall that success
came to us when the troops joined the insurgents. This is the

critical question." I did not know this answer for sure, though reports reaching Moscow indicate that many Hungarian border troops have indeed joined the insurgents and that one Soviet air field has been seized by Hungarian troops who promptly burned the planes and hangars.

October 30 : Every two or three weeks, the Communist Party dispatches one of its lecturers to the Lenin Library to set forth the latest views of the Party on contemporary problems. The lecturer tonight was a young, thin, nervous type, who wore a black suit with two medals on his lapel, and his topic was "international affairs." The lecture hall was the main reading room in the old building of the Lenin Library, the former Pashkov House that the Sheremetyevs lived in for over one hundred years, and it was crowded. All the seats were taken, the aisles were overflooded with young and middle-aged listeners, and the back of the room was a cozy sardine can where the rest of us were packed. I came upon this lecture by accident. The reading room happens to be located in between the check room and the Manuscript Room, where I do my research, and since it was impossible to get through this mob—nor would I have tried—I decided to listen to see how the party attempts the difficult job of keeping the Russian university youth informed of the Party position on all contemporary issues. The gist of the lecture was that the Soviet Union has maintained and will continue to maintain a firm policy of peace and cooperation with all countries, regardless of the social or political systems of the countries involved.

"Just today," the speaker went on, "the glorious Communist Party and Soviet Government expressed their unyielding devotion to the Bandung Conference and the spirit of Bandung, in a talk with Mohammed Daud, Prime Minister of Afghanistan." He continued much in this vein, using the phraseology of the Soviet press, when it dispenses the Party line daily to its readers. Whenever the speaker used a very typical phrase like "the glorious, mighty, genius-like Soviet people, who are the builders of a new society, who are constructing communism," all of the listeners about me, almost without exception, either yawned loudly and rudely, made sarcastic comments, or continued to read their books, magazines, or newspapers. It struck me that possibly 95% of those present were bored, while the other 5% exhibited an arresting display of cynicism and disbelief.

After about one hour of this sort of diatribe, the speaker finished on a high note of Socratic eloquence. "Who," he asked, "consistently struggles for peace?" He answered: "The mighty, brilliant, genius-like Communist party and the Soviet Government (which are almost like the gold-dust twins), inspired by the great decisions of the twentieth Congress of the Communist Party and its Leninist Central Committee." Everyone yawned, or scratched imaginary bug bites, or shuffled restlessly.

At this point, the speaker called on everyone who had a question to note it on a piece of paper and submit it to him. About 50 pieces of paper were submitted. The speaker flipped through them quickly, then made the sad announcement that they all concerned one subject: Hungary or Poland, Hungary and Poland, and Hungary and Poland and their relation to the Soviet Union.

"Comrades, would it not be better to discuss the meaning of the twentieth Congress, or the denunciation of the personality cult, or the decisions of the July Plenum of the Central Committee?"

"No," was the unanimous answer.

One young man arose: "We want to know about Hungary and Poland. Tell us the truth about these two countries."

The lecturer answered: "Comrades, the Soviet press has reported the full facts about the recent events in these countries."

Everyone started to shout aloud that they were not interested in what the official line was; they wanted to know what the facts were. One man about 35 standing near me mumbled to his friend: "He's in a spot now. I don't envy him. He had better answer."

But the speaker kept insisting that a better topic for discussion would be the twentieth Congress of the party.

This was unsatisfactory.

One student arose and speaking loudly, clearly and fearlessly, said: "We are all literate. We read the papers. We know the official line. Now, we want to know the truth. We want facts. We want to know what is happening there. Don't repeat to us the phraseology of the press. Tell us what is going on there." Everyone burst into applause. The meeting was almost completely out of control. Over the racket of 200 young people shouting for the "truth," the speaker appealed for order and then, picking out what he thought was his trump card, he asked over a hubbub which would not subside: "Would any comrade suggest that the Soviet press does not print the truth, that there is a truth outside the statements of the press?"

He was to be disappointed, for another student arose, and seemingly expressing the sentiments of most everyone present, shouted: "We asked for the truth. We did not ask for a recitation of the press. We all read. Give us the truth now."

The speaker forlornly admitted: "I am here to give you the Party line on these matters. Please hear me out."

Calls of approval went up all over: "Let him speak. Let

him speak." A student asked: "Where was Gomulka for the last five years?"

The speaker stammered senselessly in answer to this question, as everyone started laughing and stamping their feet.

"Comrade Gomulka," the speaker started, "committed many errors. Five years ago, he favored the kulaks, did not support the correct line of the Party."

His voice was drowned out in a chorus of boos.

"Does the Sejm rule Poland, or does the Party rule Poland?" one student asked.

"The Party is the expression of the will of the people," the speaker answered, mouthing another Communist cliche.

This answer too was drowned out in boos. Finally, with the meeting in complete chaos, one student got to his feet, in disgust, and, turning his back on the speaker, said: "I've wasted enough time tonight. I came here for answers, and as usual I'm not getting them. I'm leaving." He made his way through the crowd towards the back door. No sooner had he started to depart than everyone, as though by command, followed his lead, picked themselves up, and left the room. Inside of two minutes, the speaker was left alone in the hall, holding the fifty pieces of paper which demanded an elaboration of the Polish and Hungarian problems outside the framework of the "official Party line," which they obviously do not believe.

"What a waste of two hours." "What sort of answers is he giving us?" "We can read the papers anytime. Now we want answers to our questions. These are not answers." I heard these remarks from three different students who side-stepped me to get out of the hall. This meeting was the most astonishing exposition of cynicism and disbelief that I had ever witnessed. As I walked off towards the Manuscript Room, I doubted very much if the Russians could construct their new society with this mass of "future builders of Communism."

By the way, for the sixth day running, the Russians in *Pravda* have claimed that the Hungarian "putsch" has been defeated. This undoubtedly is a record number of defeats, and I can well understand the cynicism of the Russian youth.

November 4 : For a few days this past week, Russia was crowded off the front page by the Suez crisis, precipitated by the movement of Israeli troops into the Sinai Peninsula and by British and French bombing of the Canal Zone area, but today it shot back on to the front page with a resounding and disgusting roar. For, today, the Kremlin in effect declared war on the Hungarian people. A three-column, banner, front page, *Pravda* editorial screamed in the most vicious language of the Soviet press since the days of the Korean war that "fascist, counter-revolutionary forces" had attempted to gain an upper hand during the "putsch." "These elements, which are hostile to the people and alien to Marxism-Leninism," must be eliminated, and increased concentrations of Soviet troops and forces have been moved into Hungary in order to crush the Hungarian "fighters for freedom."

Pravda also announced that Imre Nagy, who, just three days ago, was called a fine fellow who had the support of the Hungarian people, was actually in "connivance" all along with foreign "capitalist, imperialist powers and agents." Thus, his doom was forecast. Soviet military leaders apparently went into conference with him (presumably about the withdrawal of Soviet forces, in accordance with the wishy-washy Soviet Declaration of last Wednesday). During the conference he was arrested. A new government, led by Janos Kadar, was formed, which is obviously Communist-led and Moscow-directed. It promptly proceeded to invite Russian soldiers into Hungary for the purpose of stamping out the "counter-revolutionary" elements. This they are doing, and they are undoubtedly converting *Pravda's* verbal viciousness into physical slaughter. The freedom movement of Hungary will surely be crushed under the tread of the Soviet tank and under the hoof of the Soviet soldier.

The deceit and hypocrisy of the Soviet peace campaign is nowhere more grimly pointed up than in today's *Pravda.* Alongside the editorial calling for open and merciless war against Hungary is a article on the Afghan reception last evening in the Kremlin, which, it is stated, is further proof of the Soviet desire for peace and friendship with all peoples. Inside *Pravda* are the world reactions to the Wednesday declaration calling for relations of "equality" between the satellite states, for respect for national integrity, for non-interference in the internal affairs of one country or another.

Moscow today was calm. The weather was brisk. Children played in the streets, laughed and shouted. Students worked in the Lenin Library. Parents pushed their baby-carriages. The red banners commemorating the 39th anniversary of the Communist Revolution, which will be "staged" on November 7, have appeared on the fronts of all prominent government buildings. The major theme of these banners is pride in the accomplishments of the Soviet system. The Soviet people, who were today informed in the curious language of the Soviet press about the events in Hungary, are supposed to be inspired towards even greater heights. Can they be proud of their soldiers in Hungary today? Can they be proud of this latest atrocity?

November 5 : This afternoon, Russian youth staged a wild kind of protest on the street in front of the British Embassy.

This, like most of the demonstrations in Russia, was not spontaneous. It was planned. Demonstrations also took place this afternoon in front of the French and Israeli Embassies.

November 6 : Taking a lesson out of Dulles' book, the Soviet Union late last night embarked on its own brink-of-warmanship, rattling their rockets in sharply worded notes to Mollet of France, Eden of Britain and Ben Gurion of Israel, warning that the Kremlin is prepared to use its troops, together with those of America, and functioning in a United Nations context, to halt the "aggression" in Egypt. Bulganin also sent a personal letter to President Eisenhower suggesting collaboration of American and Russian forces to crush the "aggressors." In another strongly-worded message, Shepilov asked the Security Council to take immediate action against Britain and France and volunteered the deployment of Soviet forces in this United Nations endeavor.

The effect of this shift was immediately felt here in Moscow. At the Anglo-American school, children were sent home well before the gong sounded the end of classes. Some British children remained at school, because they could not get through the mobs of demonstrating Russians who were posted in front of the British Embassy.

The demonstrators, holding aloft their signs and placards, calling for the downfall of the "aggressors" and "invaders" and "interventionists," were permitted to crack through the gates and flood the courtyard of the Embassy, which theoretically is British property. On one occasion, the demonstrators actually entered the French Embassy, and, hours later, entered the British Embassy. Despite the assurance of *Pravda* that the demonstrations are spontaneous, these demonstrators were "spontaneously" demonstrating on government time. I have it on good authority that these workers, students and housewives were ordered to "demonstrate," that their signs and posters were painted and prepared on government time, that one group spelled another group quite systematically, and that the MVD officer who stood guard over the mobs knew exactly when the demonstrations would be called off, at least temporarily. The demonstrators themselves were not in the least antagonistic, despite the posters they carried. English personnel entered and left the Embassy, almost freely. They were never disturbed. The Russians were drinking vodka quite liberally throughout the demonstrations, and, at one point, a French correspondent walked out into the mobs surrounding the Embassy. A heavy-set Russian grabbed his arm: "Who are you?" he asked belligerently. "A French correspondent," was the answer. The belligerency melted, and the "insurgent" smiled and said: "Good." At the Israeli Embassy, things were a little rougher. The door was smashed in at one point.

There were reports that meetings were started throughout the country—protest meetings, they are called—in an attempt to whip up native enthusiasm for the strong stand the Russians have taken on the Suez question. The Russian who told this to me said that so far as he could tell the party leadership thus far has been unsuccessful in fully diverting the attention of the "thinking Russian" away from the events in Hungary, despite the vigorous and costly efforts to make the Suez the crucial aspect of modern-day international life. In any case, the extent of these protest meetings indicates that the demonstrations in front of the three Embassies were only one part of a major campaign to rivet the attention of Russia and the world on Suez, not Hungary.

Those of us living in the Embassy compound were restricted to the compound for about three or four hours this

afternoon. Apparently, this was a strictly precautionary measure. There was the feeling that the Russians might well de-
cide to stage one of their "spontaneous" demonstrations in
front of our Embassy. The tension was very high this afternoon, when the order was put into effect. Only Americans
on important and urgent business could leave the compound,
and those only in a car. One foreign service officer, who was
here also during the height of the cold war, told me that the
feeling of that period has returned to Moscow with drastic
suddenness. This particular officer even feared the outbreak
of a major war. Thoughts such as these passed through people's minds, as the snow came tumbling down upon an already
white city, chilling it still more.

Finally, late this evening, I heard a fine story about the
"spontaneous" demonstrations in front of the British Embassy. It seems that some of the Russians managed to break
through the guards and enter the building. Of course, they
were soon ejected from the Embassy, but the British Ambassador, Sir William Hayter, tall and very distinguished, walked
out into the mob of screaming demonstrators, and asked the
MVD colonel "in charge" of the "spontaneous" demonstration, with beautiful British understatement, "Could you tell
me please when these demonstrations will be over?" Not
thinking, the colonel glanced at his watch, looked up at the
Ambassador, and answered, simply: "In half an hour."

November 7 : Today, the Russians and Communists
throughout the world celebrated the 39th anniversary of the
Bolshevik Revolution. In 1917, a small, determined fistful
of diehard revolutionaries "picked up" the power, which
Lenin said was lying in the streets and built the state we
oppose today. I was opposed to it for other reasons today. I

had to get up at 6 a.m., in order to make it down into the Square before the troops, as they did on May 1, blocked all roads and entrances leading into this central area of Moscow. I was in no mood for celebration. The sun had not even come up. But thousands and thousands of troops had. They formed human walls against the traffic of people and cars and very thoroughly blocked off the Kremlin from the rest of the city. At 10 sharp, the parade started. The military part was fast and unattractive. No planes flew overhead, possibly because of the low overcast. What they call the "popular" part of the parade lasted only through 12:30 but it was colorful. The people were almost all very high, and on occasion the huge lines which snaked through Red Square swayed from side to side. Some of the marchers carried signs condemning the aggression against Egypt, and once again the Kremlin rattled its rockets as Zhukov spoke of continuing aggression and the availability of Soviet troops not only to defeat the aggressors around Suez but to crush the Hungarian revolution as well.

It snowed for the rest of the day, but this did not disturb the Russians who flocked into Revolution and Red Squares by the thousands, most of them drunk, dancing, delighted, and not in the least concerned about Suez or Hungary. This was their holiday. They do not have to work tomorrow, and the band played catchy tunes from an open bandstand opposite the Kremlin, across from the old American Embassy on Mokhovaya Avenue. The Russians danced in the streets, in the snow, and they tipped their vodka bottles continuously. Many extra platoons of militia patrolled the streets. They were very severe with the drunkards, and there were many drunkards.

While the masses of people walked and danced in the heavy snow, the Soviet aristocracy was at the Bolshoi Theater watching the Glière ballet, "The Bronze Horseman." This is more spectacle than ballet, and certainly Pushkin would not have recognized his poem, from which the ballet was adapted —but there were floods on the stage of the Bolshoi, it rained on the stage of the Bolshoi, and there was an enormous hurricane on the stage of the Bolshoi. Every now and then, a *pas de deux* was performed. Members of the Soviet elite, who pay as much as 35 roubles for one seat (about $8.75 at the official exchange rate) wore evening gowns and tuxedoes, and there were many foreign Communist delegations present.

November 14 : It has always been the endeavor of this diary to stick as close to the popular pulse as possible. This has been very hard the last few days. Russians simply are not talking as much as they used to. They apparently sense a strong shift in policy and feel the chill in the international climate.

Here, in Moscow, these are dark, frightening and tragic days. Today, for example, journalistic sources uncovered a story of mammoth proportions. Cairo has apparently requested its Moscow Embassy to take up the Russians on their offer to send "volunteers" to Egypt. The Kremlin had proposed in clear terms that if foreign troops were not withdrawn from the Suez area, it would place no obstacles in the way of those "volunteers" who wished to help the Egyptians "defend their sovereignty." Yesterday, Peiping said it was willing to send 280,000 "volunteers," a la Korea, to Egypt for similar purposes of "defense." If Communist forces of this dimension were actually dispatched to Egypt, this would constitute a strategic and military challenge greater than any the West has had to face in the last ten years.

Much of the recent about-face in Soviet policy, from the happy grin to the unhappy grimace, stems of course from Hungary, which followed close on the heels of the Polish events leading to the resumption of power by Gomulka, the dedicated Red nationalist. These twin attacks have had a major effect upon the situation in Russia.

November 16 : Cab drivers are still among the bravest citizens of any society. They are outspoken, and they are the last vestige of solid individualism in the Soviet Union. The following is a conversation, which took place this afternoon:

"Could you please take me to the American Embassy?"

"Hop in."

"Awful weather, isn't it? Constantly snowing, grey and miserable."

"Yup!"

"Been a cab driver long?"

"Listen, do me a favor?" he asked, without answering my question.

"Yes."

"What's going on in Hungary?" I was shocked by the suddenness with which he raised this question.

"Well, of course it is a horrible story, and we don't have all the news."

"Yes, but at least you have more than the Soviet papers. That's all we've got is the Soviet papers. Please, tell me the truth. What is going on there?"

I then proceeded to tell him in as great detail as possible some of the events. As he heard about the atrocities, he shook his head and mumbled how terrible is war. Then, I continued: "And probably most important is simply that the Hungarians didn't want you there. They wanted to live independently. They did not want Russians telling them what to do all the time."

"Exactly," he shouted, jumping on a theme he apparently had mulled over, "exactly, what I have been thinking all the time. I told my wife just the other night that we should never have gone into Hungary with the troops, that we should have tried to solve the problem peacefully, and if they wanted to live independent of us, then they should have been given this right. We should not make people live in fear of us. That only makes the other people hate us, and we are not a bad people on the whole. We want peace. We enjoy peace."

"Why is it," I asked, "that your newspapers are trying to stir up a kind of war psychology?"

"Listen," the cab driver answered with a fine twinkle in his eye, "the newspapers are run by the government. They write what the government wants them to write. They can write this business about war from today until tomorrow. We don't want it. We, the simple people, don't want war. Leave us be. There simply is not the feeling for war. There is no mood in this tired country for more and more sacrifices. You had to live in Russia during the war to know what suffering really is. We don't want that again. No matter what the newspapers say. We just can't be made to think in terms of conflict now. We just can't. Like the government says about the fascists in Hungary, they 'suffered a complete defeat' in their endeavor to make us think in terms of war." I was amazed at the extraordinary sophistication of this Russian proletarian.

Later, this evening, I had a conversation in the library—in the men's room, of all places—with a fairly young historian. He is working on his thesis for his master's degree, and he told me that he is 30 years old.

"What is the subject of your thesis?" I asked.

"I am writing a small part of a general history of the civil war in Russia, following the Revolution. A group of us have been told that the Institute of History leaders are desirous of having a new history of this period of Russian history. They said that they want the history completed by the celebration of the 40th anniversary. There was an article about this recently in the papers."

I told him I had seen the article, and that I had become very much interested in two major problems. "How are you going to handle the role of Trotsky in the civil war and how readily do Soviet historians gain access to the state archives?"

"I should like to answer you very frankly. As yet, we do not know what role Trotsky is going to play in the Revolution. His role has not yet been decided. And as regards the archives—unfortunately, this situation too is a difficult one to pin down. Of course, we have access to various data which is located in the Central State Archives, but first we must make sure what line the work will follow before we know exactly what material will be useful to a rendering of a history of the civil war."

"I don't follow your reasoning. What do you mean?"

"Well, when a historian sits down to write a work about a certain period, he is not told exactly what to write. This is quite obvious, but the historian must be fully abreast of the latest zigs and zags in the party line. If he writes a work which clearly moves too far in advance of the line, then the work will not be accepted and he might end up in some kind of disfavor. Therefore, he must be sure that he writes a history which will be acceptable to the Institute of History. Of course, things along this line have noticeably improved. In the past, all history simply glorified Stalin's role or else almost made up a role for him. Now, we have much greater leeway. We can actually delve into the real situation. In fact, we

believe that things are going to get so much better that soon
we will be able to write really objective history."

"Is there any real guarantee that this move in the direction
of greater democracy will continue?"

"We feel that the new leadership could not possibly go
back on its word at this point. We feel that things will continue to get better and better. We feel that soon we shall
truly be able to write a history of the civil war which even
gives Trotsky the credit which he deserves—at least, in this
period. With Trotsky, one can never forget that he was an
opportunist and he committed many drastic mistakes. On
this score, Stalin was right."

"But how do you know if he made mistakes, if the history of the last twenty years has been so badly distorted by
the Stalin personality cult? How can you check on your
facts? How do you know what his real role was?"

He let his eyes wander around the ceiling, searching out
small nooks and cracks. He shifted uneasily. "We don't really
know, you are right on this issue, but we do know that things
will get better and better. At least, we hope so." He did not
look at me for a moment or two. He looked at the floor; then,
he said: "You know, to tell you the honest truth, nobody
can tell what is going to happen even tomorrow. The events
in Hungary have had a profound effect upon my friends. We
have very little access to real news. We have only the Russian
papers. We know that we are not being told everything. We
know we are being shortchanged. What are we to do?"

November 18 : Here in Moscow three weeks ago, for reasons,
I understand, which have nothing to do with the events in
the satellites, there was a two-day strike at the Kaganovich
ball-bearing plant. Though this rumor can not be checked

absolutely, very reliable sources have heard from Russians that this strike was in the nature of a sit-down strike and was provoked by the management simply not paying the workers on time and going back on its word in regard to bonus payments. But a strike apparently did take place, which is unprecedented in this country. This is really one of the best indications so far of the extent of the relaxation in the system, the down-grading of the MVD, and the bravery of the Russian proletariat. Certainly, when the iron hand of Stalinism ruled Russia, this would have been impossible. Striking is not a right which this proletariat possesses. The pot is boiling, but whether it will bubble over or simmer down is still not clear.

November 19 : Today's *Pravda* published the text, shamefully expurgated, of Khrushchev's speech last night at the Polish Embassy. It contains one significant paragraph: "There can be no question of whether or not peaceful coexistence of the various states is needed. Coexistence is an acknowledged fact which we can see before us. We say to the representatives of the capitalist countries, if you wish you can come and visit us, if you don't wish—you need not come. This will not grieve us particularly. But it is essential for us to coexist. The fact that the Great October Socialist Revolution was carried out, that the Soviet Union and the whole system of states of the socialist camp exist, does not depend on you, after all. Such is the law of social development; furthermore, this law is operating in our favor. We Leninists, are convinced that our social system, socialism, will be victorious over capitalism in the long run. Such is the logic of the historical development of mankind."

There are few clearer statements of a Communist's dedication to socialism, which appears to be a constant, fixed dream, a star for every wavering Communist intellect. And it binds Communists together, frequently regardless of nationality or upbringing. Many Westerners simply cannot understand that people believe in communism. They know that these people exist, but somehow they feel that their dedication to Marxism is a kind of false, protective shield against doubts and frustrations. This may be true. But there should be no doubt that communists believe in their cause, and they are convinced that their cause will triumph, despite our haughty conviction that their cause will surely fail, that indeed it has no chance.

This evening, I spoke with a young student of the Institute of History. The student was a short, rather stubbily-built woman in her early twenties, with a wide, full handsome Slavic face. Her face looked like a picture of all of Russian history. We'll call her Maria. I spoke with Maria about Khrushchev's speech, and I asked her how Khrushchev could be so cocky, so absolutely sure, that socialism will triumph over capitalism.

"Oh, but you are wrong," she answered, a smile on her broad face, "he is not cocky, he is not as you say absolutely sure. It simply will be. Comrade Khrushchev merely repeated something which we Communists all know, all accept, all believe. So, you see, it is not a question of cockiness. We are merely stating a fact."

"But, how do you know that it is a fact? How can you be so sure? You might die this moment. Tomorrow, there might be a revolution in Rumania. You might never defeat the Hungarian rebels. How can you be so sure? How can you ignore other possibilities?" I asked, almost plaintively.

Maria looked at me, as my mother used to, when she tried to explain an obvious truism to me and I could not accept it, could not understand it. "These things you just mentioned —they may happen. I might die this moment. Rumanian fascists may stage a counter-revolutionary putsch. We may not be able to crush the fascists in Hungary tomorrow, or the day after, but we will. We will, eventually. You see," she continued, very patronizingly, as though she were explaining the most elementary abc's to me, "there are laws of social development, which you and I can do nothing about. Even if I decided that communism were a bad thing, that I wished to fight against it, all I would be doing would be fighting against inevitability, and this is stupid. History is moving according to these laws, and these laws indicate that communism follows capitalism, just as surely as capitalism followed feudalism."

I interrupted Maria. I thought I had finally found a flaw in her logic. "If indeed, history does move according to this inevitable timetable, if communism must inevitably follow capitalism, if these historical changes always take place, if there is a constant flux in history, then how can you be sure that the flux will stop with communism. How can you be sure that a different type of system will not follow communism, and make communism as backward and regressive a doctrine as you think capitalism is today. How do you know that this won't take place?" I thought that I had Maria. For a moment, I saw a flicker of doubt pass through her eyes. Then, her eyes sparkled again with a wicked brightness. She fell upon the inevitable "out."

"You see, one of the basic reasons for the change in social structure is the class struggle. In all preceding systems, this struggle is never-ending and firm. There can be no change, but under socialism, under communism, there is no class struggle, because there are no antagonistic classes. They are all harmonious. Therefore, with the end of the class struggle, there is the end of this historical development." She folded her arms across her chest and looked up at me. "Do you understand now?"

I threw my hands up in helplessness. "What can I say to you, Maria? Your mind is closed to other possibilities. You feel you have the key to history. I think there is no key to history. I think that you simply must open your mind to possibilities of change."

"Change there will be, but communism there will be too, just as surely as we are speaking together now. Communism will be."

Maria returned to her book. Before I left, I glanced over her shoulder. She was reading a Russian translation of Keats.

November 20 : In an attempt to follow up on the intellectual ferment among the youth of Russia, I returned this evening to the Lenin Library. Last week, the announcement was posted on the bulletin board that another Party lecturer was to come to the library to deliver the Party line on another problem. This time, the theme was "The Vigilance of the Soviet Man." When I arrived for the lecture the information bureau denied that it had ever been scheduled. Two librarians also denied that a lecture was to be held. Yet, the fact remains that I saw this sign on the bulletin board on Sunday evening. That's two days ago, and it had been there for at least a week previously. I asked one librarian for an explanation. "All I can tell you is that this lecture was not scheduled." As she made her statement, she did not look at me. She looked at the floor. No one would even admit that the lecture had been postponed, if not completely cancelled. "When will the next lecture take place?" I asked. "This I cannot tell you either," she answered, her eyes still on the floor. It is tempting to draw the conclusion that the Communist group at the library had cancelled this lecture, as well as future lectures, for fear of a repetition of the demonstration of disgust and skepticism which took place three weeks ago.

November 24 : Greater detail on the strike at the Kaganovich plant. What occurred there at the end of October writes a new page in modern Russian history. Since the late twenties, nothing like it has been seen here. It all started in the forging workshop of the plant, where 450 men, underpaid for the last four or five weeks, arrived at work on October 23, checked in, and sat down. They did not work. Local plant managers raved and ranted, threatened and shouted, but the men did not budge. They wanted to be heard. On October 24, they continued simply to sit and not work. A party leader, who has been unidentified, came to the plant to talk to the rebellious workers. He told them to return to work immediately. The workers insisted on being heard. The party leader succumbed. He asked for a volunteer to express the sentiments of the workers. A man arose and related that he had been released from a corrective-labor camp only six months ago and that for the past three months the manager of the workshop had held back on wages, had given but 200 or 300 roubles a month to his men and squandered the rest of the money on himself. The labor spokesman demanded that this manager be released from his job. He warned that until such time as this happens, the workers will not go back to work. The forging workshop, one of the most critical in the plant, had held up plant production as a whole. The party leader said he would consider the situation. He was about to leave, when this same man arose again and repeated his warning that the workers would not go back to work until this manager was removed. Within hours, he was. The following day, the workers checked in, as they had done on the two previous and historic days, and went to work. The manager was replaced, and for the next two weeks, the workers received double and triple pay in compensation. The proletariat had risen against the leadership and in brave defiance had challenged the manager of the plant in front of the party. The party, which theoretically is the expression of the workers' interests in a communist state, was forced to retreat.

Another story: Within the past two or three weeks, students at Moscow University who lived in a dormitory near the Sokolniki Park in Moscow, went on a kind of hunger strike. They were objecting to the low quality of food. They wanted to eat and live better. They refused to eat in the dormitory lunchroom. Chinese students, who lived in the same dormitory, continued to eat in this lunchroom. Some of the Russian student strikers strongly suggested that the Chinese stop eating there. They refused. The next day, they stopped. The previous evening, they had been severely beaten by a group of the striking students. Rumor has it that the food has noticeably improved.

Another story: On the bulletin boards of the University here in Moscow, a wall newspaper is posted. This paper, which gives the Party line on major current issues, had been running stories on the Hungarian events straight from the BBC newscasts, which the editor of this newspaper had been listening to. When this came to the attention of the Party cell at the University, a leading Party worker scheduled a major meeting. The Party representative demanded that the students unanimously approve that this student be dropped from the editorial board of the newspaper and from the University. The students refused. The Party worker insisted, made dire threats. The students refused. At last report, the editor is still in school, still putting out this newspaper, and the students are still reading it.

November 25 : In a clear attempt to regain the strong control characteristic of two or three years ago, *Pravda* today lashed out against students who do not occupy themselves with "socially-useful labor," which is the Communists' way of saying that these students are not thinking or behaving in a communist way. These students, the newspaper continued, must take up "concrete duties and tasks," by which *Pravda* means work on collective farms or in factories. Moreover, *Pravda* admitted, there are "a great many" students who do not work at all, who occupy their time in abstract reasoning. Yesterday, *Pravda* mentioned that "certain comrades" in universities have ideas which are "just like a bourgeois ideology." It did not point out any special ideological denomination, but the point is clear that too many of Russia's youth think and act in a "bourgeois" manner, and this must be eliminated. This is simply not the youth out of which communist tomorrows are built.

November 27 : A Russian told this story today: Three Hungarians met in Moscow's Lubianka Jail. "What are you here for?" one Hungarian asked another. "I was for Nagy," he answered. "And what are you here for?" he asked. "I was against Nagy." Both Hungarians then turned to the third Hungarian and asked why he was in Lubianka. "I am Nagy."

November 29 : I saw an interesting movie this evening. It is called "The Forty-First," and it is a story about a woman partisan during the Civil War. Unlike many Soviet movies,

"The Forty-First" has little propaganda, and it is beautifully filmed and imaginatively acted.

It is the story of a "Red" partisan who is charged with guarding a "White" officer during the Civil War. The partisan —an attractive girl—has already killed forty "Whites." The officer is young and handsome, and they upset the Marxist format by falling in love.

One morning, the two lovers, who by an odd circumstance have been deserted on the shores of the Aral Sea, spot a boat in the distance. The officer is first to see that the men on board are "Whites." In a fit of happiness, he runs toward the boat, as it approaches the shore. The "Red" tells him to stop. He keeps running. She picks up her rifle, fires, and kills him. She got her "forty-first," but no sooner does she kill him, than she is overcome with remorse. She rushes after him, and raises his dying body to her breast. She is in tears. She feels she has done wrong. Love conquers even ideology. Love is stronger than the doctrine, which is one truth. Love is a truth too.

In a country where all media of entertainment are supposed to instruct, to teach people, "The Forty-First" succeeds in teaching that love is as powerful a truth as the one-truth communist doctrine, that possibly there are other truths, that possibly the "White" officer was right. "The Forty-First" is a beautiful and surprising film. It is another indication of the healthy change which has taken place in Russia over the past year.

December 2 : Since the twentieth Party Congress, the Communist leaders have reversed their field on one crucial issue. Rather than remain silent on "shortcomings" (a word the leadership loves to use these days to explain away every inadequacy), they have decided to speak about them openly, on the assumption that it is far better to talk about issues which everyone knows exist than to let the pot of discontent boil, silently and ominously. *Komsomol Pravda,* the organ of the Young Communist League of Russia, true to this new conception, today ran a long, lead story, entitled: "Graduates remain in schools." The essence of the story is that a great many young students, who have finished their training, cannot find jobs. This is an economic heresy in a socialist society, because, as the writer explains, "There are no superfluities in our labor force." Every student presumably can find a job. Unemployment, as such, simply does not exist. Yet, *Komsomol Pravda* today admitted indirectly that unemployment does exist.

The Soviet Union has a vast system of trade schools, which are administratively subordinate to the Ministry of Labor Reserves. It is the function of this Ministry not only to train young mechanics and combine operators but also to find jobs for them. Various ministries apply for so many mechanics, and it is the duty of the Labor Reserve Ministry to fulfill these requests. But, in point of fact, it has not. In 1952, 7,600 students finished their training but found no jobs. In 1953, 14,000 finished schools and found no jobs, and last year, more than 18,000 students, diploma in hand, went about without work. This, of course, is not a large percentage of the 585,000 young specialists who were sent to work at various jobs last year, but the fact remains that the figure of unemployed young specialists rises from year to year. And, it must also be borne in mind that the majority of the 585,000 specialists were sent to work on new construction sites in Siberia and on the virgin and idle land developments in Kazakhstan and southern Siberia. The article points out that this "shortcoming" costs the state a great many roubles every year, without compensation.

In conclusion, it strikes at the principal worry of the leadership in regard to the youth. "There are losses which cannot be measured in roubles," the writer states. "Deficiencies in planning are reflected in the fate of the young workers, enforced idleness pushes them along an incorrect path and beclouds their first days of independent work." It is not only the disillusionment and unrest which ensue from the revelations of the Twentieth Party Congress but also a certain amount of economic discontent which produces unhappy thoughts and ideological vacillation among the Soviet youth.

December 6 : On October 30, I attended a meeting at the Lenin Library. At that time, a young Russian Komsomol told me that the meeting was a regular thing for the Library. He said that every two weeks, a Party lecturer comes to the Library to give the students the latest Party line on current topics of interest. I found out tonight that this is not true. That was the first meeting of its kind to take place at the Library.

Tonight, the second such meeting took place. The scene was once again the Periodical Room of the library, but tonight there was one outstanding difference. There were about half the number of listeners, and very few students were standing in the back of the room. On October 30th, the room was packed to capacity. I barely had standing room. Tonight, there was all the room in the world to stand. As before, those who were seated paid very little attention to the speaker. He spoke, in flowing cliches, about the necessity for a strict vigilance on the part of the Soviet citizen. He said that any attempts to subvert or undermine the system must be suppressed, mercilessly. He called on all Soviet citizens to stand on guard of socialist victories and achievements. In this respect, there can be no wavering, he said. The students, who were supposed to be listening to him, were busily doing their lessons, reading magazines, yawning shamelessly, shifting their feet restlessly. As before, they appeared not in the least interested in what the lecturer said. They were waiting for the occasion to ask questions. When the speaker finished in a fine flourish ("We must stand on guard of our victories. We are the builders of a great communist society. The future is in your hands."), everyone started giggling. Some laughed aloud. Others chattered noisily with their neighbors. The speaker prepared to leave. As he was gathering his papers, one young man in the back of the room stood up and said: "I thought we could ask questions." Others joined in assent. "We want to ask questions." The speaker, obviously disappointed, forced a weak smile to his blank face and agreed that he would answer every question they raised. A student in the back turned to his friend and said: "What do you bet he doesn't?"

"We have heard reports of anti-state hooliganism. Is there any truth to them?"

"To speak truthfully, comrades, I have never heard of such reports. Therefore, I cannot sensibly answer any questions in reference to them."

"I told you he wouldn't answer any questions," a student said to his neighbor, as he picked himself up and stomped out of the room, in disgust.

"You have been speaking about the vigilance of the Soviet man this evening. Do you admit that there is a lack of vigilance? Do you admit that people permit anti-state sentiments to gain power over them?"

A murmur of excitement shot through the crowd. The students moved forward in their seats.

The lecturer answered: "Comrades, vigilance is a very important aspect of our march towards communism. A lack of vigilance could lead to harm for the people."

The speaker was interrupted by a short, stubby figure in the back row who stood up and shouted: "Will you simply admit that people have anti-state sentiments?" The speaker shuffled back and forth nervously but did not answer the question. "Are there any further questions?" he asked meekly.

"Where are Rakosi and Gero?"

"I have no information on that question," the speaker said. Students around me laughed out loud. "He won't answer you," one man said. Another remarked, jokingly: "They're in Yalta resting on the beach." "No," another student shouted, "they're in Sochi at a comfortable *dacha*, just taking it easy."

"Comrades, I must ask you to stick to the topic at hand. We are speaking about the vigilance of the Soviet man."

A young Central Asian, who looked like an Uzbek, ignored this appeal. "I would like to ask this question of you. Everyone knows that the press has blamed the Radio Free Europe station, the BBC, and the Voice of America for inciting false propaganda. But we all know that propaganda and agitation have some basis in fact, have some core of reality. What have we done to eliminate the core? What have we done to get rid of the reasons for the putsch in Hungary? What happened there which made the putsch possible?" As the young Uzbek raised his question, he was greeted by murmurs of approval. "Answer this question," a young man insisted.

"Mistakes had been committed. As we know."

The speaker was interrupted by cat calls and shouts of disapproval. "Don't tell us again and again about mistakes. We know about mistakes, but mistakes don't answer all questions. What really happened? Why was the putsch possible?"

When the speaker started to talk about mistakes once again, the students grew so restless that he stopped speaking. "Are there any other questions?" he asked. "No," everyone said in unison.

"Then, the meeting is over."

No sooner had he asked his question about further questions than everyone rose from his seat and walked out of the room. Once again, the Periodical Room was empty within a matter of one or two minutes. The party lecturer stood in front of the room. His face was a study in dejection and failure. He slowly gathered his newspapers and walked from the room. Before he did, he looked quickly at a picture of Stalin that hung behind his podium, shook his head, and left the room, walking mechanically, stiffly.

I followed one young student down the hall. I asked him if he could explain to me why the emphasis upon "mistakes" was not satisfactory. He looked at me through a pair of thick, smallish glasses. "After the Twentieth Congress, mistakes satisfied many of us. It seemed right that mistakes had been made, that these mistakes had to be corrected. We had known about the mistakes for many years. Now, finally, the leaders themselves started speaking about mistakes, so we did. But gradually, we began to realize that 'just mistakes' is no explanation for things like Hungary, and I think it is no explanation for things like the excesses of the personality cult. No, I think that the reason lies elsewhere."

"Where?" I asked.

"Where do you think?" he answered, and he turned his back on me and walked away.

I think that this near-sighted student, as well as many others, with whom I've spoken, is beginning to think that possibly the fault lies somewhere in the system itself. When a student body has been brought up on Marxism—which stresses that phenomena are explained by the nature of the system in which they exist—it begins on occasions such as these to think that something is wrong with the system, if it could produce Hungarys, Polands, and Stalin's personality cult.

December 11 : For the past three months, a major intellectual battle has been storming around the question of freedom of the arts. There appears to be a very clear difference of opinion on this critical problem. Some writers and artists believe that the Party should have no control over the arts. And, for a while, it looked as though a natural sequence of events would lead eventually to the independence of art from politics in the Soviet Union. But, on November 20, *Soviet Culture*, an official Soviet newspaper, ran a long report on a meeting which took place of artists and writers, at which Molotov was present. Molotov made it very clear that art would remain subordinate to the party.

Five days later, *Pravda*, on November 25, 1956, ripped into the article which sponsored freedom of the arts. Three authors took turns destroying this "alien" thesis.

Since that date, numerous articles have come to Molotov's support, and, with each day, it appears more and more certain that the party will retain complete control over the arts today and tomorrow, as it did yesterday and the day before.

In the center of this fierce battle is a book called *Not by Bread Alone*. This book was written by Vladimir Dudinstev, and it was published in *Novy Mir*, in August, September and October, 1956. The story is rather complicated. It is about a young inventor who in his endeavor to get his invention accepted runs up against the stubbornness and intransigence of the Soviet bureaucracy. He is arrested, spends time in prison, and, upon his release with the 1953 amnesty, takes on the bureaucracy again and wins. He battles alone. He is a

strong individualist, an egoist, who shows little need or in-
clination to turn to the Party for help when he is rejected
and sent to jail. Not only is this an uncommon thesis for a
Soviet novel, but Russians say it is a first-rate work of art.

Dudinstev is young, probably under forty, with a shock of
dark hair, which looks as though it hasn't been combed in
weeks. During the thirties, when Stalin unleashed the bloody
purges, Dudinstev was a young Komsomolist, with a fierce
and dedicated allegiance to the Soviet system. He took time
out from his "great cause of building a new world" to study
writing under Lev Kassil, a Russian Jew who ran a small
Komsomol literary circle in Moscow. Dudinstev studied law
at the Moscow Institute of Jurisprudence, and during the
1939-1941 Hitler-Stalin honeymoon, he completed his course
and became a lawyer. But, before he could begin to practice
law, Hitler ended the honeymoon, and Dudinstev started a
military career. While serving in the army, he was wounded
in the leg. Because he could no longer participate in active
combat, Dudinstev was transferred to Siberia to serve as a
military procurator. This division is the legal arm of the
Red Army, which, through the curious machinations of a
totalitarian state, is also competent to trying and investigate
civilians. Lopatkin, the young, driving inventor of the book,
was also tried by such a procurator.

Meanwhile, gathering hard and very necessary experience,
Dudinstev was always writing. Or he was reading. He con-
fesses a special fondness for Joyce and Proust. He said that
he wrote one other book before *Bread,* which was called
Rovesniki (people of the same age). The book won him
an unimportant prize and the jocular criticism of his teachers
who spoke of the "liveliness of my pen and the thinness of
my material." "I was a formalist then," he confessed just
recently at a meeting. During this period, he became very

interested in Russian classical literature, and he became in-
trigued with the idea of being able to handle a major theme
himself. He tired of short stories. He longed for majesty and
depth, size and feeling, awe and power. Yearning for a large
theme, he read, read and reread Gogol, and the influence of
the writer of *Dead Souls* is very clear in *Not by Bread Alone*.
Dudinstev must have promised himself that when he sat down
to write his "big book," it would have a big theme, one which
would embrace the entire Soviet system.

Dudinstev says that he started writing *Not by Bread Alone*
in 1952, and he made his first attempt to publish the book
after the Twentieth Party Congress. I heard from a Russian
the other day that he had great difficulty in getting the book
published. I was told that Dudinstev went from publisher to
publisher and was invariably told that the book would be a
great success but was somewhat too controversial. In desperation, he turned to Konstantine Simonov, editor of *Novy Mir*,
and Simonov accepted the novel for publication.

Simonov's acceptance of the book, after everyone else had
turned it down, is interesting. Simonov is one of the old party
hacks. His works rarely exhibit a spark of originality or a
flight of fancy outside the narrow, cramped quarters allowed
by the party for "free" literary expression. Why then should
Simonov have published the book? It is the feeling of some
people in Moscow that Simonov thought that the book was a
kind of literary Twentieth Congress. It condemned bureaucracy, which the Congress had done. It favored initiative from
below, which the Congress had favored. It called for spark
and drive, which the Congress had urged. It was a bold book,
but the Congress was bold too. It is quite likely that Simonov
felt he could read the political line so much better than other
editors that he would be making an editorial coup by print-

ing Dudinstev's book. Moreover, it did have literary merit, and even Simonov could see that.

Unwittingly, in university circles, Dudinstev and Paustovsky (who wrote a wonderful book in 1952 called *The Golden Rose—Zolotaya Roza*) have become the spearheads of an amorphous youth movement which favors far greater freedom of the arts, a return to Leninist democracy (whatever that means), a repudiation of all bureaucracy, and unlimited foreign contacts.

It is quite possible that *Not by Bread Alone* does not really satisfy the unspoken sentiments of all the Soviet intelligentsia, but it is different. It is new. It is good. It is art. And, most important, it obviously is not Party trash. In one other respect, Dudinstev's book differs from most other Soviet works. It gives no answers. Soviet literature, like all forms of art, is called upon in this system to play an instructive, educating role. Books should have a moral, a point, which strikes home for the Soviet leadership. It should not encourage you to think after reading the book. Rather, it should leave you aware of a new or old social "truth," like "the party is tops," and "the collective farm is just a heaven on earth." *Not by Bread Alone* does none of these things. It has so many aspects. It raises so many questions. It poses so many possibilities, that it leaves the reader excited on the one hand and questioning on the other. For, there is no one answer.

December 12: It now seems obvious that *Not by Bread Alone* will not be published as a separate book. It should have been three weeks ago. It won't now, and *Izvestiya* warned Dudinstev "to draw the proper conclusions from this objective critique" in any of his future works. *Izvestiya* says

that Dudinstev did not really portray a real Soviet man, because not once does Lopatkin turn to the collective of the
plant, university, or party for assistance and guidance. Moreover, Lopatkin is an individualist and an egoist. This is very
bad. He must be a collective person in this socialist society.

Last night I attended a meeting at the Lenin Library. This
was the third in a series of meetings on problems which seem
to disturb the Russian youth today. This evening's concerned
the "Latest Tasks of Modern Soviet Literature." The speaker,
a man named Brovman, identified as a "laureate critic" of
the Soviet Union and a member of the Union of Writers, was
a tall man with obvious self-confidence. A receding hairline
accentuated an already large forehead, and his small, horned-
rimmed glasses sat low on his heavy nose. His audience tonight was mixed. There were students, librarians, teachers
and professors. Like the first meeting, this was a standing-
room affair. Brovman insisted that there be no reading during his talk, which brought on groans of displeasure. "If you
want to read, go outside now, before I start. If not, sit still
and listen." His tone was harsh.

He began his discussion by admitting that many of his
theses may be mistaken, may not be accepted. Yet, he added,
he would try to be objective. He started with a dull and hackneyed summary of the "great" events which have taken place
this year in the Soviet Union. He stressed that 1956 has been
as significant a year for literature as it has been for politics.
"A more objective approach to modern Soviet literature is
the most outstanding feature of 1956," he said. Ilf and Petrov
are being published. So is Bunin. Numerous writers, who
were suppressed during the period of the personality cult,
are now being published, and modern writers are writing
about the "little" person, not "the big man," as was characteristic of Stalin's day. The masses have begun to appear in

novels, the proletariat is again the vanguard of the socialist movement. Errors are being corrected. "Those who continue to speak about old truths do not deserve our respect." This comment sent a ripple of happy anticipation through the audience. A student to my right mumbled: "Maybe he's going to say something, maybe he's different."

The speaker droned on, in a loud, bombastic voice. "There have been many books published this year, comrades, which continue to echo old truths. These are poor books. One must regard literature as the expression of new, dynamic truths." Students around the room rose to their feet and clapped their hands. They were smiling. They were anticipating an off-beat delivery.

"One writer of note is Vladimir Dudinstev, who wrote the book which has raised so much clamour and fuss and hulla-baloo. *Not by Bread Alone,* which was also published in *Novy Mir,* must be discussed seriously. It is a fine piece of writing and it has a provocative theme. Dudinstev is a writer of very considerable talent." Brovman ranted on about the book in very general terms. The students all sat at the edges of their seats. Like me, they were hoping for some comment on the December 2 *Izvestiya* article, condemning Dudinstev's lack of concern for the collective, and stressing the social purposes of literature. Brovman did not disappoint us. He started speaking about the article straight away. He said, however, that the article, like the book, must be approached objectively. He said that "Dudinstev is a very exceptional writer. His characters are varied and brilliantly portrayed. He paints a very good picture of Drozdov, the bureaucrat, as well as Lopatkin, the inventor. Some of his chapters are absolutely wonderful and rank with the finest in Russian literature."

As the speaker continued, students turned to their neigh-

bors, smiling, pleased with the favorable critique their favorite book was getting. "Anyone who seeks to find a simple and
clear solution to questions raised in this book will be disappointed. There are no simple solutions in life, and there are
no simple solutions in this book. People simply are not that
simple." The students applauded once again, and the applause rocked the hall for about five minutes. Then, Brovman
continued: "One thing, however, is clear, and in this respect,
we must all be keenly objective. The book has a major shortcoming of considerable importance. It is the fact that over the
span of eight years, Lopatkin did not once turn to the collective. We know that as a fighter, Lopatkin can at times struggle
alone, and this is satisfactory. But over eight years, certainly
once, twice, he should have been moved to turn to the collective." The students grumbled unhappily, but did not do
or say anything.

"Surely, comrades, in Lopatkin's place, would you not have
turned to the collective at least once in eight years? Yes, of
course, but Lopatkin does not, and this is a very bad feature
of this book. One must in this country turn to the decisive
truth of life, the party, once in eight years. It is only normal.
By not having the character to do this, Dudinstev created a
non-Soviet type, an egoist, an individualist, of major proportion. This is what I disagree with." The speaker was well
aware of the fact that he could not hope to convince the students of his viewpoint, but he was trying to have them see the
viewpoint of the party. He kept repeating that it was urgently
important for all students to realize that Dudinstev must be
approached objectively. His appeal for objectivity was almost
justified, since he appealed for a more balanced view of *Not
by Bread Alone*. He was not in effect appealing for student
agreement with the *Izvestiya* line; he was hoping at best to
get them to modify their own views on this novel. "Whether

we say that *Not by Bread Alone* is written in the style of socialist realism, or not, is not very important. Large-scale discussions of whether a volume is socialist realism or not is
child's play, for which we do not have time."

December 13 : I heard today that many students are now
toying with the idea of university autonomy. This means that,
taking a page from nineteenth century European and especially Russian history, modern-day Soviet students are con-
templating universities which are independent of the state's
wishes and dictates. This sentiment has nothing whatsoever to
do with communism; it is antithetical to a centralized state
and the concentration of power in the hands of a few for
exercise over the many. Obviously, this is not a goal which is
capable of immediate or even possible realization under the
present circumstances. However, it is tremendously significant
that Russian students think far more in terms of concepts
like university autonomy than in terms of "the building of
communism."

I was also told of a far more dramatic and meaningful
sentiment. I was told that numerous Komsomol organizations
have held meetings, during which the possibility of the Komsomol, as an organization, breaking its ties with the Communist Party, and, as a consequence, disassociating itself from
the political direction of the Communist Party, was discussed.
I have known of skepticism on the part of the youth toward
communism. I have also seen major exhibitions of political
cynicism. On one occasion, I even heard a young student say
he would gladly lead a revolt if he thought it would do any
good. But I never heard, nor suspected, that the dissatisfaction would lead to an organizational overhaul. I do not believe that this is anything more than a dream. I think it is

quite beyond the realm of possibility, under current circumstances, but I find the fact of the existence of such sentiments challenging and hopeful.

December 14 : The discontent which has been bubbling in Russia these past few months, and which recently reached major proportions, is not limited to the Moscow students. Today, *Leningrad Pravda,* the party paper for the Leningrad region, ran a long article in which the university youth were taken to task for possessing "incorrect, mistaken and unhealthy" views and sentiments. It is particularly significant that this article, which was a report on a meeting of the Leningrad Party Plenum, dealt almost exclusively with the problem of a rebellious university youth and ignored economics and party activity, which is what most plenums generally talk about.

December 22 : Yves Montand, the fellow-travelling French cafe crooner, arrived in Russia a few days ago, and he has caused a major sensation. His concerts are jam packed, and Russians are scalping on tickets with reckless abandon. I went to the theater of the new Lenin Stadium this evening just to get an idea of what all the fuss is about. 17,000 hysterical Russians turned out to listen to Montand sing songs "about the loves, joys and miseries of the simple person," as *Pravda* billed it. They sat in rapt attention, as though they were listening to a Bach recital. Thousands of Russians crowded around the stage, cheering wildly, applauding madly. Montand loved every clap of the thundering applause. He

bowed a million bows, and kissed a million imaginary kisses
to his moon-struck audience.

I took a Russian friend to this concert, only because she
pleaded with me that listening to Montand would be a great
thrill for her. I was surprised when she made this admission,
because she is usually a solid citizen type, a dedicated Komsomol who never yet has deviated from the established party
line in her talks with me, and moreover she didn't seem like
the "crooner" kind of music lover. Anyway, I asked her afterwards, as we walked to her house through Moscow's dark and
cold streets, why the Russians were going off their heads for
Montand. "He's just not that good," I said. "We Russians
always receive foreigners well. We are a hospitable people."
I admitted that there was great truth in what she said, but I
insisted that there was a little extra in their reception of
Montand. "Well, I guess it might also have to do with the
fact that he might be the last Westerner to come to Russia
in some time. At least, that's what my friends seem to think."
The look in her eyes was so sad that I could not force myself
to continue this theme, and we did not mention it again the
rest of the evening.

December 24 : Outside of the foreign Embassies, there's
hardly a trace of Christmas in Moscow. The Russians walked
through the streets as they always do. The traffic proceeded
quickly, dangerously, through the wide avenues and narrow
streets. The stores were not packed, and this afternoon, GUM
did little business.

But in Spasso House, where Ambassador Bohlen, and his
family reside, Christmas was everywhere. The huge ballroom
was decorated with angels, red and green and smiling, and a
Christmas tree—at least thirty feet tall—stood in the middle

of the room, a resplendent tribute to a joyous holiday. All
the personnel of the American Embassy, and some from the
British and Canadian, gathered in the ballroom, around the
tree, some of us seated on the floor, and we sang Christmas
carols till past midnight.

December 28 : Sol Steinberg, the *New Yorker* cartoonist and
an astute observor of foreign cultures, mentioned when he
was here in Russia during the summer that he has never
seen a Russian artist who draws with an economy of line. I discovered this evening that there might well be such a person
in the Soviet Union. His name is Alexander Zverev, and I
hear he is young, eccentric and wildly dissipated. When he
was sixteen, he was a student of a Moscow ten-year school,
which specialized in art. But Zverev was unhappy with the
art and the school, and he quit. He started painting in an
absolutely heretical fashion for this country. His drawings
and paintings are beautiful and striking. They remind you
sometimes of Van Gogh, sometimes of Toulouse-Lautrec,
sometimes of Kathe Kollwitz. Yet, according to people who
have spoken with him, he had never seen an exhibition of foreign painting until the recent Picasso exhibit at the Pushkin
Museum. He apparently paints in this style because he feels
like painting in this style. His paintings and drawings have no
special message, except the message of the grotesque in human
suffering. They are definitely not socialist realism. He has
never had an exhibition of his work; yet he is very popular
with the students of Moscow. Definitely avant garde for the
Soviet Union, he paints refreshingly and excitingly, and he is
a young man who has been rejected by his family, who does
not work, who lives on the mercy and charity of his friends,
and who is almost mad. Yet this same young man will have his

first exhibition—it is rumored—sometime during the World Youth Festival next summer in Moscow.

December 30 : *Pravda* today revealed that Joseph Stalin was not really such a bad guy, after all. When the Twentieth Congress started to denounce Stalin, one Communist leader after another leaped on the bandwagon, and, for a while, it appeared almost a contest as to who could slander Stalin the most. Khrushchev won with his now-famous secret speech to the membership of the Communist Party. Stalin was accused of murdering thousands of innocent people, violating socialist legality, drifting towards madness, destroying the efficacy of the Red army just prior to the Nazi invasion of the Soviet Union—his crimes were summed up under the title "personality cult." His self-adulation was attacked daily in the press. Lenin's modesty was the necessary antidote to excessive praise of individuals.

In other words, the "dark" side of Stalin was illuminated, though it was also not denied in subordinate clauses that he had made important contributions to Marxism-Leninism. When Poznan erupted, followed by the "peaceful Polish revolution," and topped off by Hungary, a noticeable change took place. Stalin was no longer dubbed as evil. His contributions were given greater coverage in the press, and the Soviet leaders did not rant and rave about the personality cult as much as they did during the spring and summer.

Today, *Pravda* reprinted a very long editorial which appeared yesterday in *Jen Min Ji Pao*, the Chinese Communist equivalent of *Pravda*. The importance of the editorial was highlighted by the very great prominence it was accorded in all the papers and by the fact that the Soviet translation service had worked through the night to release a full text translation by 10:30 a.m. this morning. *Pravda's* publication of this editorial was tantamount to *Pravda* approval, and *Pravda* is the official press organ of the Soviet Communist Party.

Stalin, *Pravda* proceeded to point out, was a "staunch and very devoted Communist." He made numerous contributions to communism. Stalinism, as a doctrine, does not exist, and, if reactionaries insist that it does, then Stalinism is nothing more than Bolshevism. Secondly, *Pravda* mentioned that Stalin had committed mistakes, as everyone knew, but that his mistakes were minor compared with the great contributions which he made. Thus, Russia announces an about-face on its official position toward Stalin.

Pravda raises another fundamental question. What is the relationship of Stalin's mistakes to the Soviet system? Many intellectuals and students with whom I have spoken have asked this very question, and I have heard them begin to question the nature of the system itself. Marxism, which is the ideological backbone of the Soviet Union, is like a religion. It must remain unquestioned to be vitally effective. This, it is not. It is being questioned vigorously, and the structure itself is beginning to groan and moan under the pummeling of doubt. I think that *Pravda,* in raising this issue before the public, recognizes the seriousness of the situation and would like to do something about it before it gets out of hand. So, *Pravda* followed up its question by answering it in roughly these terms: "If democracy can be used for anti-socialist activities, can be used to weaken the cause of socialism, then this so-called 'democracy' can have nothing in common with socialist democracy." In other words, "socialist democracy" means freedom to function within the boundaries established by the party. If the Party determines that the boundaries must be cut back, then they are, and everyone will have to follow suit. Idle discussion among students is bad; these students should be made to work.

December 31 : New Year's Eve in Moscow, and the Russians are taking advantage of their biggest holiday. A Russian told me today that New Year's is far and away the brightest, gayest, happiest holiday of the year. "It is much more popular than November 7 and May 1. Those are political holidays." The Russians really did celebrate this evening. Enough vodka to float a battleship was consumed today throughout the Soviet Union.

The entire foreign colony, which gathered at the American House Club, also did itself proud.

January 1 : The Embassy was very quiet today.

This evening, I found out that Vladimir Dudinstev, who wrote *Not by Bread Alone,* has suffered a slight heart attack. He is very ill. His health, badly impaired during the war when he was injured on the Leningrad front, has not been good, and the attacks against his book, which have been noticeably stepped up, have affected him noticeably. Since the December 2 *Izvestiya* article, Dudinstev has not appeared in public, and he now lies ill and morose. I am also told that the Russian intellectuals and writers are all being squashed. Molotov's direction of the arts has been dynamic and firm. Socialist realism is being reimposed. Magazines have been warned to publish only "reliable" articles.

Stalin must be very pleased. His ghost walks triumphantly throughout the Soviet Union, a smile across its waxen face, confident that a soft line could not yield positive advantage and that the hard line is the only line. Stalin had a bad year in 1956, but he seems to have recovered handsomely in the last few months. 1957 looks much more promising for him. But 1957 will also pose the problem most arrestingly: Can the leaders reinstitute a hard domestic and satellite policy on the one hand and pretend to be peaches and cream to the outside world on the other? The answer to this question may be one of the most significant of the 20th century, for the consequences will have a most telling effect not only upon the Russian people and the Russian intelligentsia but also upon people throughout the world.

IV · SASHA AND A DOUBT

January 5 : I arrived in Leningrad today for a short holiday. The *Red Arrow* express departed from Moscow at 9:20 p.m. last night and then rocked-'n-rolled its way northwestwards to the former capital of Russia. The night was cold and snowy, but the compartment was stuffy and hot. After a rather uncomfortable evening—my bed was at least a foot too short for me—the *Red Arrow* shot into Leningrad on time. It was 8:20 in the morning, but it might just as well have been the middle of the night. It was pitch dark. A porter took my bags from the train to a taxi stand, and I had to pay him ten roubles. This was no tip. It was a charge. (Theoretically, there are no such things as tips in "Socialist" Russia.) There was a long line waiting for taxis this dark, cold morning. After a half-hour wait, I set off for the Astoria Hotel, where most foreigners are quartered in Leningrad. It was impossible to get an impression of Leningrad, because it was simply too dark. The cab cut merrily through crowds of early morning Leningraders hurrying to work. The driver did not once slacken his speed as he approached a corner. Throngs of people rushed across the street as we barreled our way towards them. I would invariably and involuntarily close my eyes as we approached a crowd of people, wait five seconds, then slowly open them in amazement, looking back to check for signs of blood. There weren't any.

It was 9:20 a.m. when we finally arrived at the Astoria, but the dawn had not even come up. I felt as though something had gone wrong with my watch or my calendar, that possibly it was still Friday evening in Moscow and not Saturday morning in Leningrad. When the dawn finally did come, it was 10:30 a.m. After a quick breakfast, I set off for my first real glimpse of the city. I had been in Leningrad once before, but then it was only for an hour. When I first arrived in the Soviet Union, last January 27th, I passed through Leningrad on my way to Moscow from Helsinki. I remember walking out on to Uprising Square and gazing at huddled masses of people, fighting to keep off the cold, while waiting for their train. I remember that I was impressed by the number of military uniforms, and I remember clearly how people stared at me. This morning, I saw almost the same thing. I was not near the station, when I took my walk—I was near the Astoria —but there were the same huddled masses, fighting the cold, rushing about the streets, in that quick, yet seemingly pointless, panic in which Russian crowds move. The military was still in evidence. And the people still stared after me as I walked down the streets.

But though there were these same, quick impressions, a year of Soviet Russia made me realize almost immediately the uniqueness of Leningrad. For Leningrad is a Western city. Its streets could be transplanted to West European capitals without a feeling of strangeness or dislocation. The people seem to dress in a more Western fashion. The buildings recall an age of Russian imperial might and stature and reflect the strong influence of the Italian architecture of the 16th and 17th centuries. The buildings are yellow and light green, and they are heavy with columns. The sky was a deep charcoal today and the snow on the streets a dirty grey, so that the entire city gave one the impression of a somber Ivy League suit.

In Moscow, as you pass old churches, you can almost imagine the deep, rich tones of the bells sounding out a scene for Boris Godunov. Leningrad does not seem to have this feeling. In comparison with the other cities of Russia I have seen, Leningrad seems like an architectural accident, the physical manifestation of Peter the Great's drive and determination. Built in the swamp lands of northwestern Russia, where the winding Neva River runs into the Finnish Bay, Leningrad was Peter's window on the West, and its Western heritage is still manifest in its architecture, its mood, its feel, and its people.

A young man approached me this afternoon, when I was walking around the Hermitage (where Russia houses its brilliant collection of Western art) and asked me where I was from. When I told him "America," he was nonplused. He confessed that he had not expected to meet many Americans in Leningrad these days. "You know, the international situation has got very bad. Very bad. During the summer, and in the early fall, we had many visitors from America. I would meet them on the street, but one sees very few people from the West now. I really hope that things get better. It is always more pleasant to have foreigners in Russia. I am an average person, a simple person, and I always gauge how friendly my government is with the West by the number of Westerners we see here. Lately, there have been very, very few, even taking into account that it is the winter and not a very pleasant time of the year to see Leningrad." We walked along together for a few minutes without saying much, simply exchanging innocent reflections on the Hermitage and Peter the Great. Then, he asked the inevitable question: "How would you compare Moscow to Leningrad?" After I told him that I thought

Leningrad a more Western city, his face beamed. "You know, everyone says that, and it is very true. I was born in Leningrad, and I have lived here all my life, but on my two trips to Moscow, I noticed the same thing. Moscow is really Eastern. We (he said this with great pride) are Western."

His attitude towards Moscow and his pride in Leningrad were things which I had heard about, and read about, but I had never known that it had struck the pulse of the ordinary working man in Leningrad so deeply. He was sincere, almost passionately so, in his loyalty to Leningrad, and spoke of it almost as a city apart from the Soviet Union. "We fought like devils here when the Germans wanted to take our city, but we wouldn't let them. Leningrad is our city. It is a great city."

The first performance in many years of Gorky's *Lower Depths* took place this evening at the Pushkin State Drama Theater, which was built in 1828-1832 by C. Rossi, who, it seems, built every other famous building in Leningrad. Nicholas I ordered the construction of this theater for performances of Russian opera and drama. In this play, which I am told was last performed in the Soviet Union in the late thirties, Gorky presents a stirring and powerful tribute to the indomitable spirit of man struggling against incredible odds. His message of the dignity of man shot through the audience like a bolt of lightning, and the audience responded by interrupting the performance with repeated applause and shouts of approval. "Man is the only truth," Gorky had written. "There is no other. Man means pride and conscience. No person has the right to offend another. No person is better than another simply by his station in life. Man can be subordinated to no end but man himself, for man is the end of life."

"This is right. This is truth," one man shouted in the middle of the play. Another cried: "Man is the only truth, there never has been another truth, and there never could be." The actors were called back for 10 curtain calls. The actors sent kisses to the audience and the director of the play was called out for a personal curtain call. It was an impressive and moving performance, and I got the distinct impression that the acting here in Leningrad was in many ways more honest, more direct, more powerful than that in Moscow.

January 6 : Today was the day before Christmas by the Russian Church calendar, and I went to the Nikolaevsky Cathedral this morning for services. The sky again was a deep grey, and the Nikolaevsky Cathedral stands against the sky, arrestingly, its aqua walls and golden domes a beautiful foreground for the wintry greyness of Leningrad. The service was conducted on two floors. The first had small, group services which centered around individual ikons. The second was the scene of a mass turnout of people, both young and old, who stood patiently in their heavy coats listening to the chanting of a lovely choir and to the powerful, bass voice of the priest. Some young mothers held bundled infants in their arms throughout the ceremony. It was so crowded that it was impossible to get closer to the ikons or the priest.

The mood of serenity of this Sunday service was upset, though, by an incident which took place in the restaurant of the Astoria Hotel, where I had returned for breakfast. The dining hall is very large. I'm sure there are at least fifty tables there. Only two of them were occupied. Two waiters were working. A group of about eight other waiters and waitresses stood off to one side of the restaurant, engaged in a heated discussion. Their arms flailed, and their voices rose and fell with irritating monotony. I sat down at one of the tables and caught the eye of one of the waiters. He saw me, and then he turned away. The argument was obviously more interest-

ing. I waited for ten minutes, glancing at my newspaper and
trying not to be too impatient.

I waited another ten minutes, but still no one approached
me. I was beginning to get a little annoyed, for I had an appointment and did not want to be late. When I caught the eye
of the same waiter once again, I asked: "May I have the
menu?"

He gave me the menu. I looked at it, made my selection,
but when I looked up, he had rejoined his companions and
was paying absolutely no attention to me. By this time, I had
waited close to half an hour. Finally, I could no longer hold
my temper in check: "Who is going to wait on me?"

"Just a moment," came the reply of an unimpressed waitress. I waited one moment, two, then a few minutes, then
again, I shouted, "I want some service here!" This waitress
asked one of the waiters in a very bored tone if he would wait
on me. He consented grudgingly and finally, after I had been
there close to an hour, he took my order.

At this point, a young man, his wife, son, and mother entered the dining hall. They sat down at a table. My waiter,
who was very unpleasant, told them that they would not be
served because there were no free tables. "But the entire
dining hall is free," the man objected. "That's right, but all
the tables are taken. We will not serve you." The mother
asked her son to leave. The wife agreed, but the husband
was infuriated. "Why must you waiters here always be so rude?
Why are you so impolite? This is terrible. The entire hall is
free, only three tables taken, and you tell me that there are
no free tables. Just what is this? If you are unhappy and don't
make enough money, argue with your trade union, but now
I am going to be served." He sat down at the table with his
family, who continued to object. It took me twenty minutes
to eat. During this entire period, the family was not ap-

proached once. It was as though they were not there. The
tables were all empty. The waiters and waitresses continued
their animated discussion. My waiter completely ignored
them. When he brought me my check, it came to 10 roubles
85 kopecks. I gave him eleven roubles, and when he turned
his back on me, I called him back and demanded the 15 kopecks change. His service wasn't even worth that small a tip.
He was furious. As I left the dining hall, he shouted: "Why
should I work? Why should I? For customers who won't even
leave a fifteen kopeck tip!" He threw his napkin on the floor
and stormed over to his waiter comrades. I left. The family
still had not even received a menu.

The Central Lecture Hall in Leningrad is located on
Liteiny Avenue. It is an old, attractive building, and I am
told that many of the scenes of Pushkin's "Queen of Spades"
were fashioned from real incidents which took place in the
main ballroom, which is now the main lecture room. In this
lecture room, this afternoon, at 1 p.m., the Leningrad Division
of the All-Union Society for the Dissemination of Political
and Scientific Knowledge scheduled a lecture called the "International Position of the USSR." A man named V. D. Smir-
nov was supposed to lecture, but I am told that at the last
minute a top-flight lecturer from Moscow named K. P. Vosh-
chenkov was appointed to this task because of the seriousness of the topic. The speaker started promptly at 1 p.m.
and he looked out over a large audience composed of young
and old people, most of them devout Communists, for they
all took notes diligently, were attentive throughout the talk,
laughed when they should have, frowned when it appeared
right to do so, and applauded dutifully.

The following is a rough outline of the lecture, based upon
the notes I took: Voschenkov started right out by recalling a
dispatch from Tass which appeared in all central and provin-

cial papers this morning. From January 1 through January 4, the Communist Party leaders of the Soviet Union, Bulgaria, Rumania, Czechoslovakia and Hungary met in Budapest to discuss the Hungarian situation and the world situation in general. (Poland was not present.) Khrushchev and Malenkov represented the Soviet Union. This, he said, was proof of the good relations among all Socialist countries. He spoke repeatedly about the "imperialist reaction," the "black forces of fascism," and "American connivance" in reference to the Hungarian revolution. The "peace loving forces of socialism" will give a "vigorous and decisive rebuff to the intrigues of the imperialist camp." He cited Lenin time and again to prove his points. He castigated America in the most vicious terms I have ever heard since I came to the Soviet Union. America was responsible for everything. Its capitalists and monopolists dictate all policy. They want capitalism back in Hungary. They wish to destroy the achievements of the Socialist system in Hungary and elsewhere. They wish to establish military bases in Eastern Europe for use against the Soviet Union. They are planning a third World War.

1956, he said, was the year of the Twentieth Congress. Heavy industry will be stressed, and, at the same time, new resources will be exploited to raise the "material level" of the population, meaning consumer goods. Our socialist system, he continued, has proved its superiority over the capitalist system. 1956 also confirms the "correctness" of the policy of the Soviet government and the Communist Party of the Soviet Union. "We have given a decisive rebuff to the forces of imperialism and fascism, led by the United States of America. Many say that the events in Hungary have weakened the camp of socialism. This is false. They have weakened the camp of capitalism. They have dealt a crushing blow to American monopolists. The camp of socialism, on the contrary, has been considerably strengthened by these events. But we have learned an important lesson. We thought we could get along with the capitalists, but we have erred. It is impossible to get along with capitalists. They will stop at nothing. They wish to restore capitalism in Hungary. But the putsch did not have a broad base. Only the fascists supported the revolt. Horthy and his men equipped with American arms participated in the revolt—not the honest workers. The Americans wanted to create a military base in Hungary, bring war very close, but we have stopped these vicious intrigues, and we will continue to crush these attempts. With the failure of the events in Hungary, the American monopolists have changed their tactics, but their aim remains the same."

The speaker gave the impression of the Soviet Union being surrounded by a rapacious band of capitalists and imperialists who are poised to spring upon the "peaceful progress of the socialist camp." This line recalled the late Stalinist line of "capitalist encirclement" and partially repudiated the 20th Congress pronouncement that this situation had been changed by the growth and development of the socialist camp.

"The attack and aggression against Egypt is just another link in a major imperialist conspiracy against all peaceful countries, against the Soviet Union, and the Bandung countries. Even in Indonesia, the Americans are trying to convert the country into an American military base. Churchill, who takes an active, back-stage role in instigating the West against Russia, is just as bad as Hitler, and you all know what happened to Hitler! The Dulles-Eisenhower doctrine is nothing more than another American attempt to convert the Middle East into an American stronghold, taking advantage of the weakened position of the British and the French. There is a constant threat against the Soviet Union, and its purpose is a third World War."

The lecturer finished amidst a burst of applause. Shouts of approval echoed in a hall which once had resounded with Viennese waltzes and Pushkin's poetry. The question period which followed went something like this:

1. Why did someone read a newspaper while you were speaking? *Answer:* I don't know why, but he should not have.

2. What role did Kadar play in the Rakosi government of Hungary? *Answer:* He was a Minister.

3. Why weren't Yugoslavia and Poland represented in the Budapest meeting you mentioned? *Answer:* Comrades, I don't know. I only found out about the meeting this morning from the papers, just as you did, so I cannot answer this question. (One woman near me turned to her friend and said: "Maybe they couldn't make it?")

4. Why doesn't Hungary let United Nations observers into Budapest? *Answer:* If you read the papers, you know the answer to this question. (Approval of this answer was evident in the hall—some nodded—others said "Yes.")

5. Why did Nagy go to Rumania and not Yugoslavia? *Answer:* He wanted to. (Woman to my left: "Of course, if he wants to go to Rumania, are we like capitalists? Do we force him to go to Yugoslavia?")

6. Was Nagy connected with the counter-revolutionary forces? *Answer:* Yes, he was, and this point must be stressed again and again.

7. Is Tito a good Marxist? *Answer:* No, he is not. He does not know the principles of Marxism-Leninism well at all. (Woman to my left: "That's right, he really isn't. And how could he? After all, he was fighting throughout the war. He didn't have a chance. That's right, I guess he is a bad Marxist.")

8. Why are Jews such a warlike people? *Answer:* It's hard to say, comrades.

9. Talk to us about Sumatra and Sukarno! *Answer:* Read the papers.

What was surprising about the reactions of these communists was their complete ability to rationalize their way out of any ideological problem. Combined with a surprising lack of political sophistication and an unfortunate inadequacy of information, these young and old Communists compose the foundation upon which this country is ruled. How different from the reactions of the Moscow University students to the same kind of Communist reasoning!

The lecture, which lasted three hours and was interrupted for a ten-minute intermission, concluded at 4 p.m. and Leningrad's streets were already dark. A light snow had begun to fall, and Liteiny Avenue, which is a major street, was crowded with people, who rushed eagerly forward in no particular direction. Pushing is common on the streets, and one rarely hears an "Excuse me." If you should stand aside for a woman, chances are excellent you won't hear a "Thank you." I turned right on the Nevsky Prospekt, which is the Broadway of Leningrad, as Gorki Street is the Broadway of Moscow. The crowds were even denser. The shops were all open, and trading was vigorous. Old houses and churches front on the Nevsky—the old Duma building, the Saltykov-Schedrin Library, and the impressive Kazan Cathedral, which, in the thirties, was converted into an anti-religion museum.

As I passed the *Europa* Hotel, I thought I would stop in at its restaurant for dinner. I had heard that the food was good there. The dining hall was crowded, and I spotted a lone figure seated at a small table off to the left of a four-piece orchestra, which insisted upon butchering American songs. I asked if I might join him, and he consented. About one-half hour passed without a word between us, until he finally broke the ice.

He asked me if I were from America, and he asked this question in fluent English. His accent was so slight that for a moment I thought I was hearing things. When I told him I was, his face lit up like a Christmas tree. "Oh, I am so delighted. How long it has been since I have spoken to an American!" His face was filled with sadness for a fleeting moment, but he recovered his composure and started asking me at least one hundred questions, which ran from New York City, where I was born, to Washington, where I worked, to Cambridge, where I studied, to baseball, to music, to pop songs, to Averell Harriman and Dwight D. Eisenhower, and finally to American poets.

He dwelt in great detail upon these poets. He loved Carl Sandburg and Robert Frost. He thought Conrad Aiken was brilliant, and he worshipped T. S. Eliot, whom he regarded as an American, even though Eliot regards himself as English. "My greatest delight is to read American poets. Many evenings when I come home from work, I pick up an old 1927 anthology I have, with an introduction by Aiken, and read the poems over and over again. They pick me up and transport me to a dream world."

I soon discovered that I had stumbled quite accidentally upon a teacher of the English language in a small technical school in Leningrad. Sasha Ivanov, as we shall call him, is about 45 years old. He was born in the Ukraine. When he was 6 years old, his parents moved to Moscow, where his father got a new job. In 1928, the family moved to Leningrad, and Sasha has not wandered from Leningrad since. "This is the closest I can get to the West. It is the most Western city in Russia, I would say." During the war, Sasha met an American who was in Leningrad, and this American gave

Sasha the anthology of poetry and a love of English. Sasha
then studied the language in an Institute and did so well that
he was given a job teaching English soon after. He's been
there ever since.

During the course of exchanging biographical information, I mentioned to Sasha that I was very interested in Russian history, and that I thought the Soviet period a most in-
triguing chapter. I mentioned in this connection the lecture
I had heard in the afternoon, that I hadn't heard anything
as violent since I'd come to Russia about a year ago, and that
I'd be interested in his reaction to the new hard line in Soviet
politics. "To be completely truthful with you," Sasha said,
"I pay very little attention to politics. Maybe that's why I
love your poetry so much. A great deal of it is so light, so
tender, so individual, so loving, that it lifts me from this
world and brings me to a sweet and fragrant paradise." Sasha's
English was like poetry. He always spoke in flowing similes
and metaphors, and I'm sure he was quoting Sandburg half
the night by heart. He'd always interrupt himself to pull an
Aiken or an Eliot quote out of the air to reinforce his point.

"The only issue which made me raise my eyebrows a little,"
Sasha continued, "was Hungary. The effects of Hungary have
reverberated not only throughout Russia but also throughout the world. It has made many of us think, think real hard,
for the first time in years. I think it has had as great an effect
upon the Russian intelligentsia (he smiled as he used this
word) as the death of Stalin. Our information, of course, is
inadequate, but I think that the government probably did
the right thing."

I objected that I could never agree that the Russian government had done right in Hungary. "Sasha, the facts about
Hungary are very clear. The majority of the people simply

rose against socialism and the Russians. They did not want either. This might be hard for you to swallow, but the Hungarian people will never accept socialism or the presence of Russian troops in their country. They hate both, and just remove the troops and you will see how quickly the people will remove the vestiges of the socialist system. Socialism rests in Eastern Europe on the bayonet points of the Red Army soldiers, on nothing else."

Sasha raised a mild objection. He said I was exaggerating the situation. "You know, I think that even in the ugliness of the situation, there is still beauty. It is like Macauley's essay on revolution when he writes that the ugliness of revolution can yield beauty in the long run, and we must not be blinded by temporary darkness to the possibility of a bright future."

"Sasha, you are a confirmed romantic, but your argument only sounds nice. The facts are that the Hungarians don't want the Russians there. You can't export revolution with the Red Army. Surely, this is not orthodox communism."

"No, it isn't. But it is orthodox bolshevism."

His voice was cold and hard for the first time during our talk. I suddenly realized—as he did almost simultaneously—that we had been arguing, and I apologized. "But I can't understand how you can condone what the Russians did in Hungary," I added.

"What else am I to do?"

We drifted on to the subject of the student body in the Soviet Union these days. Sasha spoke in very general terms that the students want more information and more freedom, but he did not think that this desire had got out of control. He felt rather that it was a good thing, that this new longing re-establishes their faith in the future. "They now have something to look forward to, to have confidence in. Before, things were stagnant. Now, they are fluid." I asked Sasha if he had heard of the illegal newspaper *Fresh Voices,* which some Leningrad students had been circulating. "I have never heard of such a newspaper." When he saw the look of incredulity which came over my face, he swore to me that he never had.

Sasha then launched into his sole attack on the government. He said that the Russian people deserve a better fate. He said that his friends want books from the West, free intercourse and exchange between countries, and a critical evaluation of the arts without any dependence upon socialist doctrine. "We all believe that socialism is inevitable throughout the world. This is a law of history, and it is inexorable. But we do not feel that art also follows inexorable rules. We believe that socialist realism should be abolished as an artistic doctrine. It is harmful and restricting. You simply cannot imagine how happy we were this past summer, seeing so many foreigners in Russia, hearing and enjoying your great artists, like Isaac Stern, Jan Peerce, and the Boston Symphony Orchestra. We would like all of this to continue. We don't want a change to the old days." I mentioned at this point that if the lecture I heard this afternoon were any indication, it looked like we were headed for another period of tension.

Sasha replied: "I think you are too pessimistic. This won't happen. It can't."

We had been talking for almost five hours, and the waitress was beginning to give us dirty looks, when I suggested that we might go for a short walk. We left the restaurant, walked up the *Nevsky Prospekt* for a few blocks, took a bus towards the Astoria, and Sasha walked me to the door of the hotel. He told me how grateful he was for our talk, and he promised that he would call me during the week.

January 7 : The weather was even worse today than it was yesterday. A stiff wind cut through the streets of Leningrad, bringing snow and a biting cold. Early this morning, I went to the Saltykov-Schedrin Library to see if I could get additional material for my thesis on Uvarov, who, by the way, was once the assistant librarian there. I had been told by the librarian at the Lenin Library that she had written a note of introduction for me to the head of the Manuscript Division of the Saltykov-Schedrin Library, and I made my way to this division immediately. When I entered the room, I was told by a short, thin, nervous man that the head of the division was not in, that he did not know when he would return, but that if I wished, I could wait for him. I thanked him and sat down. Within about ten minutes, he returned and asked where I was from. When I told him America, he literally began to tremble. He stammered that he did not know when the head would return, possibly not at all today, that it would be "more convenient" if I went to another library. I asked him why he was so nervous, but he did not answer. He only managed to repeat once more that I should leave the room, come back tomorrow, the next day, any time, but leave now. He was so frightened that I agreed that possibly it would be best if I returned some other time.

I decided, in this case, to try my luck at the Institute for Russian Literature, a branch of the Soviet Academy of Sciences, which is located in the Pushkin House on the Makarov Embankment. Here, the environment was completely different. I was received very warmly, and when I mentioned that I was an attaché at the American Embassy, the Director of the Institute, with whom I had a short talk, seemed very delighted, even flattered. The only thing which disturbed him was why anyone should bother with Uvarov. When I gave him my usual answer—I thought that all sides of Russian history should be studied—he smiled, and said that he agreed. He gave me a letter granting permission to use the Archives of the Institute, which has a great deal of information on Uvarov. And I spent the rest of the morning and afternoon, going through the Uvarov archive, which had been accumulating dust for over 40 years, ever since the Communists had the power to implement their theory that only "progressives" should be studied.

When it dawned on me late in the afternoon that I would not be able to go through all the material, the Director gave me special permission to have many of Uvarov's personal papers and letters microfilmed. And when he discovered that there were many orders in ahead of mine, he put my order on top of the list, and guaranteed that before I left Leningrad, I would have my microfilm.

The contrast between my reception in the Saltykov-Schedrin Library and in the Institute for Russian Literature was startling. It did not make any sense, but neither do so many things about Russia.

At dinner this evening, I heard one young man tell another that he has heard that *Amerika* magazine would no longer be published. He blamed the Soviet government, not us, for this possibility. A copy of *Trybuna Ludu,* the Polish communist paper, which is now so hard to get in Moscow, was stuffed into his jacket pocket. Unlike most Soviet youth, he had long sideburns, and his pants were pegged slightly. His feet beat out a tune to the rhythm of the Astoria's band, which was trying to sound like Glenn Miller.

After dinner, I took a walk to the *Dom Knigi,* a huge kind of Russian Brentano, which is located opposite the Kazan Cathedral on the *Nevsky Prospekt,* where the latter cuts across the Griboedov Canal. The *Dom Knigi,* which I had

been told is the greatest book store in the Soviet Union, was
a disappointment. It had very few books of any merit, though
it had a great many books of little merit.

January 8 : I returned to the Saltykov-Schedrin Library this
morning in order to see the Head of the Manuscript Division.
I had called yesterday, and a woman told me he would be in
his office in the morning. He was, but he did not give me permission to use the Uvarov materials. He apparently was interested in receiving clearance from his superiors, because he
told me that it would be "more convenient" if I returned
later in the day. I told him I would return about 3 p.m.

I went back to the Institute for Russian Literature, where
I had been received so warmly yesterday. The old man in
charge of the check room, was like a person from the distant
past, polite, curious, charming. He asked me the price of my
coat, my hat, and my boots. When he converted 75 dollars
into 300 roubles (the exchange is four-to-one), he was dumbfounded. "We could never get this coat here for 300 roubles;
more likely, it would cost 3000 roubles." I could of course
have told him that the exchange rate was artificial, that 10-to-
1 was a more sensible and realistic exchange, but I thought
I was doing a good turn for American capitalism, which, after,
all, has been coming in for a drastic attack of late in the Soviet press. (On second thought, even if I had mentioned that
10-to-1 would be more realistic, my clothes would have cost
750 roubles, and this too is well below the 3000 roubles it
would undoubtedly cost in any Soviet store.) He called a
friend over, told him that in America, my clothes cost 300
roubles, and asked him what he thought of that. The friend, a
whimsical smile on his face, said that he could get the same
coat for 275 roubles in Moscow. Then, he looked playfully at

the check room clerk, and both of them burst into loud laughter.

The head librarian, a tall, gracious, and fairly attractive woman, greeted me warmly and gave me the material which she had prepared for me. Before I could sit down, she asked me to join her in the vestibule for a moment. I followed her into a dark foyer, which was surrounded by book cases. There were three different pictures of Pushkin hanging on the wall. She turned to me suddenly as though she had a question or problem of enormous magnitude which she simply had to discuss. "Why are you studying about Uvarov?" The question, which has already become such a familiar one, took me by complete surprise, and I started to laugh. I explained to her why I was working on Uvarov, and we gradually came around to a discussion of America. I answered questions on the prices of consumers' goods, especially women's clothing, food, cars, houses, and finally I went into a fairly long discussion of why we do not need internal passports in the United States. This floored the poor woman. "But surely you need some identification!" she insisted. I then mentioned drivers' licenses, a draft card, a library card, "but we don't need internal passports. That's used only for travel to a foreign country." I told her that many times an American feels like a criminal in the Soviet Union, being forced at every turn to show his passport, never having his word trusted. "Well," she objected, "Russians feel like criminals whenever they have to have their fingerprints taken. Prints are for criminals, not for honest people." I countered by stating once again that if a Russian really wanted to come to America, he would not stand on ceremony concerning fingerprints. "After all, we put up with the humiliation of internal passports. Goodness, I even had to show my passport to come into your

library to work on Uvarov." She smiled, somewhat embar-
rassedly, and admitted that I might have a point.

We had got on pretty well, though, for she suggested that
I speak with a "treasure house of a man, a genius, a gift of
God," who knows a great deal about 19th century Russia—a
Professor named Alexander Naukhumovich Berkov. I said I
would love to, and she ran off and returned in five minutes
with a short, graying man in his fifties. We had a very pleasant and interesting conversation about Russian history, problems of historiography in general, and I was amazed at his vast
and very thorough familiarity with America's scholars on the
Soviet Union. He asked about Professor Karpovich of Harvard, Professor Vernadsky of Yale, Professor Kohn of City
College, and Professor Mosely of Columbia, and he gave me
some very valuable pointers on my research project on Uvarov. I spent the next four hours in the Institute of Russian
Literature working on Uvarov's personal papers and letters.

About 5 p.m., I decided to return to the Saltykov-Schedrin
Library. I went to see the library's *Ucherny Sekretar,* a catch-
all phrase which describes every Soviet institution's chief
intellect and top administrator. He was very charming, very
intelligent, and he said that I would meet no obstacles to
research on Uvarov, though he too was surprised that anyone
should show an interest in such a "reactionary." He escorted
me through a maze of corridors, each guarded very carefully
by a uniformed militiaman, who insisted upon seeing even
the secretary's documents, not to mention mine. When we entered the manuscript division once again, the little nervous
man of yesterday ducked into another office but the head was
there. He shook hands coldly and gave me a mass of letters,
which I got to work on immediately. At about 7 p.m., he
asked me how long I would be. I answered that I did not know
exactly. At 7:10 p.m., he asked me again how long I would

be, and again, I told him I did not know. At 7:20 p.m., he did not ask me how long I would be. He simply asked if I could finish up immediately. I was surprised and asked him why I had to leave so soon. He told me that he had a ticket to the movies, for a show which started at 8 p.m., and it was his duty to escort me out of the building before he could leave for the theater. I then recalled all the guards, and I cleared out.

January 9 : A sharp attack, reminiscent of the *Zhdanovsh-china* period in the late 1940's was *Leningrad Pravda* today against foreign importations in the arts. It did not have the venom of some of the late Zhdanov's vitriolic offensives against foreign art, particularly Russians "scraping" and "bowing" before Western art, but it nonetheless marked a rather sharp break from the 1956 honeymoon when one foreign artist after another appeared in Leningrad, Moscow, and Kiev. The article made mention of these appearances—made a special point of stressing Isaac Stern and the Boston Symphony Orchestra—but then lashed out at those Russians who "bow before anything Western," who prefer to sing Western songs to Russian songs, who stage Western plays in preference to native ones, who see Western movies rather than Soviet films. The writer made the startling assertion that the Italian movie industry, which produces "realistic" films, popular among Soviet people, copied the Russian style of the early twenties, that in effect the Russian inspiration for the latest Italian films, which will certainly come as a surprise to Rome, explains their vast popularity in the Soviet Union. The article concluded with a veiled, though vigorous, warning to all film producers, song writers, and the public at large that wholesale aping of Western music, drama and dance will not be tolerated much longer.

It is easy to understand the concern of the Communist leadership about the popularity of Western artists and dramas in the Soviet Union after seeing a play this evening which is a perfect example of Soviet drama. It is called "In Old Moscow." It depicts the tribulations of a pre-communist family, its financial knocks and moral destitution, and the careless, worthless, unhappy existence of the wicked capitalists. It ends with the young Communist conspirator being arrested and a young worker singing the praises of the future Communist society. The acting was competent, but the theme of the play was hackneyed and tiresome, and it put at least half the audience into a fitful slumber. The other half managed to sneak out before the end.

On my way home, the taxi driver told me that Yves Montand, who is enjoying great success in this country—everyone talks about him and he is literally worshipped—is stopping at the Astoria Hotel. As we approached the hotel, I saw a huge crowd of Russian bobbysoxers, waiting to greet their hero after his concert this evening. The taxi stopped in front of the hotel, and a tumultuous roar cut loose as I stepped from the cab. They thought I was Montand. I felt very embarrassed, said I was not Montand, but the crowd would not believe me. I was mobbed. I was asked to sign autographs. "He's so modest. He says he's not Montand." My coat hem was kissed, and young *stilyagi* grabbed my hand. The police finally came to my rescue and escorted me into the hotel, yelling that I was an American diplomat, not Montand. In the finest traditions of the "False Dmitri," who raised such a rumpus in this country 350 years ago, I rose to the throne of the "False Montand." Waving to the delirious crowd, I blew a kiss to its excited and cheerful faces, and was almost prepared to deliver an address on the hardships of singing in Parisian nightclubs, when the militia escorted me unceremoniously into the lobby of the hotel. My reign was almost as short as the "False Dmitri's."

January 10 : "Come with me," Sasha insisted, "I want to show you what Leningrad really is." He took me by the arm, and we started walking at a brisk pace down the *Nevsky Prospekt* to a bus stop. We had just spent an hour in the old Kazan Cathedral, which fronts on the *Nevsky* and is constructed after the model of St. Peter in Rome, in the shape of an enormous cross. The Cathedral is an impressive structure, built by Voronikhin, a fine Russian architect, in the early 19th century. The one disappointing thing about the Cathedral was that services are no longer conducted there. In 1929, it was given a new name. Now, it is called the "History of Religion Museum." The communists, in this museum, try to "prove scientifically" the absurdity of religious conviction, and they devote a large portion of the basement of the Museum to the "atrocities" of the inquisition and the counter-reformation.

"But where are we going?"

"I'll tell you soon enough," Sasha answered, as he continued to put pressure on my arm, making me walk at his pace, which is faster than mine. We got on a bus and started off away from the *Nevsky Prospekt*. Within five minutes, I had the feeling I was in another city. The streets became narrower and dirty. People were dressed very shabbily. We were riding down *Prospekt Gaza*, and we had obviously entered the industrial workers' section of Leningrad. "Further down the road are the Putilov Works, which played such a prominent role in the Russian Revolution," Sasha reminded me, very proud of his new role as guide to the city. We never did get to the Putilov Works, because down the road I spotted the famous Narva Gate, and I asked Sasha if we could get off the bus and look at it more closely. Sasha seemed delighted. "In the old days, I am told, the gate was surrounded by trees and parks, and it was very beautiful. Now, it is surrounded by apartment houses. It is no longer a pretty sight." The Narva Gate, which was built in the early 19th century to commemorate the Russian victory over Napoleon, is in itself attractive and sturdy in appearance. Sasha pointed to a factory on our right. "It's very important, this factory, because, in 1917, I think Stalin spoke there twice."

We walked down some of the narrow streets, crowded with late afternoon crowds of poor and shabby workers, the women in their heavy woolen shawls, the men in their fur hats and open ear flaps. Everyone seemed to be carrying a loaf of bread. The crowds moved slowly, like an enormous amoeba, through the streets and avenues. The houses were very old, small. There were cracks in the walls, and many windows were broken. Children played on the ice, sliding down little inclines on the seat of their pants and having a wonderful time. Against the grey poverty around them, they and their laughter seemed like two left shoes.

"You were spending too much time on the *Nevsky*," Sasha said, breaking gently into my thoughts, as we made our way through the crowds, which opened for us and resealed almost instantly. "This is Leningrad. These are the people who made the revolution in 1917. These are the people who are the Russian proletariat. The revolution was made in their name. Now, look at how they live!" His face was overcome by a quick anger, which seemed so out of character with his mild, poetic disposition. "How would you like to have a glass of beer," he asked. "It's not Ballantine, but it'll do." He smiled when he said "Ballantine." "I know lots of trade names, like Chevrolet, Chrysler ('Is Fritz Kreisler the manager of the Chrysler factory?'), and Coca Cola ('Have you ever really drunk Coca Cola?')."

The *Pivny Zal*, or beer hall, which we entered was very small, no chairs, just tiny round tables, and choking with the smoke of Russian cigarettes. We attracted immediate attention; my coat is a light tweed (Russians always seem to wear dark clothes in the winter), Western in design, and obviously not Russian. Many of the men who stood around the tables were drunk. They spoke loudly, hoarsely, in between large shots of straight vodka followed by beer chasers. Sasha ordered two bottles of beer, and we started to speak in English about American poetry. As Sasha spoke, we both could not help overhearing a discussion which was taking place at the next table.

Four men, very drunk, were staring at me and arguing in colloquial Russian about my clothing. They spoke in loud, uneven voices, and one of them raised his fist threateningly. Sasha got very worried, and he gestured to them that they keep quiet. Two of the men from this table began to approach us. They came close to our table. One said: "I hate *stilyagi*." He was obviously under the impression that we were both Soviet citizens, that I was very rich, thus able to buy Western clothing and speak foreign languages. "I hate well-dressed and well-fed *stilyagi*," the Russian continued. "I hate you and your Western clothing."

He leaned towards his friend and said loudly: "I wouldn't give two kopecks for his coat, or his hat, or his suit. I hate him. I hate him. And he doesn't look like a Russian. He looks like one of those Germans I used to see during the war, and I hate Germans. I hate Germans, and I hate *stilyagi*."

The situation in the beer hall had suddenly grown tense. A large crowd formed around the drunk, his friend, and us. The drunk, meanwhile, was moving closer and closer towards us, as he continued his harangue. People from the street had apparently heard the racket and had entered the beer hall. I pretended that I did not understand a word he said.

Someone then shouted out: "Maybe he *is* a foreigner!"

"No," our brave drunk answered. "He's a *stilyag*, a rich *stilyag*, who comes and boasts to me how rich he is. I know this type. They're all over these days."

His friend, though, was not so sure I was a *stilyag*. As I continued to feign complete ignorance of what the drunk was saying, his friend began to think that possibly I was a foreigner. He grabbed the drunk by the lapel—not a moment too soon, I felt—and he threw him to the floor. The drunk fell down very hard. But, he staggered up immediately, turned to his friend, without any obvious anger, and announced he would ask me. As he lurched towards me, Sasha stepped in his way.

"Sasha, leave him alone," I exclaimed in English. Sasha stepped aside with great hesitation.

"Are you a Russian?" the drunk asked me.

I looked at him, smiled, and answered in English: "I don't understand you."

The foreign words struck him like a thunderbolt. He reeled back against his friend, who was standing right behind him. "I told you so. I told you so," he said.

The drunk retreated to his table, his shoulders almost meeting in front of his chest, a figure of complete defeat and shame. He took a large gulp of vodka from the bottle on the table. Then, he retraced his steps and apologized profusely for his rude behavior. He said he did not know I was a foreigner. He seemed very shaken and visibly frightened. He went back to his table then, and the crowd dispersed.

There would be no fight between the "proletarian worker" and the "rich *stilyag*." Sasha and I finished our beer and left.

"I must apologize for what happened. I had no idea."

"Sasha, please don't apologize. I learned more about Russia in the last five minutes than I would have spending another week in the libraries and museums. I should thank you. You are very right. This is the Russian proletariat."

This evening I moved from the proletarian stratum of Russian society to the aristocratic stratum. I saw the new Khachaturian ballet, *Spartak*. It was almost impossible to get tickets, and the Intourist woman in the hotel pulled every string at her disposal to get me one. She succeeded finally, she explained, "when a Minister was called out of town suddenly." *Spartak* is the story of a revolt of Roman gladiators against the Emperor, led by the most noble gladiator of them all, Spartak, played by a giant of a man named Makarov. Spartak succeeds in rallying a loyal following, gains great military victories and poses a substantial threat to the power of the Roman throne. In the fourth act, Spartak fights gallantly against the Roman legions but loses and the ballet ends with his defeat and death.

Khachaturian explains it in this way: "Now that all peoples rise up and struggle for their independence, that colonialism is definitely being defeated, it is necessary that the people know and remember the names of those who even at the dawn of human history bravely raised their voices for freedom and independence against the enslavers. This is the theme of Rome, the theme of the oppressed slaves." Having stated his sermon, Khachaturian then proceeds to unveil a really unusual ballet. For one thing, there is no toe-point dancing throughout the ballet. The choreography is closer to modern dance than anything I have seen in Russia and this ballet thus marks an important artistic break in contemporary Soviet dance. Secondly, however, the theme, which is conventional, almost hackneyed, by Soviet artistic standards, ends dramatically with the defeat of the "oppressed slaves," which from every Bolshevik position is unheard of. The "slaves" should have won; they are always the "good guys" in this country, but the "bad guys" won.

The ballet was received with mixed feelings. I heard Russians talk of the "originality" of the conception. I heard others say they'd rather have watched Ulanova dance "Romeo and Juliette." In every case, though, the Russians knew they were seeing something new. In anticipation of the event, Leningrad's top society was there. Khachaturian and his wife and family sat in a box just to the right of the stage. Shaporov, the composer of the opera *Decembrists*, sat in the second row with his wife, and Shostakovich sat alone in the third row. Plesetskaya, the charming Bolshoi theater ballerina, sat to my left during the ballet, watching carefully every step, making critical comments to her friend, and saying nothing more than "It is very interesting," when I asked her how she liked the ballet. The friends of these famous Soviet artists were very well dressed. The women wore beautiful dresses. Their hair was attractive and well-groomed. Some wore fur wraps. The men, for the most part, wore white shirts (not the usual stripe), single-breasted suits, and their trousers were all slightly pegged. The contrast between these people and the drunk in the *Pivny Zal* was truly fantastic, and, if I had any doubt about the existence of classes in Soviet society, today's experiences would have put them to rest—for all time.

January 11 : I spent this morning at Leningrad University, located on historic University Embankment, overlooking the Neva River (which is almost at its widest at this point) and directly opposite the Bronze Horseman statue of Peter the

Great. The buildings of the university are very old, many of them dating to the beginning of the 19th century. I had a one hour conference with three of the university's top experts on the 19th century. One of them, Professor Okun, struck me as a particularly brilliant historian.

Our general topic, of course, was Uvarov. I discovered that there is not a single monograph on Uvarov written in the Soviet period, despite the fact that he was President of the Academy of Sciences for almost 40 years and a former Minister of Education. "We have very few books on personalities in history. We believe in describing mass historical movements, rather than centering attention on just one man." I felt that our talk was proceeding too smoothly to bring up Soviet historiography on people like Lenin (about whom Okun himself wrote a book), Marx, Pushkin, Chernyshevsky, Stalin, and other "progressive" figures in Russian history. They presented me with some very useful bibliographic information, and our conference was drawing to a very rapid close, when Professor Okun raised the inevitable question: "Why Uvarov?" I answered in very general terms; I said I thought all sides of every question should be studied for the sake of "pure" history. My reference to "purity" in historical writing was interpreted by two of the professors as a dig, which it was partially, and by the third as a truism. He said: "We must study all sides of all questions. With this, I have always agreed."

After the conference, I took a small walk around the campus. There were very few students about. I asked one why, and he told me that everyone was studying for exams. He was in no mood for idle chatter. I picked up a copy of the university newspaper, called *Leningrad University,* sat down in the library of the Academy of Sciences, and glanced through it. The front page ran an editorial about the shortage of library space. The last page was devoted to Yves Montand and pictures of Moscow. The inside pages contained four rather interesting articles:

First, an article, dealing mainly with a speech by Professor A. A. Aleksandrov, Rector of the University. The gist of it was that instructors must realize their duty as educators, not only as teachers. They must help the students overcome "mistaken" views, such as placing an exclusive emphasis upon "I" and "me" rather than the student collective as a whole.

Second, another article about teachers, who are told that they must take a more active part in "bringing up" the students. Questions such as "the Situation in Hungary," or "Free attendance of lectures," or "How to regard marriage to foreigners," raised by the students, must be answered intelligently. Teachers must be ideologically alert.

Third, another attack on teachers who do not show sufficient ideological and social strength to offer constructive answers to students' questions. It contains an attack upon teachers who feel they should limit themselves to subject matter and not be called upon to offer political or ideological advice. A. M. Sedova, a foreign language teacher, came in for special abuse for letting a discussion of foreign affairs turn into an "undisciplined talk about the international situation." The editorial pleads for a "vigorous assault upon high-handedness, scholasticism and dogmatism!"

Finally, there is an article about the student "wall" newspapers, which are put out by each individual student group. One of these papers, called *Catalyst*, ran what amounted to a "purely hooligan attack against the leading organs of public organizations," meaning the Communist Party. Other student newspapers are only satirical, the article continues, and they contain no political message; this is sharply condemned.

January 13 : Leningrad's weather finally cleared up. The sun rose about 11 a.m. and instantly bathed the city in pastel beauty. Once again, Russia's Western capital smiled its regal charm. The Winter Palace, where Russia's Tsars lived from the 18th century through the Bolshevik Revolution, stands along the Palace Embankment and faces out on to Palace Square. The Hermitage is located in the Winter Palace. When the cruiser Aurora fired its shot on October 25, 1917, signaling the start of Bolshevik power in Russia, sailors and workers, the story goes, stormed the Winter Palace and charged through the home of the Russian Tsar. Tsardom was crushed, but the reverence of the Russian people for royalty (or, if not royalty, for a sort of distant and omniscient ruler) is plainly painted on every peasant face which stares in adoration at the splendor of a lost age.

The enormous social revolution which Russia has experienced in the last forty years is clearly apparent in the people who visit the Hermitage. Intellectuals visit the art collection today, but they did forty, fifty years ago too. The Russian aristocracy, then based on birth and money, now on station and money, visit the Hermitage, but they did forty years ago too. But the peasants, who shuffle into the massive, high-ceilinged and -columned chambers, rarely if ever had an opportunity to see Western art or the quarters of the Tsar. Now, they can. Still, it is most unlikely if even today they enter the Hermitage to see Rembrandt or Reubens. They enter into a kind of sanctuary, a holy of holies, a sacred seat of power. Their eyes are wide-open in astonishment. Their heavy-felt boots move along the magnificent floors with the certain knowledge of treading on an earthly paradise, and, as though almost by an accident of history, they walk the same floors that Catherine the Great did. A Russian with whom I visited the Hermitage remarked: "The people come to the Hermitage to pay reverence to royalty—not to art, which they don't understand. Russian people are a simple people, and, like most simple people, they are impressed by big things, with fancy things. Most of all, they are impressed by the power and majesty that this building embodies." My Russian friend spoke of the people as though he were not a part of the people. He was in fact a teacher, and he considered himself a member of the Russian intelligentsia. The people (*narod*) were the masses, the intellectuals stood above the masses, their political and ideological vanguard. It is true that the peculiar place of the intellectual in Russian society, which he carved for himself throughout the nineteenth century, has been carried over into the Soviet period. I have heard students and teachers refer to the "inert Russian masses," and I have heard peasants refer to their Communist masters with the same reverence, born of subservience, which the peasants once reserved for the landowning masters. A social revolution has taken place in Russia, but it seems not radically to have altered the thinking processes of the people, though the framework for this thinking has been dramatically changed.

Across the Neva from the Hermitage, on one of Leningrad's 101 islands, is the Peter and Paul Fortress, built in the early 18th century, converted into a political prison in the 19th century, and, after the revolution, made into one of Russia's proudest museums. Many of the Russian revolutionaries, whose activities led to the 1917 revolution, spent weeks and years in this prison. Its honor roll includes, amongst others, Alexander Ulyanov, Lenin's older brother and idol, who was killed for complicity in the assassination of Alexander II in 1881; Chernyshevsky, the radical writer of the 1860's who wrote *What Is To Be Done?* (a book Lenin adored); Gorki; and the old anarchist, Prince Kropotkin. Our guide boasted that no one ever escaped from this prison. She denied that Kropotkin ever had, despite what he wrote in his "Memoirs." Every political prisoner was kept in a large private cell, no companions. The furniture consisted of one cot, one table, and one chair. We were told that the cells were made this spacious to accentuate the loneliness of the prisoner. Our guide, who was a short, charming Russian girl, explained every detail of the prison as though she herself were involved in an enormous conspiracy. Her eyes flashed and her voice fell to a whisper, as she explained that by a knock-knock system of communication, the prisoners were able to keep in touch with one another. She said, rather proudly, that Kropotkin once conducted a two-hour lecture on the Paris commune by means of this system.

In the evening, I went to the theater with some friends from the Embassy who have come to Leningrad for the weekend. We saw *Mazeppa,* a Tchaikovsky opera classic, at the old Marinsky Theater, but, unlike last Thursday evening, the theater was almost empty. It was as though the performers were playing for a select circle of friends. It would be easy to draw the conclusion that the Russians are tired of their own classics and prefer to see only Western art or new Soviet art. Certainly, this explains part of the reason for Russian indifference to operas like "Mazeppa" and the consequent poor attendance at theaters, but, tonight,—at least, tonight—there was another reason, for tonight was New Year's Eve—January thirteenth, by the old calendar—and Leningraders were all set to welcome in the New Year for the second time. Restaurants were jammed with dancing and drinking parties, and Western music could be heard on the streets. The Astoria's dining room, where we came to welcome in the New Year, was crowded beyond capacity, and Leningrad's smart set was celebrating lavishly. Women wore low-cut dresses, some strapless; the men dressed in single-breasted suits, and the music consisted of mambos, sambas, and lindy-hops. At exactly midnight, many people arose and toasted the New Year. January 13th, by the old calendar, probably has no religious significance, but, as one Russian said: "It's a good excuse to have a good time."

January 14 : I had an appointment this morning with a graduate student of Leningrad University. I had met him last week, and he called me at the hotel to arrange an appointment. He said that he had some information on Uvarov, in which I would probably be interested. We decided that the Russian Museum would make an appropriate rendezvous-place. At 11 a.m. almost as the clock struck its eleventh chord, the student appeared. He told me where I could get a lot of personal information on Uvarov. He mentioned the Central Historical Archives, which are housed on Decembrist Square, opposite the statute of the Bronze Horseman, in the large yellow buildings where the old Russian Senate and Synod used to convene. I told him that I could not possibly gain admittance to the Archives, because all Archives are under the direct control of the MGB (Ministry of State Security) and as such are inaccessible to foreigners except through the most elaborate and complicated and frustrating procedure. "This I cannot understand," the student said, in an exasperated tone, "what difference would it make to anyone if you saw Uvarov's personal papers? What difference at all? Certainly, Uvarov's papers would reveal no important state secret! Ah, sometimes, I get so angry!"

We drifted on to other subjects, and we spoke for about an hour about Western historiography on Russia. I mentioned that research projects are underway in many of America's leading institutions, which are examining right-wing, reactionary figures and movements in Russian history. I mentioned that my study of Uvarov was merely one of many. The student listened attentively, as I described research on Karamzin, the Slavophiles, Count Witte and Stolypin. Suddenly, the student interrupted. "This is what we need too. We need real scholarship. We must be alert to all trends in history. Sticking only to one cuts us off from the historical truth, which is made up of many different and conflicting tendencies and trends." The student was speaking in very unguarded language, and he surprised me. "What's the matter?" he asked. "Are you amazed to hear me say these things? Are you surprised that I speak what I feel? If so, you should attend some of the student meetings I have attended recently. Many times, such a tumult is raised that the professors must end the meetings, because they simply can't control them any more."

I spent the rest of the afternoon drifting from one second-hand book store to another and walking along the *Nevsky Prospekt*. The air was clean and brisk, and the avenues were crowded. In the evening, I had an appointment with Sasha, whom I would be seeing for possibly the last time. We decided to eat in one of the fine small cafes along the *Nevsky*. This one is called *The Seagull*, probably after Chekhov's play. Sasha and I had limited ourselves for the most part to literary discussions, but this evening, Sasha started to speak about politics.

"We may never see one another again, and I want to say that I shall never forget you. You are the first American whom I met, with whom I have spoken at length. You are so different from what I had expected."

"What did you expect? I mean, did you believe what you read in your papers?"

"Well, not everything, but I do believe that certain circles rule the government and determine American policy."

"Who are these circles, Sasha? Describe them to me."

"Well, everyone knows that certain circles of capitalists are interested in enormous profits and find these profits in the manufacture of military weapons and guns. These circles are on Wall Street, and they run Congress."

Sasha's entire frame of reference is a Marxist one. He sees history through the prism of Marxism. He sees huge classes of workers, growing larger and larger and poorer and poorer. He sees a small class of capitalist monopolists, growing smaller and richer, living off the sweat and labor of the worker. He sees profits as "surplus value," an old Marxist term which is not even stressed any longer in Marxist journals. He sees no difference between the Republican and Democratic Parties, since both only reflect capitalist interests, which are all the same. He sees great corruption and misery. He sees slums for the workers, Park Avenue for the capitalists, and there is no road from the slums to Park Avenue. The capitalist society is a closed one.

"But your country is technically very powerful, very progressive economically. We know that your workers live better than ours, but that is because you have a higher technology. We believe that if communism took over in America, there would be a real paradise on earth there, because you have such an advanced industry."

I explained that the average American worker was not a socialist. If anything, he was very bourgeois in his tastes and habits. He did not want socialism. I said that in this respect the American workers were like the Hungarian workers, who also did not want socialism. Sasha seemed almost incredulous. "Surely, this is impossible. Workers love socialism.

Socialism is a workers' doctrine. Socialism is made for the workers. How can they not like socialism?"

"You must try to understand that you are an intellectual. You are not a worker. You really do not share their hopes and miseries. The facts about Hungary indicate one thing very sharply: the workers did not want socialism."

"But you must admit they did not want a return to fascism?"

"I don't know what they wanted, but they did not want socialism. In this respect, the negative aspect is clear. What they wanted positively, I don't know, and it is unlikely if they themselves were aware of any long-range political and economic program. As in most revolutions, emotions and passions carried the movement, not a doctrine for tomorrow, only a hatred of yesterday."

Sasha weighed my arguments very carefully. He did not answer them directly, but when he did start to speak finally, he spoke in very general, superficial cliches. "The Red army had to move into Hungary. If it didn't, the Western armies would have. We had to stem the rise of fascism, which we hate. The workers were misled by black reactionaries. Mistakes were committed by the leadership. Honest discontent was twisted to meet the needs of the counter-revolution. Honest communists were being killed." Sasha rambled on, as though he were reciting his first grade lesson before a stern teacher. His voice was lifeless, as his arguments were bloodless. He exhibited a remarkable lack of enthusiasm for his own viewpoints. It was as though he were delivering this lecture to satisfy an intellectual need within him to cling to a doctrine upon which his entire life has been based, to cling to this doctrine because abandonment would mean ideological bankruptcy and moral desolation. It would mean ripping from him the reason for his existence.

Sasha's face suddenly lit up. He had found a good argument, he felt. "Capitalists distort news and information about the Soviet Union, about my country. The bourgeois press twists the truth almost beyond recognition. That's why you think this is a bad country. It is really a very good country. You write about a reign of terror, about fear, about misery and lack of culture."

"Sasha, let me answer your question: it is true that we have written about a reign of terror, about fear, misery, and many other things. Some of these reports have been exaggerated, but they are basically true. Are they not?"

"No, they are false," Sasha countered, "they are all false." His voice had reached a falsetto pitch.

"Sasha," I asked very quietly, "come back to the hotel with me."

My question stunned him. "What did you ask?"

"I asked you to come back to the hotel with me for a drink. Will you?"

Sasha grew defensive and frightened. "No, I don't think I shall."

"But why? Why, Sasha? In America, this would be a normal thing."

"Someone might misinterpret my visit."

"But who, why?"

"Oh, someone might. Someone might." His voice trailed off into a senseless, unintelligible mumble, his shoulders slumped forward, his proud face seemed twenty years older. He looked up at me after a while. There were tears in his eyes. His hands, trembling, reached out towards mine: "Oh, my friend, my dear friend, it is not so easy, it is not so easy. Life is very hard, very hard," and he held my hands in his moist ones for a long time, before we both decided that we needed some fresh air.

Outside we greeted the cold air, like a reprieve from political exile. We walked quickly, almost happily, down through the dark, side streets of Leningrad, past the large cathedral, built on the very spot where Alexander II was assassinated, past the Russian Museum, out towards the *Nevsky* once again. As we passed the Russian Museum, I asked Sasha if he had ever heard of or seen the Russian moderns, which are kept on the third floor, not for public exhibition, in the storehouse of the Museum. He said he had not, but he knew someone who might be able to get me permission to see them. He said he would call me tomorrow to tell me if he has succeeded.

January 15 : I visited the Repin Institute of Art late this morning with friends from the Embassy. We were warmly received by the Assistant Director, Cerebnyi—a very slick, handsome man in his forties, who spoke in a confidential whisper throughout our interview—and later by Orechnikov, the Director, whose general nervousness was accentuated by a bad stutter. Both men are Professors of Art, who are exceedingly proud of their studios, which we got a chance to see later in the afternoon.

They spoke freely about their Institute, which is one of the two largest art institutes in Russia. The other is in Moscow. They said that there are about 600 students at the Institute, which is divided into numerous faculties or departments. The most popular faculties are painting and architecture. About 200 students work in each of these, and the remaining 200 students work in less popular faculties, like sculpture and lithography. All of the Institute's students have to pass very rigorous entrance examinations, which consist of a combination of academic knowledge and artistic ability. The students apply from all of Russia's republics, and the "people's democracies." There are no Western students at either the Leningrad or Moscow Art Institute. Many of these students have received preliminary artistic training in specialized secondary schools, which are stepping stones to the Institute and a professional artistic career.

Work at the Institute lasts six years. The first three years are devoted strictly to course work and the mastering of the basic skills. The fourth and fifth year are occupied with personal instruction, and the senior year is reserved for "independent" and creative activity. The students put in an eight-hour day generally, five hours of which are dedicated to drawing. Light is a very critical factor in Leningrad, where there is only three or four hours of daylight during the winter months. As a result, the Institute encourages students to engage in independent activity during the summer months.

Cerebnyi and Orechnikov discussed in detail the Institute's theoretical orientation, and I found one of Orechnikov's remarks very revealing. When asked if the Institute is guided by the principles of socialist realism, he answered: "Why speak about socialist realism at all? One speaks of socialist realism incorrectly these days. Realism is crucial, and that which depicts socialist society is realism." The distinction between socialist realism and realism within a socialist framework is a fine distinction, but it is an important one.

We spent the next hour or two roaming through studios, looking at examples of the students' work. I must admit great disappointment. I had expected differentiation and individual expression—or, at least, degrees of this, because of the 1956 relaxation in the arts—but I found for the most part duplication after duplication, interrupted only by an occasionally individualistic canvas. I would guess that this is not what the students would like to paint but what they are required to paint. One student told us: "These canvases are for the professors. They are all alike. We do our own painting —that which we want to do—on our own time." Another student told me: "After a while, just to satisfy the professors, the students begin to paint like their professors, and I guess there are some students who actually think their way is the best way." A third student said: "Oh, how I would like to go to America and see your art. It must really be wonderful. In fact, I would just like to go anywhere."

These students, when they are graduated from the Institute, enter artists' collectives, where they receive a minimum, according to Orechnikov, of 6000 roubles a year (which at the official exchange rate is $1,500 a year), plus any private sales they might make. In regard to scholarships for students in the Institute, one professor said that about 70% of the student body obtain financial assistance, depending on (1) the financial "status of the student's family and (2) how much money parents give to the students. I found this explanation very interesting, because it was one of the first official comments I had heard about considerable financial distinctions in the Soviet society. These distinctions are well-known, but they are rarely mentioned.

We thanked Orechnikov for his tour, his patience, and his explanations, but he was unhappy. He was spoiling for a fight. He said antagonistically that "modern Western art" hasn't advanced in the last thirty years. We had the impression that he wanted us to say that Soviet painting hasn't advanced in the last forty years. He wanted an ideological tussle, but we disappointed him. We said we had to get back to the hotel to eat, pack, and prepare for our return journey to Moscow.

I wanted to return to the hotel for still another reason. Sasha had promised that he would call. He did—about ten minutes after I had arrived in my room. He said, in a quiet voice, heavy with resignation: "I saw my friend this morning, but I did not ask her for permission. I did not ask her for permission for the same reason I did not come to your hotel last night." Sasha's voice started to crack, and I assured him that I would see the Russian moderns myself, some other time, and urged him not to be upset.

"But I would have liked to help you, but I can't. You're right, and I'm wrong, but what can I do?"

Sasha started to cry. His crying continued for a few seconds, then I heard the click of his receiver. There was nothing more for him, or for me, to say.

Epilogue

I returned to Moscow in time to hear Khrushchev, in a
snappy reversal of fields, offer the ideological background for
Sasha's tormenting doubts. At a diplomatic reception, Khrushchev raised a toast to Joseph Stalin—the Georgian leader
whom he attacked a year previously as a criminal, madman,
and fiend. "God grant that every Communist be able to fight
as Stalin fought!" He actually said *God*.

His remark produced a startled hush. He continued: "For
all of us, Marxists-Leninists, who have devoted our lives to

the revolutionary struggle for the interests of the working class and its militant vanguard, the Leninist Party, the name of Stalin is inseparable from Marxism-Leninism."

Khrushchev had spoken. The line was finally set.

I packed my toothbrush and went home.